This book is a tribute to Dr Janice Martin Benario, without whose help I may never have discovered my mother's own codebreaking story.

Originally their individual secret narratives were weaved together in a work entitled, *A Tale of Two Secrets*. However, their stories were separated, and Janice died in December 2020, a month before the first book was published.

Never to be forgotten.

Dedicated to my parents and friends of the Silent Generation of the Second World War, and to a peaceful world for their families and future generations.

'What would it be like to keep a secret for fifty years, never tell your parents or your children; never even tell your husband?'
— Steve Goss, WABE, NPR, Atlanta, 2012

'You see it was during the war,' came her reply, 'and everyone kept secrets.
I was told not to say a thing, and I never did.'
— Janice Martin Benario, Atlanta, 2013

THE SECRET LIFE OF AN AMERICAN CODEBREAKER
CODEBREAKER GIRLS

JAN SLIMMING

Pen & Sword
MILITARY
AN IMPRINT OF PEN & SWORD BOOKS LTD.
YORKSHIRE – PHILADELPHIA

First published in Great Britain in 2022 by
PEN AND SWORD MILITARY
An imprint of
Pen & Sword Books Ltd
Yorkshire - Philadelphia

Copyright © Jan Slimming, 2022

ISBN 978 1 52678 415 5

The right of Jan Slimming to be identified as the Author of this work has been asserted by her in accordance with the Copyright, Designs and Patents Act 1988.

A CIP catalogue record for this book is available from the British Library.

All rights reserved. No part of this book may be reproduced or transmitted in any form or by any means, electronic or mechanical including photocopying, recording or by any information storage and retrieval system, without permission from the Publisher in writing.

Typeset in Times New Roman 11.5/14 by
SJmagic DESIGN SERVICES, India.
Printed and bound in the UK by CPI Group (UK) Ltd.

Pen & Sword Books Ltd incorporates the Imprints of Pen & Sword Archaeology, Atlas, Aviation, Battleground, Discovery, Family History, History, Maritime, Military, Naval, Politics, Railways, Select, Transport, True Crime, Fiction, Frontline Books, Leo Cooper, Praetorian Press, Seaforth Publishing, Wharncliffe and White Owl.

For a complete list of Pen & Sword titles please contact

PEN & SWORD BOOKS LIMITED
47 Church Street, Barnsley, South Yorkshire, S70 2AS, England
E-mail: enquiries@pen-and-sword.co.uk
Website: www.pen-and-sword.co.uk

or

PEN AND SWORD BOOKS
1950 Lawrence Rd, Havertown, PA 19083, USA
E-mail: uspen-and-sword@casematepublishers.com
Website: www.penandswordbooks.com

Contents

Foreword by Paul Reid   vii
Prologue   ix
Introduction   x

Chapter 1	Baltimore 1923	1
Chapter 2	Trouble in Europe	7
Chapter 3	War UK	12
Chapter 4	America Inches Forward	17
Chapter 5	A Junior in College	26
Chapter 6	War USA	35
Chapter 7	Chosen	40
Chapter 8	A Brief History of American Codebreaking	48
Chapter 9	Codebreaking in America	54
Chapter 10	Women in Codebreaking	66
Chapter 11	Signals, Operators, Poppies and WACs	81
Chapter 12	WAVES	92
Chapter 13	Going to the Chapel	99
Chapter 14	Battle of the Atlantic	104
Chapter 15	Working in Nooks and Crannies	117
Chapter 16	Handling Top Secret Intelligence	127
Chapter 17	Bombe Machines, German Codebreaking and ULTRA	136
Chapter 18	Japanese Codebreaking	160

THE SECRET LIFE OF AN AMERICAN CODEBREAKER

Chapter 19	The Workings of Secret Codebreaking	188
Chapter 20	Alien Codes?	206
Chapter 21	D-Day	213
Chapter 22	Final Battles	221
Chapter 23	War's End in Europe	229
Chapter 24	Waiting for VJ Day	237
Chapter 25	Aftermath	243
	Epilogue	251
	Afterword	255
	Memorial Day 2021	260
	Acknowledgements	262
	Abbreviations	264
	American Personnel at Bletchley Park	267
	Endnotes	269
	Index	283

Foreword
by Paul Reid

Co-author with William Manchester, *The Last Lion: Winston Spencer Churchill, Defender of the Realm, 1940-1965*

Winston Churchill once told an audience: 'History, with its flickering lamp stumbles along the trail of the past, trying to reconstruct its scenes, to revive its echoes, and kindle with pale gleams the passion of former days.'

Note the words he used: 'flickering', 'stumbles', 'pale gleams'. Churchill meant that historical truths do not reveal themselves with the absolute clarity of mathematical or scientific truth. History is shadowy, rife with hard-to-fathom motives and passions. History is messy, mysterious. It challenges us. It instructs us, but only if we actively shine the lantern on past events. A story left untold will never have any light shed upon it, pale, flickering, or otherwise. A story untold will remain forever dark, lost to the future. It may as well never have happened.

Sometimes a story is told in detail and at length and still the light flickers, pale. My bookshelves hold Winston Churchill's six-volume history of World War Two, written in the decade following the end of the war. Millions of readers worldwide read this history when it was published; millions still read it today. The index of this critical history contains no entry for 'Enigma' (the German military's encryption machine), nor does the index include an entry for 'Bletchley Park' (the secret campus where British codebreakers worked on the decryption of Enigma messages).

Churchill, you see, was constrained by Britain's Official Secrets Act, which forbade disclosure of this information for many decades following the war. In his history Churchill refers to 'agents' and 'networks' and 'sources' but he could not tell the real story. Over the last five decades, after these constraints were lifted, many books have been written about the Bletchley codebreakers, including Jan Slimming's fine addition to the genre: *Codebreaker Girls: A Secret Life at Bletchley Park*, the deeply personal story of Daisy Lawrence, Slimming's mother, and a Bletchley analyst. Slimming wielded the lamp of history, and the tale she revealed was neither pale nor glimmering, but clear and bright.

She does so again with *The Secret Life of an American Codebreaker*. Janice Martin Benario, the young woman at the centre of the story, begins World War Two as a college student and ends it working in top-secret codebreaking for Naval Intelligence. The book weaves a history of WWII American decryption capabilities and intelligence services around Benario's personal story. The reader will reap the best of possible outcomes: a compelling tale of personal transformation and a comprehensive examination of American intelligence services.

Enjoy this important book.

Paul Reid
Tryon, NC,
August 2021

Prologue

'Each day a man came; a naval officer, armed with a gun and a padlocked leather pouch. When he knocked on our door, we knew he wanted our yellow envelope, the one we had already prepared and sealed. We signed it over to him, he put it in the pouch close to his gun and left.

As a high-ranking messenger, he had a huge responsibility to maintain the secrecy, making sure messages arrived safely and reached the correct person. He walked out of the building, got into his car and immediately drove to Main Navy on Pennsylvania Avenue, where it went straight to Admiral King and the United States Submarine Tracking Room. No other place could that envelope go…'

'Nobody ever did say anything, at least not until several years later.'

* * *

1943: America was fighting on two fronts, east and west. Europe was under Nazi siege and German U-boats prowled the Atlantic attacking Allied shipping. Japan's murderous military forces ravaged the South China Seas and other territories in the Far East. In a surprise attack, Pearl Harbor had been bombed in December 1941 by the Japanese Navy Air Service, killing or maiming 3,400 American servicemen and civilians. Days later Hong Kong also lay victim to Japan's deadly rampage, then Singapore fell in February 1942 after a brutal seventeen-day battle. Wholesale massacre was widespread. The military might of the enemy had to be halted using weaponry and cunning, but this war also had secret weapons – maths, science and Intelligence.

Introduction

A thunder-bolt opportunity awakened my interest in codebreakers in 2012. It was, perhaps, a chance not to be missed and the last opportunity to delve into my mother's long-overdue story. Little did I know I was about to embark on one of the most enlightening and fulfilling projects of my life and learn, in the process, about American codebreaking.

My family had moved to Atlanta in 2000 for my husband's job. We settled quickly into our new environment and, as avid BBC Radio 4 listeners, rapidly became accustomed to NPR's global news via our radio alarm clock. That's when I first heard the voice of another codebreaker whose story mirrored my late mother's.

In England, my twin sister and I learned about our parents' war. Snippets of quickly rescinded information haunted our childhood, which resembled a mysterious fairy tale in a far-off land where we rarely heard the end. Trailing sentences of a time in Singapore – never fully explained. The phrase, 'Oh, that was a long time ago and you don't need to worry,' sufficed after we learned our father had been a prisoner of war. To us his war was black and white, on a small TV screen; nothing exotic – another war, not his, someone else's fiction because he was at home with us in Surrey.

Our home life was real, and around the time we turned six we ventured out in our new family car for a weekend trip, north of London, to an aggregates and brick manufacturing town called Bletchley. Mum also wanted to show us the place where *she* worked during the war, but it was closed, at least to her. The high chain-linked fences, topped with barbed wire, screamed high security. At the front gates Mum couldn't get in. Fifteen years had passed since she was there, and the highlight of her younger life was closed to her and the public. She said she worked there as a clerk, a filing clerk.

INTRODUCTION

A decade passed before the subject of Bletchley Park was raised again and we heard about the Official Secrets Act. My mother, Daisy Lawrence, was prone to nervous breakdowns and we were told not to ask questions. It slipped out that she had worked for the Foreign Office and as a civil servant was bound by rules of secrecy. Then further into the 1970s the secret-keeping of wartime Bletchley Park was suddenly headline news. How was she involved? She would never say but gradually, over the next ten years, thousands of others' secrets were revealed, but still our mother said little. 'It was unimportant,' she said, and my sister and I did little to delve further into this part of her life. Only after her death in 2006, did we discover wartime papers and the seeds of her story – contravening the rules of the Official Secrets Act – hidden in a trunk at the end of her bed. Her story is told in another book, CODEBREAKER GIRLS: A Secret Life at Bletchley Park.

* * *

In Atlanta, as I sat in bed that November day, toward the end of 2012, sipping my early morning cup of tea, the American woman's voice on the radio could have been my mother. My husband listened silently too. He knew this was important. The usual morning news host, Steve Goss, asked: 'What would it be like to keep a secret for fifty years…. from your parents, your children, and even from your husband!?' His words echoed around the room.

'Well, this person did, and we can now hear why.'

'You see it was during the war and everyone kept secrets', said the American woman. 'I was told not to say a word and I never did.'

My mother seemed to be speaking from the grave, but this lady did not have a London accent!

Who was this person? I had to find out. Did she know the unspoken secrets of my mother's war, the story we were not permitted to hear? Could she fill the holes in my mother's life? Running downstairs to my computer, her words rang like beautiful music in my ears. I had to find her; was there a connection? Thank goodness for new technology (I didn't know at the time how relevant and important Google was!) After a few clicks and a refined search through NPR and WABE websites I was able to trace Janice Martin Benario to Georgia State University. She was an

THE SECRET LIFE OF AN AMERICAN CODEBREAKER

American codebreaker. It was quite a moment for me as my name is also Janice and, from something my mother once said, I was convinced I was named after her.

* * *

This is the story of Janice Martin Benario, a WAVE (Women Accepted for Voluntary Service) during the Second World War. She was part of naval intelligence OP-20-G. While America's seeds in this secret community germinated from the First World War, mass intelligence collection and analysis only started to take shape in 1941 when discussions, then formal agreements, with Britain allowed access to their organised codebreaking factory. The subsequent collaboration of combined communications under their respective war offices was, and still is, one of the most amazing feats in history. What is even more remarkable is that the huge contribution of women employees – the first for women in any war system in collection, analysis and sometimes strategy on both sides of the Atlantic – was not publicly known until decades later, and that military commanders making final decisions on attack or defence, relied heavily on the secret intelligence that codebreakers provided.

Who were these people? Why were they chosen? What did they actually do?
Why were they never properly recognised?

Chapter 1

Baltimore 1923

I was grateful for NPR's lead and Janice was equally keen to tell her story. She was Professor Emerita in Classics at Georgia State University. She was born in Baltimore, worked in Washington DC, and had lived in Atlanta for a long time with her family. Her husband, Herbert Benario was also Professor of Classics at the neighbouring college, Emory University.

The administration office at Georgia State connected us, and after one hour of me hitting 'send' on my email that November day, Janice telephoned me. She said she had newspaper cuttings and book references and two days later I received a large envelope with multiple photocopied articles about Bletchley Park and cryptology. Now I really wanted to uncover my mother's story, but I almost didn't know where to start. Should I be looking at codes and try to learn about codebreaking? Or assemble old photos from my mother, that didn't mean much to me? Instead, I started reading accounts of others and wondered how my mother fitted into this.

After further long conversations, Janice and I eventually arranged to meet. I was apprehensive but delighted to finally introduce myself to the person who I was by then calling my adopted codebreaking mother. Her huge smile was infectious and almost overwhelmed her small-framed body. She was even the same height as my mother, though slimmer. We continued our discussions and Janice told me everything about growing up in Baltimore and her wartime experience. This was the first time I'd spoken at length with anyone involved in the Second World War. It was emotional and exciting at the same time. She showed me photos of when she was young and gave me a list of additional books. So, with the help of the internet, scant memories and many books, I started to piece together my mother's days at Bletchley Park. I had to read, read, read and organise a visit to England.

My research soon led me to also capture her oral history and write her story; it was an important opportunity and not to be missed.

THE SECRET LIFE OF AN AMERICAN CODEBREAKER

Background – Leading to the Second World War

Janice was born five years after the end First World War, 1914 -1918. The death toll had been over twenty-two million, and the Allies had formed the League of Nations in 1920 to prevent further wars and disastrous loss of life from ever happening again. A long period of intense patriotism ensued. This was followed by uncertainty, and then a period of economic prosperity.

In North America and Western Europe – especially in big cities such as New York, Paris, Berlin and London – cultural bias paved the way for the Roaring Twenties (or *Années folles* in France). The 'Crazy Years' emphasised social, artistic and cultural dynamism. Some events and reactions were considered extreme and hyper-emotional, but many wartime survivors were young women who had lost their fathers, brothers or fiancés and, for them, theatre and musical artistic flair was crucial to define their role as modern women. They had new freedoms in politics, the workplace, fashion and behaviour. Over-zealous young women were called 'Flappers' wearing shorter skirts and bobbed hair. They listened to jazz and flaunted their disdain for those who considered their behaviour morally unacceptable. They were called brash for applying excessive makeup, drinking contraband alcohol and expanding their sexual liaisons in a casual manner. They smoked cigarettes, drove cars and generally flouted the so-called social and respectable norms of previous years. During this time, women also won the right to vote in most major countries.

It was a period of unprecedented industrial growth, accelerated consumer demand and aspirations resulting in significant lifestyle changes. Manufacture of vehicles expanded, and a few telephones started to appear in homes leading to better communication. Electricity became widely available and radio connected towns and cities across the world. Refrigeration paved the way for convenience foods at home, then came air conditioning, and moviemakers focused on film stars and palatial cinemas. In 1923 a growing dance craze was sweeping the United States, 'dance 'til you drop'. Young couples endangered their lives by dancing for hours, hoping to win a handsome cash prize. Many were injured. One girl's ankles swelled to twice the normal size after dancing more than forty-five hours and wearing out five male dance partners. In Baltimore, a couple were stopped by police after a marathon of fifty-three hours.

* * *

BALTIMORE 1923

Janice was born on 19 February 1923. 'I was born Janice Marguerite Martin. My mother's maiden name was Gladys Kathryn Martin, and my father was J. Elmer Martin.'

That was a surprise. The 'tape' was running and I interjected to question why they had the same name.

'Yes', said Janice. 'It was a strange thing that my mother had the same married name as her maiden name. She had some difficult moments explaining they were legally the same. It was an unusual situation.'

She continued: 'I grew up in a typical Baltimore Row House. It was long and narrow with a red brick front and white marble steps. Baltimore is known for rows and rows of this type of house. Ours had three floors and a basement. My grandfather, John L. Martin had been a bricklayer and he helped build the house for his son, J. Elmer. When my parents married, his mother and father were getting old and so an apartment was made for them on the second floor. My parents and I lived on the first and third floors, plus we had use of the basement. Our address was 2923 North Calvert Street, Baltimore.'

Janice and her mother, Gladys Kathryn Martin, Calvert Street, Baltimore. (Janice Benario Archive)

THE SECRET LIFE OF AN AMERICAN CODEBREAKER

The Martin residence resembled a New York Brownstone, in the middle of a block of several houses. It was 16 feet across on a strip of land just 16 feet wide, which her grandfather had bought. 'The dwelling areas were long and went right to the back. On the first floor was a living room, a music room, a dining room and a hall which passed by the pantry to the kitchen,' Janice remembered.

'Their furniture was smart and solid. The kitchen had a large stove, a sink, a large worktable and a wall of cabinets and cupboards. There was also a small dinette where some of their meals were eaten.' Through the kitchen, a door opened to the back porch, where steps led down to the garden and a cement sidewalk that bordered a small lawn to a brick garage for her father's car. 'He was lucky to have one,' she said.

'I used to call my grandfather "Dadaddy", and with Grandma and my parents, we all lived happily together for many years. We were not rich, but comfortable; my family knew how to handle money.'

Baltimore was a large city and as the houses were close together Janice said she got to know all her neighbours and had plenty of other

Janice in the Calvert Street garden with her grandfather, 1926. (Janice Benario Archive)

BALTIMORE 1923

children to play with. 'We roller skated in the neighbourhood and threw balls around, not in the road, but on the sidewalk. We also played hopscotch but there were trees along the edge of the street which always got in the way.'

She was five-and-a-half when she started kindergarten at Margaret Brent Elementary School, ten-minutes from her home. Her father had his own law office and together they walked the three blocks, then he caught the streetcar to his office. By the time she was six or seven, she walked by herself. She went to public school all the way through to high school. 'My mother was a "stay-at-home".'

I enquired if her mother minded being a 'stay-at-home'. Most married middle-class women did stay home then, but attitudes toward women were changing. She replied, 'Well, the interesting thing about my mother's family (who also lived in a row house four blocks away) was that when she graduated Eastern High School and wanted to go to college in 1912, her father had strict views, saying, 'As long as I can support you, no daughter of mine is going to go to college.' So, her mother didn't go to college and never went to work. Janice said she didn't think her mother resented it, '...she was happy being at home.'

Her father J. Elmer, however, was pulled out of high school at 16 to work at the Pennsylvania Railroad as his father, Janice's Dadaddy, was injured and couldn't work. He only went to the second year of high school but was able to take an evening business course. Later he went to law school at the University of Maryland. After three years he took the bar exam and passed first time.

Janice's mother had married J. Elmer, at the age of 26 and he was 32. They had few relatives, but all lived in the Baltimore area. 'One aunt, one uncle and one first cousin, sixteen years older.' Consequently, Janice was brought up to be independent and safely travelled the city by herself from a young age. 'I was not spoiled in any way. I was just very independent.'

From the beginning education was important in her family and, as an only child, she spent many hours reading. 'I always had a library card for books and read magazines, *American Girl* or something similar. I went through a spell of reading *The Bobbsey Twins* and *Nancy Drew*, and liked mysteries and romances. *Little Women* by American author Louise May Alcott, published in the 1860s, was also a popular choice.

Baltimore had both a morning paper and an evening paper; my family bought them all.' Janice was well informed on current affairs.

'We were never wealthy, but if we needed a new car, we could get one, of course it helped that my parents lived in a house my grandfather built and paid for long ago. They had no mortgage.'

Her comfortable upbringing, however, indicated little of what she was to experience in later life. She did not have siblings and entertained herself playing hopscotch in the street when she was young, schoolwork, sewing, practising the piano, and playing sports. When the bubble burst in September 1929, Janice's family were able to balance on the edge of the Great Depression, maintaining their stability, and could still have vacations.

'My favourite was to Atlantic City, New Jersey, where I could swim in the ocean. My father never learned to swim but he loved the Atlantic Ocean and got me liking it too'.

Janice and her father, J. Elmer Martin, by the ocean at Atlantic City beach. (Janice Benario Archive)

Chapter 2

Trouble in Europe

Janice was an inquisitive student and read about the turmoil growing in Europe, including the complex decisions her country might have to take. At the age of 12, history was one of her favourite subjects. Through school lessons and her parents' newspapers, she learned about world events and the Neutrality Act, an ancient proclamation, which would soon be amended and affect America's decisions in global affairs.

The first mention of neutrality was in a formal proclamation issued by the US President, George Washington on 22 April 1793. He declared the nation would abstain from conflict between France and Great Britain and threatened legal proceedings against any American who aided any country at war. The Neutrality Act was formally passed in 1794, and clearly outlawed military operations against nations at peace with America.

During the early 1930s and the Great Depression, the Neutrality Act was still in force, but later amendments were passed by US Congress in response to a repeat of increased tensions in Europe. The 1935 act sought to ensure America would never again become embroiled in foreign conflicts. The amendment was spurred by strong isolationist and non-interventionist feelings, from those who remembered the country's costly involvement in the First World War, not only in lives but dollars as, two decades later, America's allies still owed huge sums of money.

An embargo on all war-item shipments was established which meant Americans were not permitted to travel on belligerent ships, and hostile countries were not allowed loans, but as the country wallowed in neutrality and isolationism, events in Europe and Asia escalated.

Totalitarianism – full government political power over public and private life – became a form of communism in the USSR under Joseph Stalin, while Spain and Italy followed the fascist ideals of Hitler, and fascism grew in Japan. As world economy slumped in 1937, America passed another amendment to the act allowing warring nations to buy any item except arms. Still Britain hoped for more from the United States, but many Americans remained reluctant to be involved.

* * *

Events abroad, however, did not prevent Janice from enjoying her early teenage years as a Girl Scout, where she earned the position of a camp counsellor at Camp Cloudmarch, 'It was a big camp in Maine. The first time I went there was the longest trip I'd ever taken alone.'

When she was 14, she attended Roland Park Junior High and later Western High. 'At that time, there were only two important women's high schools in the area; mine was one, the other was Eastern High. I learned to ballroom dance. My father played the piano, mostly hymns. I had piano lessons and often listened to the radio – Dance Time and the Hit Parade.'

Janice learned to sew from her mother who was an accomplished seamstress, and through her teenage years she made many of her own dresses and excelled at needlepoint. 'As far as clothes were concerned, I had enough skirts and blouses to wear something different every day in school.' Her favourite colour was blue.

She began Latin in Junior High and took a Modern Language course embracing Latin, French and History. Her plan was to major in history, away from Baltimore, but Goucher – a female liberal college – was just six blocks from her home and despite her independence her father insisted that's where she would go.

As well as her studies Janice enjoyed swimming and tennis and played basketball. She was part of the Freshmen team, which was a surprise as Janice is not tall. I asked her if she had won any medals. 'Well, that's a good question,' she said. 'When I was at Western, they had track and field events for girls. One thing was the Standing Broad Jump, which they don't do now. You just stood in one place and jumped – a bit like long jump, but you just stood. No running to the starting board or line. One day in the gym I jumped eight feet, three inches!'

'Everyone around me had a complete fit', she laughed. 'Nobody at my school had ever jumped that far from a standing position, and so they sent me to the South Atlantic Championships. The event just

TROUBLE IN EUROPE

Janice's winning Broad Jump Medal at the South Atlantic Championships for 1937, 1938 and 1939. (Author's photograph/Janice Benario Archive)

happened to be in Baltimore that year. I went as a competitor and won!' She still has her gold medal. 'I won three years running: 1937, 1938 and 1939.'

There was a High Jump category in the Olympics and Running Broad Jump, but Janice didn't believe Standing Broad Jump ever became an Olympic sport.

* * *

'Goucher was the number one college "down the street" and gave part scholarships, twelve each year', recalled Janice, 'four to Eastern High, four to Western High and four to one other. We took a scholarship exam and I came out as first alternate and received a Western High Alumna Scholarship. The amount I received was $350, matching Goucher's

Goucher College. (Public domain via I & M Ottenheimer)

tuition fee per year, but the fee rose to $450, therefore, my father made up the rest; $100 was a lot of money in the late 1930s.'

The college began as a small seminary and became the Women's college of Baltimore City. Its first class of five successful students graduated in 1892. The institution grew and was renamed Goucher College in 1910 after its principal.[1] It was one of seven Class 1 liberal arts colleges in America including Mount Holyoke, Radcliff, Smith, Vassar and Wellesley. Though inconsistencies exist in various lists either Bryn Mawr or Barnard College are also part of the prestigious collection known as the *Seven Sisters*.

Male ivy-league colleges including Dartmouth, Princeton, Harvard and Yale would not admit women, a commonly supported view, as demonstrated by Janice's grandfather in respect of her mother. Beliefs in the early 20th century thought higher education for women pointless and nugatory. Fortunately, his son, J. Elmer Martin, held a different view and his daughter was on track to attend college.

* * *

TROUBLE IN EUROPE

Changing the subject, I enquired if she had ever smoked. 'Well, since I was very athletic, I never smoked, but I learned to drive when I was sixteen.' The two things went together in Janice's experience. In Maryland she had learned to drive as soon as possible with a special driver's licence for a month and then passed a test. She went on to explain that she was very young when her family first owned a car, and that her father was fortunate to trade in his old vehicle for a new one during the Second World War, as car manufacturing had stopped because factories and supplies were needed for production of war materials – aircraft, weapons and ammunition to name a few.

'We had a Ford. A black Ford. You could have any colour as long as it was black! The model released after the Model-T, was the V-8.'

Chapter 3

War UK

As Janice completed her last semester at high school and prepared for college, she kept up with the escalating events in Europe. General Franco in Spain had gained control of Barcelona and Madrid with the help of Italian air force bombers, resulting in many deaths and starvation for civilians hiding underground. The Catalans, after patchy resistance, either surrendered to Nationalist troops or escaped to the borders of southern and western France. The UK Parliament formally recognised Franco in a vote of 344 to 137 which caused ugly scenes in the House of Commons. Their opposition government shouted, 'Heil Chamberlain' and 'Now the Vulture'. But Prime Minister Chamberlain justified the recognition believing that Franco possessed most of Spain and that nobody knew how many of the losing side remained or where they were. Meanwhile, Britain's Royal Air Force (RAF) enlarged its stock of air power four-fold and elevated the importance of its pilot training programmes. Germany had already increased their aircraft arsenal by six.

Dark shadows loomed and Janice wondered what would happen next after Mussolini joined Hitler in a fascist alliance. Meanwhile, North America hosted King George VI and Queen Elizabeth on 6 June 1939. The Royal Commonwealth tour to Canada, was extended to visit New York's World Fair. A visit of such extravagance displaying modern and futuristic living, in Flushing Meadow, seemed a curious decision by the royals while Britain teetered on the brink of war. However, the tour was designed to soften strong isolationist tendencies and the hospitality afforded by President Franklin Delano Roosevelt and his wife Eleanor, successfully bolstered support and friendship between both countries.

Roosevelt's fears for Europe, and ultimately his own country, meant he wanted to preserve communication with Britain. He felt US involvement was just a matter of time but needed to ensure he was still president and commander-in-chief when that occurred. However, isolationists were still a problem: 'Nazi Germany is 4,000 miles across the ocean; why should we be involved again, have more heavy losses of life and unpaid European debt?'

Congress considered again but chose to stay on the sidelines, offering only safe havens for migrants and partial help.

Then a proposed collaboration between Britain, France and Russia soured when Stalin agreed a non-aggression pact with Germany instead. The growing spat between Chamberlain and Hitler reached its climax when Germany invaded Poland on 1 September 1939. If it wasn't clear before it was now patently obvious that Hitler's dictatorship intended to spread across Europe, and even across the Atlantic. Families in Poland were slaughtered, and rumours of persecution against many populations in Germany swept through causing panic and dissent. The tyranny had to stop. Britain and France declared war on Germany, on 3 September 1939. With a crackle and a whistle, Chamberlain's announcement came over the radio:

> *'I am speaking to you from the Cabinet Room of 10 Downing Street. This morning the British Ambassador in Berlin handed the German government a final note, stating that unless we heard from them by 11 o'clock - that they were prepared at once to withdraw their troops from Poland, a state of war would exist between us. I have to tell you now that no such undertaking has been received and that consequently, this country is at war with Germany....'*

Immediately air raid sirens in London sounded and the capital's inhabitants hurriedly closed their windows thinking a poisonous gas bomb might be dropped. People were scared, but no enemy aircraft came that day. Parents prepared to evacuate their children to other parts of the country, far from large towns and cities, and barrage balloons rose eerily from their moorings over London hoping to impede enemy aircraft.

Later that same night, a British transatlantic passenger liner the SS *Athenia*, was attacked in the Atlantic and sunk – 112 sailors and passengers perished, including Canadians and twenty-eight American citizens. Kapitänleutnant Fritz Julius Lemp of submarine *U-30* was the culprit[1], but this truth was not revealed until later. Meanwhile, some said it was a deadly clandestine scheme of the British to bring America into the war.

* * *

THE SECRET LIFE OF AN AMERICAN CODEBREAKER

During the 1920s and 30s, the German military had grown, and part of their indestructible confidence relied on a new message enciphering system which they considered to be unbreakable. But Churchill had been privy to similar systems from when he was First Lord of the Admiralty in the First World War. German codebooks had been captured then and later he was informed of other advances in cryptography. From this time, he was also aware of Britain's ability to secretly intercept other powers' messages. However, it was slow work, as penetrating enemy codes and ciphers[2] often took months to break and understand. Britain needed a more proficient system for their codebreaking processes to keep on top of Hitler's plans. As a backbencher, Churchill had maintained a prominent presence in Westminster and warned Prime Minister Neville Chamberlain's government, in September 1938, against Appeasement with Hitler, calling instead for collective action against his aggression. Therefore, when Britain declared war on Germany on 3 September, he was immediately elevated and re-appointed as First Lord of the Admiralty to Chamberlain's war cabinet.

* * *

As young men in Britain complied with conscription[3], other men and women, secretly gathered at Bletchley Park for intelligence work of national importance. America watched as the reality of war started to sink in. However, the next eight months of military inactivity, became known as 'The Phoney War' marking a lack of major land operations on Germany's Western Front. The term was first used in late September 1939 by US Senator William Borah when he commented on allied European inactivity. No Western power was committed to a significant land offensive. Poland was overrun within five weeks and Britain and France did nothing despite their promises, contravening the terms of the Anglo-Polish and Franco-Polish military alliances, where Britain and France were obliged to assist.

Kapitänleutnant Lemp of the submarine *U-30* had joined the group of 'small' military actions on both sides, and when Germany further escalated attacks at sea against British aircraft carriers and destroyers, sinking several with heavier losses, there was limited defensive air action.

Roosevelt continued to be supportive of the European allies when isolationists blocked his proposals, but then the Neutrality Act was repealed and amended in Congress. On 4 November 1939, the arms embargo was finally lifted and American shipments of war items could be sold to allies. Sales, however, had to be recorded through the National Munitions Control Board and paid for on a 'cash and carry' basis. As France and Britain were considered belligerent nations, this was the only way Congress was prepared to aid in the sale of arms.

Meanwhile, Britain waited, but kept themselves informed of America's intentions via their own intelligence services, as they secretly read America's diplomatic messages. 'The cryptanalysts did not even have to furrow their brows excessively,' wrote David Kahn in his 1967 publication *The Codebreakers*. For the codes of this great power were pre-First World War…, 'and as puny as those of many smaller nations.'[4] President Roosevelt distrusted his State Department codes.

* * *

Janice read in the news that the ambassador to the United Kingdom, Joseph P. Kennedy, had shown little support for Europe and the challenges Britain faced. As Hitler invaded other lands, his defeatist attitude and acceptance of Neville Chamberlain's Appeasement policies proved him to be a selfish individual, concerned only for his own interests. After the Munich conference in September 1938, when Czechoslovakia was 'handed over' to Hitler, he gleefully remarked to the Czechoslovakian ambassador, Jan Masaryk: 'Isn't it wonderful (that the crisis is over)? Now I can get to Palm Beach after all!'

A former venture capitalist on Wall Street, and ex-chairman of the Securities Exchange Commission, he spent his ambassadorial years in London protecting his personal coffers. It was no secret. 'Wars were bad for business,' and 'even worse, bad for *his* business,' reported James 'Scotty' Reston, a prominent US journalist.

'I'm for appeasement one thousand per cent,' said Kennedy who seriously believed this and used his position to obtain sought-after cargo space to export pallets of liquor across the Atlantic. After frequent German bombing raids on London and other counties, Kennedy turn-tailed and ran home to America declaring 'England is gone.' His departure was also apportioned to his hatred of Winston Churchill whom he called 'a drunken sot' and 'a third or fourth rate man'.[5]

* * *

Chamberlain had resigned on 10 May 1940. The Phoney War came to an end with Germany's successful invasion of Belgium, Luxembourg and the Netherlands. Discredited through bungled campaigns costing many lives, the British people lost faith in his ability to lead and could only envision a mounting military catastrophe. Churchill was chosen to build an emergency coalition government; he would tell the truth, they believed.

'We shall fight on the beaches, we shall fight on the landing grounds, we shall fight in the fields and in the streets, we shall fight in the hills; we shall never surrender,' he stated in Parliament. As German forces pushed back, he later announced news of a colossal military disaster: 'The whole root, core and brain of the British Army' had been stranded at Dunkirk in northern France and seemed about to perish or be captured. Operation Dynamo, 26 May – 4 June was hailed by Churchill as 'a miracle of deliverance' when 850 little ships sailed from Ramsgate in Kent to save over 338,000 Allied soldiers from beaches and Dunkirk harbour. But the 'Miracle of Dunkirk' wasn't a miracle. It was a disaster. More than 68,000 British Expeditionary Forces (BEF) were either dead, wounded or captured. Churchill was quick to say that the 'miraculous evacuation' should not be celebrated as a victory – 'Wars are not won by evacuation.'

The country mobilised as the new Prime Minister took further stock of the manpower needed to defend the nation. More than 'blood, toil, tears and sweat' were needed. Churchill's words were gallant, but for his country to survive he knew another kind of war, far different from any before, was necessary. A report was secretly commissioned on wartime needs and the people required to meet them. He planned a war fought with intelligence and science more than vessels and gun powder, a strategy which he later referred to as a 'Wizard War'.

Chapter 4

America Inches Forward

Roosevelt had made the decision to run for an unprecedented third term, and as the presidential election approached, he promised America would be kept out of war. During this time, he maintained contact with Winston Churchill, but made him no promises.

Churchill saw America as the ally Europe needed and continued to foster good relations. As Prime Minister, he held highly confidential information in his grasp and hatched a plan to bring America to the table. On 8 July, Lord Lothian, Britain's Ambassador in Washington DC made an offer to reveal secret technical information about England's latest developments in radar and other scientific fields. Churchill believed America was significantly behind in these areas. Two days later the offer was formalised by Lothian to the President:

> *'Should you approve the exchange of information, it has been suggested by my Government that, in order to avoid any risk of the information reaching our enemy, a small secret British mission consisting of two or three service officers and civilian scientists should be dispatched immediately to this country to enter into discussions with Army and Navy experts.'*

The letter went on to suggest compensation for such secret information:

> *'His Majesty's Government would greatly appreciate it, if the United States Government, having been given full details of any British equipment and devices, would reciprocate by discussing certain secret information of a technical nature, which our technical experts are anxious to have.'*

The President brushed aside dissension from high-ranking military officers including General Marshall and, in September 1940, provided resources for Sir Henry Tizard, a chemist and adviser to Britain's Ministry of Aircraft Production, to visit. In his briefcase were MOST SECRET details regarding radar and radio interception. But one file remained under wraps, ULTRA – the confidential key to Britain's survival, the most important top-secret intelligence of all.

The Blitz in London lasted thirty-seven weeks as America looked on in despair. There were many who wanted to help as parts of London were destroyed or severely damaged. The Battle of Britain had been a pivotal moment for the RAF with nearly 3,000 serving with Fighter Command. While Londoners took shelter and watched air battles from below, the Luftwaffe battled with 2,600 fighters and bombers, as British pilots and their teams waited for their call, chain-smoking and downing a stiff whisky, knowing this might be their last. The front and rear gunners, the navigator, the pilot – it was likely that many would not survive their next assignment. In all 1,023 RAF planes were lost in the air battles and the Luftwaffe lost 1,887. Over 40,000 civilian and military lives were lost with London taking half the fatalities. It was unnerving to see the average age of a pilot was only 20. As well as the UK, many came from British Dominions, occupied Europe or neutral countries, including some Americans.

* * *

Roosevelt had been right to distrust his country's security methods. The M-138[1] flat strip cipher of the U.S. Army, was unreliable. American journalist and humourist, James Thurber, a code clerk briefly serving with the peace mission at the American embassy in Paris during and after the First World War, commented on this history in *The New Yorker*, writing, 'all our code books except one were quaint transparencies dating back to the time when Hamilton Fish was Secretary of State under President Grant', referring to a period seventy years prior in the mid-nineteenth century.[2] 'They were intended to save words and cut telegraph costs, not to fool anybody.' Little had changed.

They used GRAY and GREEN codes despite advice from cipher experts to the State Department. It was considered the most secret method of cryptography, based on the strip cipher of M-138, invented by Parker Hitt – a cipher with origins in Thomas Jefferson's time.[3]

AMERICA INCHES FORWARD

Some considered this secure for American diplomatic correspondence, but it entailed 100 strips that had to be kept secret and changed often. The State Department still used the old system to encipher a triple priority message from Roosevelt to Churchill after the Atlantic Conference in August 1941. After several security breaches, Roosevelt decided to communicate with his ambassadors in London, Paris and Moscow on 'matters of utmost secrecy', via the Navy. The State Department felt shunned and thought diplomatic matters were withheld. However, it was not Roosevelt's intention to suppress information, but to halt crucial confidential data from reaching other world powers who, he believed, had plenty of time to crack America's antiquated codes. It was common knowledge through departmental gossip that the State Department's enciphering methods were vulnerable. Indeed, the American embassy in Madrid received its most secret instructions in British code.

* * *

After Henry Tizard's September visit to Washington, Churchill learned America had broken a high-level Japanese diplomatic code. He was impressed and considered revealing Britain's own secrets for breaking German diplomatic codes but needed to wait until Roosevelt was re-elected President for a third term.

On 5 November 1940 that happened, and Churchill wrote to Roosevelt.

> *'...I prayed for your success.... We are entering a sombre phase of what must inevitably be a protracted and broadening war....'*

Roosevelt did not respond, but subtly engaged in preparations for America's entrance into the conflict. Four days later, on 9 November 1940, Britain's former Prime Minister, Neville Chamberlain, died of cancer. He was 71. Though haunted by 'appeasement' and the 1938 Munich Agreement controversy, his country and world leaders paid tribute to a great patriot and devoted servant of the nation, and his struggle to preserve freedom and world peace. His words 'Peace for Our Time' still resonate. It just wasn't to be in his.

* * *

In 1940/41, during Janice's early college years, it was possible US troops could be involved at any time. Eventually, complacent America became sympathetic toward Europe as they recognised a German victory would pose a deeper threat to their national security. The Martin family kept abreast of the devastation in Europe, but life carried on in Baltimore. Janice, now at Goucher, had a part-time Christmas job at Hochshild-Kohn, selling gifts. Another holiday season she also helped in a bookshop. She liked to keep busy, but also listened to the radio.

'This is London,' announced Ed Murrow, to America. Broadcast journalism had been born. Radio had become an effective source of news and propaganda on both sides of the European conflict. Murrow from America's CBS had reported from London since 1937 and was one of the first to arrange multiple-subject broadcasts outside America, covering European culture, education and news. At the beginning of his journalistic mission, he operated a one-man show to record debates, strategic interviews with international figures, concerts, and even dog shows. But as Hitler marched across the continent, Murrow added other journalists to his CBS news programme such as veteran correspondent William Shirer, based in Berlin, and Ellen Wilkinson, a British Labour MP,[4] along with others in Paris and Rome. Together they became established as important reporters capturing history in a round-up of events. The last report always came from CBS in Washington.

It was a major success; radio not only revealed information as it occurred but also relayed news from afar with speed and immediacy. The sound of London being bombed by German air raids was widely covered bringing reality to American ears. This was not fictional drama. Now they heard overhead aircraft, wailing sirens in the described darkness, exploding bombs, buildings crashing, shouts and screams and cries for help. No other news media portrayed the grim truth of brutal attack in such a powerful way.

The regular reports became a national listening habit. With each broadcast Murrow gained American trust while signalling with increasing severity that 'England couldn't go it alone; America would have to join the fight'. Hundreds wrote letters indicating their opinion had moved from neutral support for Britain to positive. A 1940 Gallup Poll indicated that 39 per cent favoured more US aid. After Murrow's reports, this increased to 54 per cent. Ed Murrow became the best-known

AMERICA INCHES FORWARD

American in London; many thought he had more influence on America's reaction to foreign news than anyone.

Murrow was also a useful conduit for Roosevelt to Winston Churchill, as he and his trusted aide Harry Hopkins, a former social worker from Iowa, worked hard to intimately understand the predilections of the British leader, his family, people in the British government and those on the periphery of parliamentary officialdom.

On 29 December 1940, the re-elected President addressed America in one of his usual fireside broadcasts. He began, 'This is not a talk about war, but a talk about national security. If Great Britain goes down, the Axis powers will be in a position to bring enormous military and naval resources against this hemisphere. We are the Arsenal of Democracy. Our national policy is to keep war away from this country.'

The President believed, the best way to avoid direct war with Germany, was to send military aid to Europe to keep the enemy at bay. America would expand and implement a new way of providing military hardware and shipping to Britain without monetary payment. Roosevelt then persuaded that repayment for this costly service would instead take the form of defending the US in a Lend-Lease programme. This seriously stretched the notion of a 'neutral' America, but the people and Congress were beginning to agree. Known as his Arsenal of Democracy Speech, Churchill was relieved by Roosevelt's broadcast.

Meanwhile, Harry Hopkins championed the Lend Lease scheme he created after the First World War and was ready with a similar plan. During the first three months of 1941 American, British and Canadian military staff held secret talks in Washington. Their brief was to agree a basic outline for military co-ordination, should America enter the war. Their help was crucial. Hopkins' scheme became formal on 11 March 1941, in 'An Act to Promote the Defense of the United States'. This supplied Free France, Britain and the Republic of China with food, oil and matériel. In a subsequent period (until August 1945) they also supplied provisions to the USSR and other Allied nations, including warships, warplanes and weaponry. The aid was free, though some hardware such as ships, had to be returned after the war. In exchange America leased land for US bases in Allied territory: 'Destroyers for bases.' The programme effectively ended the United States' position of neutrality and was a decisive step away from non-interventionist policy.

As well as Hopkins and Murrow, help also came from other American officials in London. The new Ambassador to Britain, Gil Winant – who replaced Joseph Kennedy – and Averell Harriman, directed Lend Lease in London. Each official had a stepping-stone directly to allied war leaders, particularly Churchill, and felt comfortable in bombed-out London. They used their connections to broadcast the plight of European people and consistently helped the President convince Americans their country should participate in the war. Europe needed America, but America needed peace in Europe. German U-boat attacks on Allied merchant ships and supplies were taking their toll.

* * *

Liberty Ships were built to replenish destroyed merchant vessels and in 1940 Britain ordered sixty more Ocean class steamers from American shipbuilders. The British design, originating from the First World War, was basic with just one coal-fired reciprocating steam engine replicating 2,500 horsepower. Coal-fired steam engines were old-school but reliable, and Britain had large supplies of coal, to which America would later add. The US Maritime Commission adjusted the initial design to accelerate production and reduce costs – welding seams instead of riveting was less expensive. A system of mass-producing prefabricated components was developed at various factories which were then transported to shipyards for assembly within record time.

Women helped build them and fourteen ships were launched to great acclaim. They were a good omen for Europe at a time when liberty from Nazi oppression was deeply needed. Each merchant ship had five cargo holds for 10,200 tons, deck houses amidships and aft, and carried around forty sailors. For defence, an aft machine gun was mounted and anti-aircraft defences were added later. To meet production demands new yards were built on the east and west coasts of America, and the Gulf of Mexico. Construction took place in Alabama, California, Florida, Georgia, Louisiana, Maine, Maryland, North Carolina, Rhode Island, Texas and Washington DC. Some states had two or three shipyards.[5] Britain's sixty ships were just the tip of the iceberg as the US commission ordered 260 vessels, a procurement that later doubled under the Lend Lease scheme.

* * *

AMERICA INCHES FORWARD

Meanwhile, at Scapa Flow, Orkney in Scotland, on 6 February 1941, an important group of North American personnel had arrived for their first official journey to the British Isles. In September 1940 General George Veazey Strong, labelled a 'senior American observer in London', had approached his British counterparts to see if they would be open to discuss cryptanalysis problems. One imagines their answer at first was 'no', but certain supporters demonstrated this could be a good idea if something valuable was put on the table in exchange for 'full information on German, Italian and Japanese codes and cryptographic information' and 'to make a continuous exchange of important intercepts'. The American Navy was reluctant to share for fear of British attacks on American systems. However, American Army intelligence (under William Friedman) was far less proficient in German and Italian cipher systems and regarded this exchange as 'absolutely essential to their National Defense'.[6] The exchange visit went ahead a few months later. The weather was terrible when HMS *King George V* anchored in a snowstorm that afternoon, and its guests were swiftly transferred with their luggage and special crates, to a cruiser destined for the Thames estuary in London. They sailed by the east coast of Scotland and England, where they witnessed the reality of war. Multiple sunken vessels lay damaged and abandoned in the shallow waters of the North Sea, their funnels and masts still visible. En route they experienced an assault by a German bomber, but the attacker missed his target. One could say they had a difficult journey as the visitors, under veils of strict confidentiality, came to exchange secret techniques and information with the British government. They were met at the London dockside by Deputy Commander Edward Travis and Colonel John Tiltman, Foreign Office officials, who took charge of their luggage and crates which contained a strange machine and highly classified papers.

The men were Abraham Sinkov and Leo Rosen both from US Army's Signals Intelligence Service (SIS), and two navy officers, Lieutenant Prescott Currier and Lieutenant Robert Weeks. The group was swiftly transferred to a dimly lit mansion in the countryside, north of London. They were met by a commander and his staff and, over a glass or two of warming sherry – a quaint, but typically British thing for American whiskey drinkers to experience – they settled in. They had come to learn about Britain's intelligence operation to bolster American intelligence departments. They also brought a valuable gift. An analogue cipher machine where, in return, Britain provided knowledge on the Enigma cipher machine and plans for a faster codebreaking machine. It was the start of a renewed trust between Britain and America.

Meanwhile, the Luftwaffe continued to bomb Britain, and despite warning signs, Hitler's Panzer Divisions hurtled into Russia in June, contrary to the promise of non-aggression made to Stalin two years before. The Russian Commissar for Foreign Affairs, Vyacheslav Molotov, told the Russian people in a radio broadcast, that the action was 'an unheard-of attack on his country… without example in the history of civilised nations'. Stalin set up a Committee of Defence to run the Russian war effort during the next month of July, and retaliated by bombing Finland, East Prussia and the Danube oil ports.

* * *

The next month Roosevelt set off on a secret rendezvous, code named RIVIERA, in Newfoundland, the future tenth province of Canada. On 8 August, shrouded in early morning mists, the British battleship HMS *Prince of Wales* sailed into the seaport of Argentia, a US navy base in Placentia Bay. On board was Winston Churchill. The British Prime Minister had left Scapa Flow four days earlier to speedily cross the Atlantic, escorted by destroyer convoys to ensure the group's safe arrival. His entourage included the First Sea Lord Admiral of the Fleet Dudley Pound; Chief of the Imperial General Staff Field Marshal Sir John Dill; Vice Chief of Air Staff Air Marshal Sir Wilfred Rhodes Freeman, the Permanent Under-Secretary of State at the Foreign Office Sir Alexander Cadogan, Churchill's scientific advisor Lord Cherwell, journalist and travel writer Henry Vollam Morton, novelist Howard Spring and Harry Hopkins, President Roosevelt's closest advisor.

The secret Atlantic Conference had been passed off as a ten-day fishing trip for Roosevelt. Without delay, Churchill transferred to the USS *Augusta* for talks on enemy matters with the President, and during the period 8 – 11 August, American and British ideals for war were aligned on international trade, with agreed proposals for a conference on Soviet aid to bring Russia back in the Allied loop. The joint declaration of the Atlantic Charter was issued on 14 August and by 29 September 1941, an aid conference was planned between Lord Beaverbrook, Churchill's Minister of Supply, Stalin, Avril Harriman and Vyacheslav Molotov. The first Moscow conference was code named CAVIAR.

AMERICA INCHES FORWARD

The Atlantic Conference aboard HMS *Prince of Wales*, 12 August 1941: Franklin Roosevelt and Winston Churchill flanked (L-R) by Harry Hopkins, Averell Harriman, Admiral King, General Marshall, General Dill, Admiral Stark and Admiral Pound. (United States Navy)

Chapter 5

A Junior in College

Janice Martin only knew what she read in the newspapers about the war, but behind the scenes deeper trouble was brewing. At almost 19 she was having fun. She would support a war in Europe, but it was not at the forefront of her mind while college life was exhilarating. 'I loved to dance. I learned in ninth grade and danced all the way through high school and Goucher. Johns Hopkins University was about six blocks from our house in Baltimore in the other direction, so I lived right in the middle of both colleges. There were many dances with big bands, including Tommy Dorsey and a number of other stars.'

Janice didn't have a special boyfriend, but she admitted, 'when I got into college, I did meet some Hopkins boys, and there were some who invited me to their prom…, if I was around.'

She could never have imagined that her life would be so different a year later, and that her day-to-day tasks would be connected to tracking military submarines in important world history, after an extraordinary turn of events in the halls of Goucher College.

* * *

All of England was elated at the arrival of John Gilbert Winant the new American Ambassador. He arrived on 1 March 1941 and was met by King George VI at the railway station close to Windsor Castle. 'I am glad to welcome you here,' said the King. 'There's no place I'd rather be at this time, than in England,' replied Winant for the press. It was an obvious reference to Joseph Kennedy's gloomy departure.[1]

Ambassador Winant was keen to separate himself from the defeatist views of his predecessor, but his mission was tough. His goal was to maintain a considerate level of discussion with the British government while explaining to his host country that America wanted to help but

A JUNIOR IN COLLEGE

President Roosevelt signs the 'Lend Lease' bill formally entitled *An Act to Promote the Defense of the United States*. (Public Domain via Associated Press)

would not fight – a dilemma, when so many had lost homes and family to Luftwaffe bombs in Hitler's plan to conquer Britain.

Further diplomatic efforts followed when Averell Harriman, Special Envoy to Europe, started to oversee the flow of American aid under Lend Lease and, with Winant and Harry Hopkins, offered the spirit of American friendliness and support. However, the parameters of Lend Lease were insufficient for Churchill. Britain needed urgent help with defence: weaponry, ammunition, and troops. This he eventually obtained, but if it hadn't been for Roosevelt's representatives, the Allied push and presence of Generals Patton and Eisenhower in Europe leading to D-Day's victory might not have happened as it did.

* * *

Janice's newspapers in July 1941 did not report that American troops had landed in Iceland to repel a German invasion. The year before the country was occupied by Britain to prevent German harassment of vital British and US shipping. Roosevelt had extended the Pan-American Security Zone in April, to just 50 miles short of Iceland and, from subsequent intelligence reports, decided in June to thwart a Nazi attack by quickly installing 4,000 marines. Britain welcomed the move, which released 20,000 of their men from the British garrison and aided Allied convoys.[2] At the same time the group of North American intelligence professionals gathered to improve their codebreaking operations, using as a model Bletchley Park's covert operation. Utilising key British personnel's advice and guidelines from their February visit, a recruitment plan was drawn up to employ suitable Americans for another massive intelligence factory.

The US military officials mulled over the needs of such an 'industry', realising that training and shortcuts were vital to speedily build on British success – or learn from its failures. Some foreign language ability, history and science were important, as was meteorology. The weather, it was explained, had a huge impact as many intercepted messages originated from weather ships and aircraft. Day to day forecasts, were central in collecting intelligence via signals, as well as for planning attacks. Germany craved this information for their air attacks on Britain's defences to pave the way for a full invasion, and beyond to America. But they were disadvantaged as weather moves from west to east – a huge obstacle.

For most land-locked Germans to understand the science of meteorology they had to penetrate the might of the North Atlantic, an area dominated by British navy ships for centuries. They had begun their weather reconnaissance over the airwaves with three planes in 1940. Over time their capacity grew to a full squadron, but repeat observations were limited when they could not fly the longer distances from ground-based weather stations and a few sea-based weather vessels. Air pressure reports from 5,000 feet – temperature, humidity and wind at sea level 300 miles away – could not replace the twice daily reports of various heights, water temperatures and sea conditions in good or bad weather from places farther than German airplanes could achieve. The inefficiencies of aircrews and their imprecise estimates of light surface winds – often tested by firing a burst of ammunition from a forward machine gun to see which way the spray drifted – did not help.

Germany then reverted to a relay of ships for weather observation. This strategy also included submarines, much to their commanders' objections, who insisted U-boats should not be endangered by the secondary mission of weather reporting: 'the task of buoys and fishing trawlers', and 'U-boats were for sinking enemy ships'. But they were overruled and U-boats were ordered to transmit regular weather reports. However, the system lacked regular reporting from a single location and so a move to requisition German fishing vessels went ahead to provide Germany with information for raids on British shipping. Once seized, the fishing vessels were kitted out with the necessary accommodations and provisions for extra men and radios, a 150-watt transmitter and a 40-watt portable transmitter, two portable receivers, one panoramic and one broadcast receiver. German naval high command declared that weather ships were non-combatant, therefore not warships. They retained existing civilian sailors and fisherman but added navy (*Kriegsmarine*) radiomen and a machine gun for protection. They were also equipped with cipher systems to report their observations.

One cipher was the *Wetterkurzschüssel*, or Short Weather Cipher, a 21-page pink booklet consisting of tables, where each reported weather observation was translated into a corresponding letter. The pink book was made of absorbent paper with water-soluble ink for fast destruction if needed. But Germany knew the meteorological cryptanalysts in Britain would quickly determine the valuable information and took a further encryption step using an Enigma cipher for additional security.

Kriegsmarine weather vessels in the Atlantic, including requisitioned fishing trawlers, were secretly issued with manuals and monthly cipher keys to set their Enigma machines.[3] This was known as the Home Waters Cipher. During May 1941, the *München,* received orders to relieve another vessel north east of Iceland. They were to patrol 54 square miles of freezing ocean on the *Kriegsmarine* grid, square AE39. The crew consisted of fishermen and a few hurriedly trained meteorologists from the German navy. As their assignment straddled two months, they not only had cipher keys for May but also June.

Harry Hinsley's team at Bletchley Park assumed this might be so and suggested the vessel be captured. Previous captures had yielded rotors and secret papers that assisted in breaking Enigma intercepts, but more were needed. With approval from the Admiralty at London's Operational Intelligence Centre (OIC), a plan was hatched with a Captain Haines, for the British Home Fleet of Vice Admiral Holland to lead three cruisers and four destroyers to grid square AE39.

THE SECRET LIFE OF AN AMERICAN CODEBREAKER

A young weatherman, on the *München,* from Wilhelmshaven, was in the middle of transmitting a report in his radio shack, when his crew spotted the advancing convoy. Hurriedly, he collected secret papers and instruments, as they tried to run. Aided by an officer, he stuffed everything into a lead-based canvas bag and together they threw it overboard. The trawler made no attempt to scuttle, partly as its seacocks were blocked with cement that had been used as ballast instead of sand. The British had no resistance from the *München's* crew but found little in the way of papers. But then a second boarding party from the cruiser *Edinburgh* arrived with Captain Haines. He knew what he was looking for and where to find it, and it wasn't in the radio shack. Instead, he disappeared into the depths of the ship to the officers' quarters and emerged clutching a duplicate sheaf of nondescript papers.

Haines was swiftly transferred to the destroyer *Nestor* and immediately ordered to Scapa Flow. Three days later, he arrived at Bletchley Park with the Short Weather Cipher and Enigma settings for the Home Waters key. Holland had called them 'rather undistinguished documents', but they bore with them the seeds of power,[4] and became perfect up-to-date materials for new recruits to codebreaking.

* * *

Now ordered to send weather reports by German Navy high command, U-boats transmitted their observations across the airwaves. These were picked up by random shore-based German radio stations where the cryptogram was immediately acknowledged and the Enigma encipherment removed. The Short Weather cipher message was then forwarded to German central meteorology where the data was decoded using the pink book to return to the plain text of the original meteorological readings.

Germany believed their method of encryption unbreakable, as the Enigma machine had enciphering possibilities of 3×10^{114}.[5] They never reached that theoretical level of security, but neither did they consider the cryptanalytic abilities of their adversaries. Along with random German stations the British also listened. Interception, decipherment and cryptanalysis had been part of their intelligence process for some time, and now with the pinch of 'bland but valuable' up-to-date documents from the *München*, they could swiftly decode to find the intelligence they needed. The intercepts were sent to Bletchley Park for registration and analysis, and the bulk of messages provided many clues, keys and identifiers to other messages. This was achieved initially by reading regular header information dubbed 'cribs', or sometimes operator sign off signals, 'kisses'. With this basic knowledge, further codes were broken, and messages read to produce a massive collection of useful leads.

One civilian cryptanalyst from the Air Ministry, Percival Archer (known as Philip), was so prolific with cribs in Bletchley's Huts 10 and 8, that in true Bletchley nomenclature his successes became known as 'Archeries'. With so many Enigma cribs the analysts could work backwards using obvious short messages – standard weather reports and terminology – to find the likely key settings. When the messages were read the information was reported to the Submarine Tracking Room at the OIC, where locations of weather ships and submarines in the Atlantic were tracked on a pin and flag chart system.

There watchkeepers moved markers on nautical charts following intercepted U-boat and weather ship reports. The charts included the most valuable vessels of all – Allied convoys traversing the Atlantic. Each coloured flag or pin indicated a vessel's movements and its possible outcomes and were moved around according to instructions by women in uniform. Eight or nine vessels or convoys could be crossing the ocean in each direction at any one time. Protection of Allied cargoes was paramount for, as well as supplies, convoys often carried troops. The Submarine Tracking Room aimed to be ahead of the German U-boats called 'wolfpacks', as their patrols of stretched-out U-boats hunted Allied convoys en-masse.

* * *

Janice read about the 'Joint declaration by the President and the Prime Minister' where clarity was established between Roosevelt and Churchill when America announced support for Britain in the war. The 1941 Atlantic Charter 'turning point' and policy statement defined the goals of both countries and presented unity in respect of mutual principles, hopes for a post-war world, and agreed policies after the defeat of Germany. OIC London would also provide guidance on proposed routes for future convoys. America was still not 'in the war' as they maintained an 'armed neutrality' but provided cargo and convoy escorts with limited military protection to Britain and its allies crossing the Atlantic. Enemy reports of U-boats started to be sent to the Navy department in Washington regularly from the OIC. Coastal listeners had originally intercepted their weather reports and codebreakers at Bletchley Park had decoded and provided the intelligence.

German submarine positions in the north Atlantic, came from sightings, torpedo engagements, direction finding and – though not explicit – the U-boat's own messages indicating their position. In October 1941, an allied convoy of 54 ships, HX155, was to sail across the treacherous Atlantic from Halifax, Nova Scotia, to Liverpool following a route recommended by the Admiralty. The US Navy concurred a few hours later, observing a series of latitude and longitude points, identified by a letter, which would guide the convoy to a mid-ocean meeting point (known as MOMP). There the US escorts would transfer their responsibility of protection to a British convoy (and vice versa for westbound routes). The time was given in Z time or GMT, pinpointed by the letter P.

On Thursday, 16 October, the convoy risked leaving Halifax and sailed at 8.8 knots. Clear of the coastline they assumed sailing positions in eleven columns, of four, five or six vessels each. The *City of Bath* carried copper and general cargo, the *Coulberg* held sugar, the *Margarita Chandris*, grain. The *British Chemist* conveyed oil and was one of many combustible fuel ships in the convoy. Early on Saturday morning the designated American Task Unit 4.1.7. of five destroyers left Argentia to join them. At 9.30 in a calm swell, under pleasant weather of high cloud and gentle winds, the unit joined the merchant sea vessels as they entered the Atlantic, to follow the route agreed between OIC and OP Nav (the operations division of the US Navy): D 47-00 north 51-00 west, E 54-00 38-00, F 58-50 30-00; 1000Z/25 October; P 58-50 22-40; Q 58-50 20-00, R 59-50 07-00.

Close to midnight the convoy turned north following a north-easterly course to pass through point D. Meanwhile, in London's OIC Submarine Tracking Room Captain Charles Rodger Noel Winn read the teletype reports of enemy U-boat intercepts. Some gave submarine locations, and direction-finding also provided bearings. Peter Kemp, head of department, plotted these on his own chart and between the two emerged a U-boat course. On the 16th, seven were in the east central

A JUNIOR IN COLLEGE

North Atlantic, and four appeared to form a thin straggly line from the tip of Greenland's Cape Farewell. The next day this number expanded to eight or nine submarines, north and west. A few days before convoy SC48 had been torpedoed in the area, and escort ship USS *Kearney* was hit, therefore, their information was plausible. Eleven men had lost their lives and twenty-two were injured. The incident was a huge worry for escorts and almost saw America declaring war on Germany. Codebreakers felt they were failures.

Winn and his team carefully rerouted the convoy. With understandable jitters, sightings of searchlights and reported gunfire, they proved to be false alarms for Convoy HX155 as it continued northeast. His report presumed submarines pursuant of SC48 southeast of Greenland, would take up new positions and the OIC recommended the convoy change its route through two new points and not point E: H 50° 00' north 46° 30' west, and J 57° 30' north 40° 00' west. The shift would put the convoy 165 miles to the west of Point E, but away from the dangerous U-boat concentration. However, HX155 did not make the diversion until noon on Monday, 20 October. Instead, the timing of the change took them closer to four U-boats southeast of Cape Farewell, but their distance apart averaged 75 miles which seemed less of a threat to the mass of other U-boats that Submarine Tracking aimed to avoid.

That Monday, they reported, '5 or 6 submarines between latitude 55/57 N west of longitude 15 W, moving west', and, probably referring to the line of four, reported: 'Subs in Northern Atlantic appear to be proceeding west'. The data also indicated a U-boat at 55° north 42° west – right in line with the convoy's new route. A message was rapidly transmitted:

> *'HX155 to increase clearance from suspected U-boat area recommend change route from H to 56-00 north 42-30 west then to J'.*

The line of march was now even further west. At 8.8 knots on Tuesday, under cloudy skies and with a moderate gale pushing from starboard, the convoy swung due north.

On Wednesday morning the U-boat report declared ten enemy submarines west of the east central North Atlantic, the area where so many ships of SC48 were sunk. Now HX155 turned east once more for its British destination. The US Navy radioed Task Unit 4.1.7. recommending they proceed at 'utmost speed for the next 48 hours'. Raised to 10 knots the convoy turned northeast to pass above the sub-infested area.

Over the next two days the convoy made several turns to starboard, but the period was uneventful. By Friday they were steaming due east. On Saturday, a few hours after fog had lifted, they finally reached the mid-point meeting place, south of Iceland – MOMP. The American escort returned home, and British escorts took over protection responsibility. Eight days later, on 3 November, OIC messaged 'HX155 met as arranged. All ships now arrived. No stragglers.' The crews and cargoes of sugar, oil and grain had arrived safely.[6]

Chapter 6

War USA

After the Atlantic Charter, British and Soviet troops marched into Iran to dislodge the Nazi German Fifth Columnists and halted an attempted coup by the Axis powers. Toward the end of August, Gurkha troops aided in crossing the Iraqi border, while British Indian troops seized seven Axis merchant vessels and airborne troops dropped in on oil fields to protect Britons and prevent sabotage. Most Iranians looked on with 'benevolent interest', while in the north Russia carved a convenient route from the Caspian Sea to the Turkish frontier, capturing Tabriz and securing the supply of war matériel to Russia. A month later 21-year-old Mohammad Reza Pahlevi, swore the Oath of Office before parliament while British and Soviet troops occupied and protected the fringes of Tehran. As a 'completely constitutional monarch', the new Shah of Iran promised a fair government, unlike his unpopular bullying father who was forced to abdicate.[1]

* * *

On 25 November 1941 Averell Harriman indicated that US involvement was real. The U-boat war was escalating and had seriously involved America's military when a German torpedo sunk the first American warship in the north Atlantic. The destroyer was one of three that disobeyed orders in taking a proactive stance, violating US neutrality laws. USS *Reuben James* was employed as one of twenty-four from the US Navy for convoy duties between Halifax and Iceland,[2] but in the cold morning mists off the coast of Iceland the *Reuben James* exploded. Reports said the ship set out to hunt submarines using precise map co-ordinates provided by intelligence, only to become the exact target for *U-552*. Kapitänleutnant Erich Topp commanded this U-boat, one of several German VIIC submerged workhorses that terrorised the seas. It held the moniker 'Red Devil Boat'. A *U-552* torpedo struck the port side of the American destroyer and penetrated its forward stash of ammunition. The resulting eye-burning explosion on 31 October cut the ship in half killing 115 of the 160 crew. Whether Topp deliberately fired, or the destroyer sailed into the path of a torpedo, has never been proved.

* * *

American intelligence sources were wary of fomenting conflict with the Japanese, but weaknesses and leaks in their personnel and systems were damaging. A massive leak had compromised the State Department when Tyler Kent, a dashing young man whose father had connections in the State Department, worked at the American Embassy in London. He was a cipher clerk with diplomatic immunity, but his loyalty to America was hampered by his friendship with White Russians and his twisted view that impending troubles for his country were generated by a Jewish conspiracy pushing America into an unwanted war. Thinking he was protecting his country, he passed secret and sensitive documents to a disbanded British anti-war group called *The Right Club*.

This was one of many small anti-Semitic associations opposed to war. One of its members was William Joyce who later defected to become a Nazi propaganda broadcaster in Germany and was notorious in Britain as Lord Haw-Haw (he was hanged for treason in January 1946). The group was identified by British counter-intelligence and kept under surveillance. Using undercover agents, MI5 infiltrated their meetings which led to the arrest of White Russian Anna Wolkoff and Kent in May 1940. They were tried for espionage, after trying to pass documents to the German Abwehr via the Italian embassy. Kent's rooms were searched and over 1,500 American embassy papers and telegrams were found, together with duplicates of keys to certain parts of the embassy. He was convicted and sentenced to seven years in prison under the British Official Secrets Act. When asked why he betrayed America, Kent explained that giving the documents to Germany would have helped keep America out of the war.

Reading about the fiasco in the newspapers, Janice would never have considered this as part of her future.

The case compromised the confidential communications systems of America and brought into question the security of secret ciphers. 'Because of Kent's treachery all diplomatic communications of the US diplomatic service were blacked-out at a crucial time,' namely during the days leading up to Dunkirk. The shutdown affected all American embassies and missions throughout the world and lasted two to six weeks, until multiple special couriers delivered new codes from Washington.[3]

Meanwhile, lack of efficient American cryptography led to weaknesses in the State Department when it came to negotiations with moderates in Japan. The main codes used by the US Embassy then were GRAY, BROWN, A-1, B-1, C-1, D-1, and M-138 as its most secret method, but Ambassador Joseph C. Grew might have helped Japanese interceptors when he wrote:

> *'One of the high officials of the Japanese Government wanted to send a secret message to our Government which they did not want the Japanese military to see, and in passing this on they asked me to please put it in our most secret code. I said of course I would do so.'*

However, Japan failed to penetrate M-138.[4]

This laissez-faire attitude to code security was not addressed. Grew's 1 August 1941 diary note indicated that Japanese premier, Prince Konoye, knew Grew wanted to speak with him often, just as FDR did with Admiral Nomura, but Grew's 'fear of leakages and publicity prevented such interviews'. It was known within the US embassy that official communications with Washington, would soon be known by Japanese authorities through the less secure codes. Grew noted that Japanese spies understood the US embassy had 'one confidential code', M-138. But the President did not bother with a safer code either, for certain messages. In a dispatch appealing for peace to the Emperor of Japan, he sent a handwritten note on White House stationery to Secretary of State Cordell Hull: *'Dear Cordell, Shoot this to Grew – think can go in gray code – saves time – I don't mind if it gets picked up'*. These dispatches on 6 December 1941 were crucial. Grew afterwards thought that if a tighter code had been used the message may well have reached the Emperor of Japan earlier. Instead, it is said, the Emperor did not receive the message until ten hours *after* it was received in the Tokyo Communications Ministry. Grew thought the GRAY code had not saved time but cost time and lives, because Japanese militants had intercepted the message, solved its contents and deliberately delayed it to hinder any peace effort. The real reason, however, was not the code or the militants, but a full embargo placed on all Japanese military incoming diplomatic messages.[5]

* * *

Janice and the rest of the United States woke to shocking news on 7 December 1941, when American planners were caught completely off guard by the searing attack of the Japanese Navy Air Service on the US Pacific Fleet at Pearl Harbor. Tipping the balance, now America really was at war. The population listened incredulously to the news that the US base in Hawaii had been decimated. NBC's reporter H.V. Kaltenborn delivered the startling news that Sunday, via CBS. The attack was at 7.48 am Pacific Time (18.18 GMT), six hours behind Washington.

> 'Japan has made war on the United States without declaring it. Airplanes presumably from aircraft carriers have attacked the great Pearl Harbor naval base, on the Island of Oahu in the Hawaiian Islands, and have attacked Manilla, capital of the Philippines. There has been damage; some fires were started; about fifty planes participated in the attack on the Hawaiian Islands, many, according to a bulletin that has just come in, were shot down. This attack occurred at the very moment when Ambassador Nomura and Special Envoy Kurusu were at the State Department discussing the possibility of peace between Japan and the United States. We know that Japan set a precedent for this kind of attack in the Russo-Japanese war, when she attacked the Japanese… (corrected)… Russian fleet without a declaration of war while that fleet was not expecting attack. However, the United States was not unprepared for attack. Anti-aircraft guns went immediately into action and were responsible for bringing down many of the Japanese planes.'[6]

They were unprepared for the attack as it was Sunday and all retaliatory ammunition was under lock and key as required in the rules for inspection. Three thousand naval servicemen died. America and Britain declared war on Japan immediately.

WAR USA

Four days later, Germany declared war on the United States citing the country as a belligerent against Japan. As the Allies struggled to keep Hitler at bay, a European War had become a World War. The Allies had been ambivalent to the threat of Japanese invasion in the Pacific and Far East, but with the attack on American soil, attention moved to the new conflict. More manpower, fighting ships and weaponry were needed, not just on one front – but two. Some say that after Pearl Harbor, Churchill's first thought on hearing the US declaration was: 'We've won the war!'

* * *

Discussions between Allied leaders covered war policies over twelve strategic conferences, including refining the Atlantic Charter and the strategy of Europe First, which culminated in a United Nations Declaration. On 25 December Hong Kong fell to the Japanese after a seven-day battle, when more than 6,000 defenders were forced to surrender unconditionally. The next day Churchill addressed US Congress. He received wild cheers after a rousing speech, raising American opinion to a new level of enthusiasm to support Britain's war. Churchill and Roosevelt seemed to have everyone on their side.

On 29 December the text of the declaration was drafted by Churchill, Roosevelt and Harry Hopkins, and on New Year's Day, 1942, twenty-six countries gathered in Washington to affirm their opposition to the Axis Powers of Germany, Italy and Japan. The first four major participants to sign were America, Britain, USSR and China. Representatives of a further twenty-two countries signed the next day, including Australia, Belgium, Canada, Czechoslovakia, El Salvador, Greece, India, Netherlands and New Zealand.

> *'In days to come the British and American peoples will, for their own safety and for the good of all, walk together in majesty, in justice and in peace.'*
> – December 1941, Winston Churchill.[7]

Chapter 7

Chosen

Divisions, however, between British and American military chiefs surfaced almost immediately. America was not prepared for war and questions were asked about what they knew about waging war. Winston Churchill advocated for a unified command, while a Washington-based committee wanted to plan strategy. British top brass was aghast.

Field Marshal John Greer Dill had served in South Africa in the second Boer War and France in the First World War. Highly decorated and a gifted army instructor, his reputation led him to army staff colleges including India. By the early 1930s he was Director of Military Operations and Intelligence at the War Office in London, and produced a controversial memorandum advocating the use of chemical warfare against a German landing. Realizing this first use of a chemical weapon would alienate America and encourage Hitler to retaliate, he justified his suggestion saying, 'that at a time when our National existence is at stake…we should not hesitate to adopt whatever means appear to offer the best chance of success'. Under criticism from most government offices, he withdrew his suggestion, but the idea was largely supported by Churchill, and the RAF prepared to deploy a mustard gas. However, they knew Cabinet approval was needed.

Dill gained a reputation as an unimaginative obstructionist, but despite his opinions, by the end of 1941 he was posted to Washington as Churchill's personal representative to the British Joint Staff Mission, where he was seen to have 'great flair for diplomatic military presence'. He became friends with army General George C. Marshall and Roosevelt said, 'he was the most important figure in the remarkable accord which has been developed in the combined operations of our two countries'[1]. Ultimately the Combined Chiefs of Staff (CCS) set all major policy decisions, subject to approval by Churchill and Roosevelt.

It was clear to Dill that America was unprepared: 'I have never seen so many motor cars, but I have not seen a military vehicle,' he wrote to Alan Brooke, his successor as the chief of Imperial General Staff in London. 'And yet amid all this unpreparedness, the ordinary American firmly believes that they can finish off the war quite quickly – and without too much disturbance.... This country has not – repeat not – the slightest conception of what the war means, and their armed forces are more unready for war than it is possible to imagine.'

Dill would also have been shocked on 8 December 1941, if he'd been in DC the day after the Pearl Harbor attack, when US Military officers were ordered to report to work at the Army and Navy Munitions building in full uniform. The picture was a complete rag bag of ill-fitting or incomplete regalia, mostly from the First World War.[2]

* * *

America's intelligence community was under question. The department's whole being – cryptanalysis and its value – was in doubt. Military commanders protested that even when intelligence did work the process was slow for use in any battle. In 1919 Will Rogers had said, 'the United States never lost a war, nor won a peace,' but according to David Kahn, they may well have assisted in losing the peace in December 1941.[3]

The US War Department had been headquartered on 17th Street NW, Washington, since 1888 in the State-War-Navy Building, next to the White House. However, their intelligence department was squeezed out in 1918 by the Department of State, to the Munitions Building – an insect-ridden temporary construction on B Street (now Constitution Avenue and Constitution Gardens). A small number of cryptanalysts were employed in these Main Navy and Munitions offices, but after Pearl Harbor some were stumped as to how to revive faith in American intelligence. However, the small group of US military representatives who visited Britain's growing intelligence factory in February 1941 had already seen a way through. Code-making and codebreaking of US intelligence was about to undergo a huge make-over, especially as Britain and America could now join forces in almost every aspect of defence.

Against the military backdrop of Dill, BJSM and CCS, America increased recruitment for its intelligence sections for the armed forces. Inexperienced, but handsome young male officers, not yet destined for Europe or the Far East, stood in hotel lobbies or on station platforms finding young women for war work. They were not privy to the tasks the women would fulfil, but their rate of recruitment was impressive. Janice couldn't help but notice them and the striking posters of smart uniformed women that blazoned, *'For your Country's Sake Today; For your Own Sake Tomorrow – Go to the nearest recruiting station of the armed service of your choice.'* Men knew their responsibility was physically fighting for their country, and there was a system for this, but women too? What would she do? She was a student.

Surprised, mostly female, college professors started receiving confidential letters from the US Army and Navy. 'Cryptanalysis' was something few knew of, but they in turn would introduce hand-picked students for Essential Work of Major Importance. The letters were sent to colleges as early as November 1941, seeking educated, trustworthy women for intelligence work. The plan was to follow the 'Most Secret' example already operational in Britain at Bletchley Park. Candidates met in private to receive an outline of the 'Top Secret' course they would undertake. It was clear from the start the unmarried females should utter nothing to anyone – not their parents, siblings, friends or boyfriends. The US Navy and US Army oversaw their work at the highest level of government confidentiality. If they passed, they would be sent to a government department in Washington – 'something to do with the war'.[4]

* * *

A thousand US troops landed on British soil in Northern Ireland on 26 January 1942 – unprecedented since the First World War. The mission held the highest level of confidentiality that even the band of the Royal Ulster Rifles were unaware. However, theystill managed a rousing welcome and an acceptable rendition of *The Star-Spangled Banner.*' The Secretary of State for Air, Sir Archibald Sinclair, flew in from London:

> *'Your safe arrival here marks a new stage in the world war. It is a gloomy portent for Mr. Hitler, nor will its significance be lost on General Tojo, the Prime Minster of Japan.'*[5]

The capitulation three weeks later, however, by British troops in Singapore to the Imperial Japanese Army on 15 February 1942, shocked everyone. Newspapers gave incomplete reports of a negotiated truce and indicated Japanese forces had taken thousands of soldiers as prisoners of war. All their families heard were ranting reports of surrender to Japan. Churchill said the Fall of Singapore was the 'worst disaster' and 'largest capitulation in British military history'. The devastating military surrender was a national controversy. The Fortress of Singapore, a British naval-base stronghold for many years, was thought to be impregnable. Many months, and years, passed before the full story was revealed.

The Pacific War escalated, with fierce battles as Japanese armies advanced through the islands. America bombed Tokyo in April 1942 and the following month American and Japanese navy vessels fought, using air combat weapons over the Coral Sea. The fight demonstrated that naval battles could be won at sea using aircraft carriers, where the opposing vessels never saw each other. Both sides claimed victory, but the Japanese were prevented from landing on the Solomon Islands and New Guinea. The battle of Midway Atoll took place in June, a turning point, which historians called 'the most stunning and decisive blow in the history of naval warfare'.[6] The victory for America was made possible through intelligence collection and analysis at Hypo, the US Naval station in Hawaii. But there was still the war in Europe to fight, with the RAF and United States Air Force broadcasting to the German people to expect devastating air raids every night.

Production of ships, weapons, munitions and aircraft increased, and women were encouraged to join men in the military or replace male factory employees. Governments advertised: 'Women, you could hasten victory by working and save your man.' Another slogan bellowed: 'The more women at work, the sooner we win.'

* * *

Winston Churchill made several hazardous trips across the Atlantic, and a second Washington Conference was hastily arranged, when he and Roosevelt met again in June 1942. This meeting was to discuss military strategy rather than a formal conference but at 2am on 23 June, a broadcast announced that Britain and America aimed to apply 'the earliest maximum concentration of Allied war power upon the enemy'. The President's closest adviser, Harry Hopkins, confirmed:

> *'If necessary, second, third and fourth fronts will be opened. America is not training three million troops to play tiddlywinks with Germany. We will pen the German army in a ring of steel.'*

Major General Dwight Eisenhower was given command of all US Forces in Europe, establishing his main headquarters in London, with satellite operations on the outskirts of the capital, closer to the English Channel. One was Southwick House five miles from Portsmouth in Hampshire. The war in the Pacific was holding its own, and now the priority was for Churchill and Roosevelt to open another front in North Africa before a cross-channel invasion. Harriman then accompanied Churchill to a Moscow Conference to explain why the allies were carrying out operations in North Africa instead of opening a promised second front in France. The Anglo-Soviet talks resulted in exchanges of information on technology.

* * *

Janice Martin was still a student in Baltimore, and unaware of older women in education and their students undertaking secret intelligence work in government departments, instead of factories. But it wouldn't be long before she would join them.

Goucher College was a front runner to find educated women for intelligence work, mirroring GC&CS at Bletchley Park. Goucher's dean was Dorothy Stimson. Her older cousin was former Secretary of State, Henry L. Stimson, who was reinstated in 1940, at the age of 73, for a second term to the US War Cabinet as Secretary of War. Curiously for the intelligence world, during his first term he had disbanded the government department of MI-8 (a version of MI-6), citing its inappropriate function for the diplomatic arm because apparently he thought gentlemen should not read each other's mail. Though in a different twist he might have said, 'only gentlemen read other gentlemen's mail'[7]. Some thought Stimson was too old to revisit the task, but he proved everyone wrong with his gusto and energy, often rivalling men twenty years his junior. Dorothy Stimson was well placed to source students of a high calibre.

*　*　*

In the autumn of 1942, Janice was a senior at Goucher, a Latin History Major. One day, as she walked through the hall between two classes, an English professor whom she knew but didn't have classes with, asked her to enter her office. Janice went in and sat down. The professor came in behind her and firmly closed the door. The first thing she said was: *'What I'm going to tell you now is all a secret and you don't tell it to anybody.'*

Dr Winslow wasn't going to have anyone breaking into the conversation and continued to stand steadfastly against the door. She said the US Navy was giving a course in cryptology at seven women's colleges and Goucher was one. She revealed that she would teach the course and asked if Janice would like to take it. 'Of course, I didn't have to tell her that instant. She said it was secret work in communications intelligence in Washington DC.'

Janice went home to persuade her parents this was what she wanted to do, but she could not disclose details. If asked she could say she was studying Communications. Her father had always wanted her to go to

A Senior photo from Janice's 1943 Yearbook at Goucher College. (Janice Benario Archive)

Graduate School, but this was 1942 and by then most professors were recruited to military service.

'One thing about the Second World War was that everybody was in it or wanted to be in it; every man, woman and child wanted to help. And so, they said 'all right' since Washington was just 40 miles from Baltimore.'[8]

Janice agreed to take the course. Ola Winslow, professor of English at Goucher College, had won a Pulitzer Prize the year before, for her biography of Jonathan Edwards, an 18th-century theologian whose texts she edited for Signet Classics. Whether this alone gave her the credentials to teach the cryptology course – she seems to have had no prior knowledge – is uncertain, but Janice felt the power of her popularity was a deciding factor.

'Dr Winslow was a favourite of many students, both those in her class and outside. She was an excellent judge of character, understanding, and a mentor to many.'

Professor Ola Winslow. (Photo by Cecelea Eareckson, Goucher College Special Collections and Archives)

CHOSEN

Janice had known her from when she was a counsellor in Maine at summer camp for a Mrs W. Guth. Ola Winslow's summer home was nearby and, as well as in Baltimore, the professor always welcomed students to her office or apartment. Attending the course, Janice recalled:

'A small group of us met once a week on a Friday at four o'clock in a locked classroom on the top floor of the building. If anybody asked where we were going and why we were hanging around Goucher Hall at four o'clock we had to make up some story or go the other way because you couldn't say you were going up to take a Navy course. I don't remember my story, but people didn't hang around that building at four o'clock on a Friday and I don't remember if there were any problems. However, I probably did have to make up something. We met for ten to fifteen weeks and apparently I passed the cryptology test.'

Chapter 8

A Brief History of American Codebreaking

Janice had entered the world of intrigue. Puzzles, codes, enciphered messages and interceptions, though she didn't know the full extent initially. Several other recruits from Goucher also took the course. Their classes covered the history of codes and ciphers and explained the differences in terminologies. A code is where *each word* is replaced with a different word or symbol, but a cipher is where *each letter* in a message is replaced with a different letter, number or symbol. However, most people use the word 'code' when they actually mean 'cipher.' Generally, it is an accepted error.

Every week number sets – ciphers – were provided and, with strips of paper containing printed letters of the English alphabet, each had to be solved and returned to Dr Winslow. Students were permitted to assist each other in groups of two or three as they tackled their lessons from a workbook learning different ways to approach a secret message, and how to write one. Janice remembered, 'the messages ranged from easy, by letter count, to harder. The book, of course, had to be disguised and could not be left just anywhere.'

The instruction, via Ola Winslow, was conducted by CRE (Chief Radio Engineer) S.B. Berkowich from the US Navy and WAVE Katherine Fowler. US Naval Reserve Officer, Lieutenant Commander Leon P. Smith (a former college professor) was often present to remind them of the programme's strict secrecy requirements. Pressure was applied to bring them through quickly, but Dr Winslow was often no more than a chapter ahead of her students. In a system resembling a correspondence course the tests were taken to Washington for acceptability. The word 'Cryptanalysis' was drummed into them with warnings never to utter this or its theory to anyone.

Other Goucher cryptography students were Frances Steen Suddeth Josephson, Jaqueline B. Jenkins-Nye,[1] Charlotte Anderson Stradford,

A BRIEF HISTORY OF AMERICAN CODEBREAKING

Gwyneth Gminder Wilson, Doris Voyce Hewitt, Irene Hussey Butterbaugh, Marianne Porter Dodge, Helen Kent Longley, Judy Froelicher Keyser, Constance McCready Rush, Joan Richter, Lillian Zimmermann Draper, Frances Flynn Milgroom, Edith Hyde Russell and Emmy Lou Hutchins Russell. Another was Janice's good friend Jane Thornton Apostol. One by one they all passed the code and cipher tests. Lieutenant R.B. Heckman, another former college professor, worked with Leon Smith regarding their placement.[2]

* * *

Enciphering and deciphering secrets is centuries old, especially between warring factions, but Britain and America were not successful at serious analysis of modern ciphers and codes, code making and codebreaking until the First World War. The British Army had solved cryptograms in the Boer War and on India's Northwest Frontier, but the navy didn't engage in detailed 'cryptanalysis' until August 1914.

Early in the First World War, after sunken transatlantic cables were severed in the North Sea, Germany needed another way to communicate and adopted a different method of encoding messages. At the time Sir Alfred Ewing, Director of Naval Education in England and a renowned figure in mechanical sciences, seemed to be the only Admiralty person interested in the idea of cryptology and set out to develop a deciphering machine to read German messages. One day he described his idea to Admiral Henry Oliver. He also spoke of modern enciphering methods. Oliver, new to his Intelligence position, took the opportunity to mention a pile of naval and commercial radio station messages accumulating on his desk that needed attention. Ewing, of course, was interested and Oliver decided to show him later that day, as there was no specific government cryptogram department to deal with their analysis. Ewing confirmed he could identify the German source and suggested their solution and content would be valuable.

They set to work with Ewing honing up on ciphers from the British Museum Library, commercial codes from Lloyds of London and messages from General Post Office files. The task was huge and help with the secret assignment was enlisted from other young naval officers. Small amounts of progress were made to distinguish naval messages from military, as well as reading 'call signs' – names of sources or telegraph offices. A methodical system of sorting and filing the data they gathered was introduced for future analysis.

In October 1914, Ewing and Oliver were lucky to acquire a German codebook from SMS *Magdeburg*. The vessel was part of a German offensive against Russia after it ran aground in the Baltic Sea. During the incident the captain decided to abandon and blow up his vessel using the explosives on board. He also tried to destroy secret documents and his ship's lead-bound books of message code keys by throwing them overboard. As he did, premature detonation of the explosives rocked the boat killing crew members. Damage to the vessel was only partial and the captain survived, but the Russian first officer who boarded found another codebook, hidden in the bows of the boat, which held the secret to Imperial German Navy codes.

Russia, then ally to the British Navy, recognised the value of their discovery and loyally notified them of the recovered cipher and, in a well-organised secure plan, delivered Codebook 151 to the then First Lord of the Admiralty, Winston Churchill. 'It was a gift more precious than a dozen Fabergé eggs: the big, fat, blue-bound *Signalbuch der Kaiserlichen Marine*,' he stated. Later, Russian divers salvaged other codebooks from the seabed thirty feet below but kept them for themselves.

Ewing and the Admiral's fledgling agency welcomed the *Signalbuch*, which provided the German key to five and three letter groups. This proved useful for weather reports and messages to auxiliary vessels, but generally only produced gibberish text. A later break via an Australian merchant ship came along with a *Handelsschiffsverkehrsbuch*, or HVB, which further disguised the four-letter code words, in a method of superencipherment.

Others joined the cramped Naval Intelligence office, including personnel efficient in German, helping to further expose the messages of the German High Seas Fleet. Their breakthroughs gave cryptanalysts plenty to think about and more thinkers were employed. Soon a large room was found for the section, which became known as 40 OB (for 'old building'), because number 40 was written on the door, but in time the department's name simply became 'Room 40,'[3] officially part of NID25.

During this time Churchill, as First Lord of the Admiralty, kept an eye on results from the new department and insisted on seeing actual decrypts as well as reports. A procedure was devised for a daily selection to be sent for his personal perusal, including main intelligence documents from all military sections in their 'original' form. These were known as BJ telegrams, or Blue Jackets, as they had blue covers.

America was not in the conflict at the beginning of 1917, but a Room 40 employee, Nigel de Grey, of the Royal Navy Volunteer Reserve, decrypted with his colleagues one of the most important diplomatic telegrams in codebreaking history. On 10 January, a communication was telegraphed by the German foreign secretary, Arthur Zimmermann, to Heinrich von Eckardt, the German ambassador to Mexico. It was a crucial time and American freedoms were at stake as the message instructed the ambassador to offer the return of Arizona, Texas and New Mexico states to the Mexican government, if they sided with Germany against the United States.

It was a pivotal moment in early decryption when Britain's signals intelligence held honesty in their hands and influenced world history. Without openly revealing the source American officials were informed and six weeks later, toward the end of February, Zimmermann admitted the telegram was true. The public disclosure of the proposed pact brought America into the war against Germany, which eventually led to a ceasefire on 11 November 1918.

* * *

During the years between the First and Second World Wars, Britain's main government codebreaking effort remained at London's Admiralty in Room 40, Old Building. Other nations, neutral and belligerent, honed their cryptography skills and, not wanting to be caught off guard, availed themselves of the fruits of valuable intelligence. From Vichy France to Sweden, and other places in the world, cryptologic bureaus were set up or expanded. Some obtained published study materials based on First World War cryptology and used these successful methods for their cryptologic bases.

Yves Gyldén, from Sweden, published his views in 1931, *Chifferbyråernas insatser I världskriget till lands*. His interest in codes and ciphers was fanatical after his father, Olaf, head of Sweden's Royal Naval School, expressed a financial interest in cipher machines. Yves studied cryptology and cipher machines of the First World War, and at the age of 36 published his findings. The work was translated into English by the US Army Signal Corps (where William Friedman is now cited as the author). In David Kahn's words, 'the book demolished the lingering myth of "chamber" analysis, demonstrated the crucial role of errors and torrents of cipher texts, generally crystallised the lessons of the First World War and catalysed the evolution of cryptology today.'[4]

Under the umbrella of the Foreign Office, as British diplomats were urged to be cautious in their use of codes, their cryptologic department expanded in the 1920s, and merged with the War Office's Cryptographic branch, MI(b). The combined section would be a unified signals intelligence agency, run by Rear Admiral Hugh Sinclair, as the non-operational director, in addition to his leading role in the Secret Intelligence Service (SIS). Sinclair was known as 'C' in government circles and his department was known both as 'C's organisation and MI(c), for Military Intelligence (c), the name of which eventually became known as MI6. Sinclair, who was also known as 'Quex', declared that the codebreaking work of Room 40 (NID25) would work beside the British SIS who would be responsible for distribution of the signals intelligence they deciphered. In return, access to their past records would be available for Room 40's research. The group became the Government Code & Cypher School (GC&CS).

Young and mild mannered, Dilly Knox was employed in Naval Intelligence from 1914. After the merger of departments, he tackled the secret ciphers of rising European dictators and eventually achieved the great feat of reading the Italian naval Enigma. Hugh Foss was also key. The animated Scotsman had an intense interest in cryptology which opened the door for him to codebreaking in 1924. Born in Kobe, Japan, in 1902 to missionary parents, his father was also the Bishop of Osaka. Young Foss was fluent in Japanese and his subsequent British education took him to Marlborough College and Cambridge. He also knew about Enigma, a commercial version of which, he said, Dilly Knox already had after buying one in Vienna.[5] By 1928 Foss had written 'The Reciprocal Enigma', a detailed paper solving the non-plug board version of the machine.

Developing Bletchley Park 1939–1943

By August 1938 as war loomed, the British government started to move their secret offices to a safer place in the middle of the countryside. Their undercover group was known as 'Captain Ridley's Shooting Party' and represented a varied collection of senior government officials. Some Admiralty departments transferred to new headquarters in London's Broadway Buildings, opposite St James' Park underground station, and GC&CS recruited certain intellectuals for the larger task in hand.

As Germany invaded Poland, Commander Denniston implemented his emergency plan and Gordon Welchman, a Cambridge intellectual, was the first of several to begin the secret journey to Buckinghamshire. The new recruits, who reportedly received a coded message saying, 'Auntie Flo is unwell' and to 'keep ten bob' (ten shillings) in their pocket for a train ticket, came to Bletchley Park. They were paid handsomely at £11.5s.6d per week. £600 a year was a large salary then (approximately $800).

* * *

Welchman, who was recommended by the physicist and novelist C.P Snow, recognised the value of all intercepted messages, but his attention to detail equalled his vision of a wider picture. He admired individual qualities in his colleagues but was frustrated by the slow pace of interception and communication and the apparent lack of lateral thinking as to how message intercepts were stored and used.

Around these parameters, he developed an efficient system to deal with the problems and created an accessible retrieval system for intelligence to always be useful, not just for a day.[6] His plan for tasks to be separated into sections, called 'Huts', quickly developed as Welchman began to increase recruitment to work on German Enigma Army and Air Force ciphers. It was known as Hut 6. Nobody outside of the department was to know they were breaking Enigma. Some of the best Hut 6 codebreakers were chessmen, who crunched through code puzzles as if they were chess moves. But more help was needed at Bletchley Park and a letter was eventually sent to the Prime Minister, Winston Churchill.

Additional chessmen were not needed, but forty-eight senior and junior women were, in addition to existing staff. They would be divided into four sections requiring an average of twenty-five in each, headed by four Temporary Junior Assistant Principals, with 100 Temporary Assistants. One-third more office space was also requested. His requests had the support of Commander Travis, but senior staff, either at Bletchley or higher in the Foreign Office, had not responded to his needs before 1942.

Chapter 9

Codebreaking in America

Janice was in her forties and had a young family when David Kahn's *The Codebreakers: The Story of Secret Writing,* made headlines in 1967. It was 'the first comprehensive history of secret communication, from ancient times to the threshold of outer space.' But she remained tight-lipped.

Kahn's, account, in 1,164 pages, starts with Pearl Harbor but has scant reference to the people and full operations at Bletchley Park. The GC&CS name is not mentioned, despite the author's words, 'It (Bletchley Park) is far and away the most history-redolent black chamber of all.' A pre-war history of the Admiralty and Room 40 is told, but no disclosure of the massive codebreaking industry in the middle of the British countryside. Twenty-two years after the war, its 13,000 codebreakers were still governed by the Official Secrets Act. Harold Wilson, Prime Minister in 1967, and his government, banned Kahn and Macmillan his publisher, from any direct reference to Britain's secret intelligence centre and its methods. But when you know and read between the lines, nuances can be glimpsed. Meanwhile, William Friedman, Parker Hitt and a few others take most of the credit as early twentieth century American heroes of breaking codes.

Overall, British secrecy and anonymity protected not only military strategy and new technologies, but also the people who worked in this environment from enemy acts of vengeance. Several new accounts have put the record straight on Bletchley Park's leading place in intelligence history, its successes, processes and organisation, however, it is important to acknowledge America's contribution.

* * *

In December 1911, Parker Hitt an older man aged 31, attended a signals training course at Fort Leavenworth, Kansas. It was the fourth conference for the small signal training school, and Hitt found he was mesmerised by the words of Britain's Royal Field Artillery Captain Murray Muirhead. His enthusiasm for cipher work 'of all kinds' grew as he found he 'had a real knack for it', which resulted in him delving into automated cryptograms and by 1914 he had developed a flat strip cipher from Jefferson's cylindrical system. Meanwhile, another course attendee, Lieutenant Joseph Mauborgne, was solving Muirhead's 814-letter Playfair code.

From Indianapolis, Hitt had left his civil engineering studies at Purdue University at the age of 18 to join the army. Having served in Cuba, he won a commission and travelled extensively in America and the Philippines. He was involved with Mexican ciphers and operated from Fort Sill, Oklahoma, receiving intercepted messages from signals people in radio trucks, placed on both sides of the border. Soon he was solving codes and ciphers used by the Conventionists, such as Pancho Villa or Emiliano Zapata and the Constitutionalists.[1] His system became known as the Mexican Army Cipher Disk, which included four numerical alphabets on revolving disks. Hitt, literally, was a hit, being a handsome tower of a man at six feet four inches and an excellent cryptologist. He went on to produce the *Manual for the Solution of Military Ciphers* of which 4,000 copies were printed and published by the press of the Army Service Schools, Fort Leavenworth which sold for 35 cents each. It was 'a mass of material on cipher work' accumulated over four years and sanctioned as a basis for future courses in army ciphers. Having enriched his base from almost zero knowledge to fanatic – using theories and information on cryptology from European books borrowed from the Army War college – he was seen as America's leading expert and later became an instructor.

Hitt's pragmatic and straightforward approach raised points such as 'why should cryptanalytic offices be attached to field headquarters, and how should they be organised?' He gave advice on how to correct errors in enciphering and transmission. He replaced worn examples of messages from other books with original cryptograms, including some Spanish plain texts, to instil reality. His observation of the four factors of successful cryptanalysis – perseverance, careful analysis, intuition and luck – often amused his followers when he recited the old miner's proverb: 'Gold is where you find it.'[2]

Genevieve (centre) and Parker Hitt. Quite possibly America's first codebreaking couple. (United States Army)

However, events in Europe had far outrun elementary notions and the book was almost out of date before its birth. Cryptograms were no longer solved using a single message and military ciphers had attained a tactical complexity not mentioned in his manual, though it was the first of its kind to be published in America.[3] Nevertheless, it was a useful introduction to cryptology for people who were stricken by the cipher bug.

* * *

Before America entered the First World War in 1917, socialite George Fabyan courted clandestine fame to offer the services of his private codes and ciphers division to the government. There was no central federal department, though the US Army and Navy had such sections at various times. The government accepted his offer but it was a strange choice, as the eccentric make-up of George Fabyan's wealthy estate in Geneva, Illinois – Riverbank Laboratories – also consisted of odd research assistants working on various obscure scientific projects.

Fabyan was a tycoon who inherited abundantly from Bliss, Fabyan & Co., enough to provide him and his wife a sizeable financial foundation. They bought 10-acres 40-miles west of Chicago on the Fox River. This eventually grew to 325 acres. He was sometimes referred to as 'Colonel' after an honorary title given to him by the Governor of Illinois, Richard Yates, at his appointment to the military guard in 1901. He spent time in Japan cultivating friendly relations with government and business representatives and was appointed liaison in Russo-Japanese peace negotiations held in Main in 1905. In May 1909 he was awarded the Order of the Rising Sun by the Japanese government.

Fabyan's estate expanded with Japanese gardens, a private zoo, a Roman-style pool, a lighthouse, grottoes, greenhouses, a farm including a prize herd of cattle, and the Riverbank Research Laboratory. The Fabyan farmhouse was remodelled by Frank Lloyd Wright, and in 1914 they purchased and relocated an 1870 Dutch-style windmill from its original farm in York Center, Illinois. The research laboratory was an outlying 'think tank' – the first of such, in America, to be privately owned. Fabyan's ambition was to 'seize the secrets of nature' and thus prove to academics that their theories were incorrect. Some say this stemmed from an insecurity rooted in his limited formal education. He appeared to obsess over anything from literary manuscripts to acoustics and agricultural experiments in Riverbank's fields.

For this work Fabyan hired young students straight from university and William Friedman was one. He had a degree in genetics from

Cornell University, but also had other interests emulating, perhaps, Cornell's founder: *'I would found an institution where any person can find instruction in any study.'* One of these was to study the effect of moonlight on oat crops.

As head of the Department of Genetics, Friedman lived in a studio on the second floor of the pseudo-Dutch windmill. As well as oats he worked on experiments with fruit flies, testing Mendelian biological laws of heredity, and developed a hobby in photography. It was this diversion that catapulted Friedman into serious cryptography when he was asked to help Riverbank researcher Elizabeth Gallup, a former schoolteacher (and by all accounts a bit of a crank) in photographing Elizabethan manuscripts in England.

William had been born Wolf Friedman in 1891, to Jewish parents who fled Rumania a year later to escape anti-Semitism. They settled eventually in Pennsylvania where his name was changed to William. As a child he was introduced to cryptography through the eyes of Edgar Allan Poe through a short tale entitled, *The Gold Bug*. The tale includes a cryptogram that Friedman was able to decipher, becoming, he claimed, his first foray into the world of codebreaking and ciphers. The adventure story is about a wealthy man who was bitten by a gold-coloured insect and, while all around him thought he was mad, the man believed he had a special power to decipher a secret message that would lead to buried treasure.

Now Friedman was part of a research project into sixteenth century coded messages of Sir Francis Bacon which allegedly hid, in bi-literal ciphers, secret texts of British royalty in the reign of Elizabeth I and James I.

During that period, he met Gallup's assistant Elizabeth Smith. William admired her vibrancy, intellect and dynamism, while she was attracted to his debonair and sophisticated character. They courted and in less than a year they married in May 1917, and Elizabeth moved into the windmill. Their union of equals was unusual at the time, in terms of working women, but together they created a powerful force in cryptology.

Their pre-war expertise was successful to a degree and helped advance a common interest in modern and ancient cryptology when, as parlour games, they pitched puzzling codes and ciphers for family members against friends and new acquaintances. Stronger challenges were later set for other cryptanalysts and movie stars as Riverbank became a famous weekend retreat.

CODEBREAKING IN AMERICA

As well as genetics, William was also director of Codes and Ciphers and wrote several papers on cryptography after the end of the First World War, known as the Riverbank Publications. These included *The Index of Coincidence* (revised several times including in 1955 by Howard H. Campaigne (See Chapter 20), which became an important mathematical tool used in cryptanalysis. Another of the Friedman's successes was to unravel a code used by Hindu radicals in America. The subversive group was funded by Germany who planned to ship arms to India to gain independence from Britain. The Friedmans' 'cryptanalysis' – a word, it is said, he coined when training students – eventually revealed their code source as a German-English scholarly publication from 1913.[4] A seven-page letter had been passed to him undercover from England and, taking full advantage of the clues and codes within, he was able to build the entire plain text of the codes the Hindu group was using, without knowing the source. Known as a book code, using numerical patterns and page numbers – a common code technique for the period – Friedman provided evidence and the conspiracists were prosecuted in mass trials held in Chicago and San Francisco. Most of the defendants were found guilty, but not before a dramatic assassination in court in April 1918, when one of the defendants killed another, and the marshal fired another shot killing the first gunman.

* * *

Across the Atlantic, Britain easily read American diplomatic messages. The consensus for several decades was that American codes were simple to break. David Kahn wrote: 'the United States must have been the laughingstock of every cryptanalyst in the world'[5], adding that 'American diplomacy must have been conducted largely in an international goldfish bowl'. European countries were ahead in intelligence collecting techniques, some of which led the British War Office and Nigel de Grey's Room 40 team to successfully decode Zimmermann's telegram, bringing America into the war in April 1917.

By that time, every major power had secret copies of America's Diplomatic codes. Foreign employees had the run of the American embassies abroad and to obtain their confidential code books was effortless. Furthermore, it was common knowledge that if Room 40 could solve two-part German codes, they could certainly read straightforward

American codes. James Thurber in Paris was astonished to see major *faux pas* in code compilations. He reported:

> 'The new diplomatic code book had been put together so hastily that the word "America" was left out, and code groups so closely paralleled true readings that LOVVE, for example, was the symbol for "love".'

Thurber went on to say that all young American code clerks in his department were happy until told by a dour senior man that Germany could read all their codes because they often sent messages taunting Washington about the childish ciphers they used. The Germans even had the audacity to suggest they should combine two codes to make the deception harder and named the two different codes they should use! Rumour or legend, six code books went missing, but a seventh was returned to another American embassy by the Japanese, wrapped and tied securely with a courteous note. They had either finished with it or already had the key.[6]

The Black Chamber

Herbert Osborn Yardley served as a cryptologic officer with the American Expeditionary Forces in France during the First World War. Born in 1889 in Worthington, Indiana, his father was a telegrapher for a railroad company and Herbert followed the same path. After dropping out of the University of Chicago in 1912, he passed the civil service exam to become a code clerk and government telegrapher in the US State Department. During that time, he made certain discoveries, including that of German spy, Lothar Witzke, who was arrested at the Mexican border with a cryptogram concealed in his baggage. The eventual translation provided evidence that Witzke was linked to serious incidents of sabotage in America, one being the Black Tom munitions explosion in New York Harbor, 1916.[7] His experience in government codes also revealed that President Wilson's code system was outdated; it was at least a decade old. Shocked at this and the other prevalent weaknesses, he started to write *Solution of American Diplomatic Codes* which eventually stretched to 100 pages.

CODEBREAKING IN AMERICA

When he accepted a US Army Signal Corps Reserve Commission as second lieutenant, he became head of the eighth section of Military Intelligence (MI-8 USA, a version of MI6 UK). Yardley was a good administrator, and MI-8 performed well but without spectacular discoveries, until he had the opportunity to turn his attention to Japanese codes.

In November 1921, the Washington Naval Conference for Disarmament took place. The forum was conducted outside the auspice of the League of Nations with nine nations attending – including Japan, an ally at the time – plus five other world powers, working to secure global peace. The focus of the conference covered major weapons in the world and naval strength. The most important, weighing in with sizeable military tonnage, was America's Navy, Britain's Royal Navy and the Imperial Navy of Japan. The British and American governments were agreed, but the Japanese had strict instructions to get as close as possible to parity with America and Britain. The two long-time allies, however, could not afford to lose supremacy to Japan, and America felt compelled to track their diplomatic messages. Consequently, cable companies were tasked to pass on copies of Japanese embassy messages from Tokyo. However, due to the lack of Japanese speakers within the US government, nobody could read them.

Herbert O. Yardley: telegrapher, code clerk and skilful cryptologist in New York's 'Black Chamber'. (Courtesy of the NSA/National Cryptologic Museum)

Instead, attention quickly turned to the charismatic flare of Herbert Yardley, known for cracking certain codes. After the war he had a small 'cipher bureau' in a Brownstone, at 141 E.37th Street, New York, where he was required to break foreign diplomatic codes and read international governments' messages, including American allies. Apparently, the US President at the time had no idea of this operation, but now he was required to urgently decipher a Japanese message. However, he had no knowledge of Japanese coding systems, nor could he read Japanese.

The message associated with the Washington Conference confirmed Yardley's skilfulness as a codebreaker, when he deciphered and read the crucial communication within forty-eight hours, revealing the Japanese would back down on parity. They wanted their Ambassador to step away from their insistence of equal naval tonnage. Knowing that Japan would concede, America and Britain put on great pressure for the country to accept almost half the tonnage limitations of the allied fleet levels at ratios of 5:5:3. The Japanese delegation left the conference shattered at the defeat but did not suspect the insecurity of their high-grade diplomatic codes.

Though pleased with the outcome, it is uncertain whether the US Government and then Secretary of State, Charles Evans Hughes, knew of Yardley's office, a clandestine agency that over-time garnered the name *The Black Chamber*,[8] – a nod to 17th century European codebreakers. It was said to be supported by a secret slush fund, possibly illicit, by the State Department and Department of Military Intelligence. Yardley might have expected a secret reward for his undercover work but instead, when Henry Stimson became Secretary of State to President Hoover in 1929 and discovered the existence of the backroom chamber, it was immediately closed. The unit of unlawful subterfuge was Yardley's downfall.

With no official recognition and at the height of the Wall Street Crash, there was no pension and no hope for the future. However, he had a wife and young family to support and decided to publish his codebreaking story. The material he revealed was explosive and of great embarrassment to the US government since everything about his work was exposed, not only about Japanese and Russian diplomatic codes, but also those of the British and French, and the full story of the Japanese deception during the Washington conference.

CODEBREAKING IN AMERICA

Janice of course was far too young to know much of this, even when Yardley's publisher serialised the 1931 book in the *Saturday Evening Post*. Pouring more oil on to fire, it became a bestseller. The Japanese were furious; their nation had lost face on the world's stage using trickery. From then they decided to invent their own unbreakable codes – not by using pen and paper, but with machines. Machines for encoding had already been invented earlier, as with Enigma, but now a far superior encipherment apparatus was planned.

Yardley was never seen to work again in United States codes. It is uncertain if he visited Bletchley Park, but he is listed on their Roll of Honour, as director of XU, the Examination Unit – a Canadian Signals Intelligence counterpart of GC&CS in Ottawa, Canada. He died in obscurity in 1958, but his standing as a remarkable codebreaker was not lost when he posthumously received recognition with full military honours at Arlington Cemetery. David Kahn conceded he was one of the most remarkable characters in the history of cryptology when he said: 'Despite being a womaniser, a poker player and a drinker, he was an extraordinarily excellent codebreaker, and even though toward the middle of his life he wrote *The American Black Chamber* – which revealed too many American codebreaking secrets – his breaking of the Japanese Naval code and Diplomatic Code at the time of the Disarmament Conference, proved an enormous boon to the United States enabling us to gain substantial naval superiority over Japan which proved of great value during the Second World War'.

The US Army replaced Yardley with William Friedman.

* * *

After the court deaths in the Hindu trial, the Friedman's cryptography tutoring reports were highly regarded. The Riverbank Publications were the main unofficial source of cryptography in America, and despite still only being in their early twenties the Friedmans quickly built a cipher department of about thirty staff, including scientists and linguists. Soon the codebreaking group was studying all types of intercepted correspondence from the Army, the Navy, the State and Justice Departments, the postal service and others – including a Czechoslovakian love letter! The technical material, which remained classified for decades, supported the Army's training programme, but by early 1918 William had also joined the Army to serve under General John J. Pershing in northern France. Elizabeth meanwhile, at half her husband's pay, ran the courses with her staff at Riverbank.

When Friedman returned from Europe after the war, in 1920, he understood more on how to disguise military communications, a skill that America needed to embrace. Consequently, he studied all manner of European traditions of cryptography while immersing himself in German codes. In 1921 he also became head of the US Army cryptographic division of SIS, Signals Intelligence Service. At this point Elizabeth and William Friedman managed to disentangle themselves from the eccentric world of George Fabyan and Riverbank Laboratories and moved to Washington to strengthen the Army signals systems. It was a position William would maintain for thirty years. Elizabeth was an accomplished cryptographer in her own right, working much later for a government agency intercepting bootleggers during Prohibition for the United States Coast Guard. Both by then had debunked the Baconian theories and, in their secret circles, later became the best codebreaking couple in American history.

* * *

Through the Prohibition years, under growing complexities of international relations, Friedman strongly believed they must develop a secure and powerful cryptology unit. He was considered after all the expert in the field of making and breaking codes. America appeared to be an also-ran, with advanced code systems barely developed from semaphore or wigwag – a signalling system with just one flag (Europe used two).

It was time for the early systems including the Friedmans' and the important work of Parker Hitt – who they later referred to as 'The father of modern American military cryptology' – to be scrutinised and updated to provide a better cryptanalysis service similar to British army systems.[9]

Now in his forties, his eye and manner for meticulous detail and precision held him in good esteem with his staff. They always referred to him as Mr Friedman, though behind his back he was affectionately known as 'Uncle Willie'. He was a sensitive person, often easily offended, while allowing members of his trusted team to tackle important jobs within their capabilities. He delegated but did not always compliment.

A fit middle-aged man, he cared about how he presented himself. He was an accomplished tennis player and excellent ballroom dancer – a necessary mainstream hobby then in the physical world of social networking. He and Elizabeth amassed one of the few known libraries on codes and ciphers, including their own publications. They also had a fine team of devoted followers and, with the abrupt closure of Yardley's bureau, extra funding provided the opportunity to hire three young mathematicians. Two were Abraham Sinkov and Soloman Kullback – friends who attended high school and the same city college in New York. Friedman thought younger candidates were more malleable and knew their assignment ahead would take years to master. The other was Frank Rowlett, a young math teacher from Virginia, who had obtained maximum marks in the civil service entrance exam. He had no idea what a cryptanalyst was, but the salary at $2,000 was more than he and his wife, as teachers, earned together and they decided it was worth a try.

Chapter 10

Women in Codebreaking

The number of female participants in mainstream cryptology has historically been lower than men, but they are not completely invisible. Elizebeth Friedman was a pioneer in developing codes and ciphers during the twentieth century, but she was not the only female interested in the science of codes, ciphers and secrecy. One imagines that, had they been so inclined, Mary Fairfax (Somerville) and Caroline Herschel would also have been in this intriguing group of women, as nineteenth century astronomers, mathematicians, master puzzle creators and solvers. Astronomy, based on mathematics, was a key naval tool for centuries. Celestial navigation relies on 'sights' or angular measurement between the sun, moon, planets, stars or visible horizons where co-ordinates are tabulated using a nautical sextant. Mary Fairfax's father was a vice admiral in the British Navy. He was certainly a navigator, and perhaps he also specialised in codes and ciphers. However, such a deceptive practice was perhaps deemed unladylike, especially as mathematics and astronomy were already a social step too far.

Mary Fairfax was tutor and friend to Ada Lovelace who, by the 1840s, was seen to be the first to recognise the full potential of the computer. The daughter of poet Lord Byron, a mathematician and writer, she was known for her work with inventor Charles Babbage, 'father of' the first mechanical general-purpose computer. Minds of mathematicians (and code and cipher analysts) could stretch to many possibilities. Lovelace ultimately developed a vision of capabilities going far beyond just calculation and evaluation, and hence is thought to be the first female programmer. Her enquiries about Babbage's Analytical Engine led to the first algorithm for such a machine. Her 'poetical science' examined how individuals and society related to these new inventions, and she developed a useful collaborative tool for this.[1]

* * *

WOMEN IN CODEBREAKING

There are other women throughout history, who helped men conduct espionage and deliver intelligence under clandestine conditions. One was Agent 355 during the American Revolution. When Independence was declared by the Patriots in 1776, all of New York and Long Island was still held by the British. However, George Washington had developed the Culper Spy Ring to uncover movements of British troops and their ammunition stores. Major Benjamin Tallmadge was tasked with operating an effective system for coding and intelligence delivery and, therefore, turned to his childhood friends whom he could absolutely trust from Setauket, Long Island. Washington had earlier been duped by a trusted officer, Dr Benjamin Church, who was caught passing secret correspondence to the British. Now it was Washington's turn for a covert operation. Tallmadge's ring of trusted friends included Abraham Woodhull, code name Culper Snr., Caleb Brewster, a whale boat operator, local publican Austin Roe, who bought supplies in the city, and Robert Townsend in New York whose code name was Culper Jnr. Townsend would deliver the intercepted information to Washington. It has not been proven who Agent 355 was, but Abraham Woodhull wrote in code, that he would be visiting New York again, and 'by the assistance of a lady (coded as 355) of my acquaintance, shall be able to outwit them all.' Tallmadge – alias John Bolton – had created a special code in the form of a dictionary with three-digit numbers representing certain words, plus a coded alphabet for words not already coded in the dictionary.

Historians say lady 355 was Anna Strong.[2] Her husband Selah was a captain in the New York militia, suspected of spying and imprisoned by the British in the Sugar House, New York City. Anna visited with food from the farmlands of Setauket, including when he was imprisoned on the prison ship HMS *Jersey*. Her visits to New York would have been a perfect cover to deliver intelligence from Culper Snr. (722) to Culper Jnr. (723). Anna Strong was able to win parole for her husband through her parent's conservative relatives, but he spent the rest of the war living in Connecticut while she stayed in Long Island. Legend also says that she sent secret messages by hanging her laundry on a line by the shore – a black petticoat indicated to Woodhull that Caleb Brewster was in town, and the number of handkerchiefs showed where Woodhull should meet him. But this is not corroborated. After the war she was known to have strong connections to President George Washington, even entertaining him at her house in 1790. However, her family had no knowledge of her spy activities.

* * *

Handwriting and drawing are forms of code. Petroglyphs in North America, Europe and Australia date back thousands of years, while Africa has the record for the earliest communicating homo sapiens and prehistoric cave paintings. Whether carved or painted, the Egyptians and Sumerians (now southern Iraq) seem to have been the most organised with their coded messages. Over 4,000 years ago in Egypt, scribes tackled stone tablets to impress their kings and pharaohs and record events. According to David Kahn, there were some that moved to unusual alternative ways to emphasise certain parts of text 'to impart dignity and authority'. For example, 'In the Year of Our Lord, one thousand eight hundred and sixty-three, equates to 1863.' This is not necessarily secret writing, but the action incorporated an essential element of cryptography – a deliberate transformation of writing. Over time as middle eastern civilisations developed, this kind of alteration became more contrived, more frequent, and more complicated as scribes replaced action hieroglyphs with others. A simple example would be a picture of a pig, which in Arabic is 'rer', to indicate that the inscribed word would start with the same letter sound of 'r' or similar. This scene perhaps, reminds us of childhood puzzle books.

There is strong evidence that some scribes in Egypt were educated female priests and doctors trained to read law, medical and religious texts.[3] From this one can deduce women contributed to the mysterious and magical powers of burial, when they wrote an obscure epitaph for a deceased female friend in a form of code for the afterlife. It is also true that Hatshepsut, the female Pharaoh (c.1473-58 BCE), left plenty of embedded hieroglyphs for archaeological decoders in the 19th and 20th centuries, elevating her out of obscurity, a desired fate forced on her by her stepson Thutmose III and other ruling successors after her death.[4]

These women are just a few examples of women in history who worked in codes and ciphers in some way. Ching Shih (aka Cheng I Sao or Madam Ching – a former prostitute) 1775-1844, was another as her fleet of pirate ships 'ruled' the South China Seas, though these were probably spoken. Over 3,000 years of history, cryptology in different forms came and went in many places as civilisations evolved, with future generations left to untangle a patchwork of strange elements.

In fiction Dickens' Madame Thérèse Defarge in *A Tale of Two Cities*, 1859, encodes as she knits in her 'tricoteuses' handiwork, the names of people to be killed. While this might be a bit far-fetched, fiction always

WOMEN IN CODEBREAKING

Coded hieroglyphic of the female Pharoah Hatschepsut? A cartouche on an obelisk in Luxor, Egypt. (Public domain)

carries an element of truth. It is said the story is based on Anne-Josèphe Théroigne de Méricourt (born Terwagne 13 August 1762, died 9 June 1817), a singer, orator and organiser in the French Revolution.

Women working as code makers and breakers in 1940 were probably seen to be 'unladylike', as it was 'a man's job' for those hired from elite colleges and universities for intelligence work. But in 1941, the developing intelligence relationship between America and Britain, revealed that Bletchley Park's secret weapon consisted of women playing a central role in almost every aspect. Prior to September 1941 there was only a handful of women codebreakers, but Bletchley's success at trustworthy female recruitment proved that women should not be disregarded.

Director of Naval Communications, US Navy Rear Admiral Leigh Noyes, was also convinced and wrote a letter to Ada Comstock, president of Radcliffe College, Harvard's female equivalent. Noyes confided that the Navy was looking for 'bright, closed-mouth native students', meaning high-achieving, sensible women, who were born in the United States and who could keep a secret. 'Evidence of a flair for languages or mathematics could be advantageous.' He added that 'any intense sociological "quirks" would, of course, be undesirable'. Without stating what he meant by quirks he offered a Navy training course to gifted seniors which, 'in the event of total war, women will be needed for this work and they can do it probably better than men'.[5] Ada wrote to Donald Menzel at Harvard, to confirm her interest in the idea and that she was happy to obey the secrecy rules. Menzel, her friend, was an astronomer and one of five professors chosen as a contact for naval recruitment.

* * *

The tentacles had not yet reached Janice at Goucher College, but another pioneer, Genevieve Young, an Army wife, was the first to pave the way for many junior recruits into the world of cryptology. Her story was overlooked for many years but is now represented in US Army Women's History. She was the wife of Parker Hitt.

Genevieve was born in 1885, to a wealthy family in San Antonio, Texas. Her father was a doctor. At high school she studied history, botany, English, chemistry and astronomy and, in the view of her principal, had 'ladylike deportment'. Her character, schooling and social acceptance – parties, dances and parlour card games – were all perfect training and acceptable attributes for a woman in the early 1900s to marry a man who would care for her for the rest of her life. She vowed never to marry an army officer but met and fell in love with Captain Hitt, an infantry commander at Fort Houston. They married in 1911 and moved to Fort Leavenworth, around the time her husband attended the Army's Signal Corps school. This coincided with the new cryptology course being offered on 'Military Cryptography by Captain Murray Muirhead' of Britain's Royal Field Artillery. When Hitt discovered he was interested in cipher work of all kinds and 'had a real knack for it,' Genevieve also became hooked on unravelling ciphers, and studied the (perhaps unladylike) disciplines alongside her husband, leading eventually to their publication of the *Manual for the Solution of Military Ciphers*, in 1916.

The following year Parker Hitt was deployed to France during the First World War and the reality of Genevieve's role as an army wife hit home. She returned to Fort Houston to be close to her family but before long, she decided to embark on additional training at Riverbank Laboratories. There she met Fabyan, the Friedmans and another accomplished female in cryptology, Agnes Driscoll. After she completed the course and returned to Texas, she started to receive personal hand-written mail attached to cipher messages from the 'Southern Department', and without further question (or pay) she routinely set about deciphering them.

By April 1918 Genevieve found herself in charge of code work for the Southern Department's Intelligence Officer, Robert L. Barnes. She was then paid $1,000 annually for five and a half days work (plus overtime), coding and decoding official army intelligence communications and it was her responsibility to maintain control of Army code books. A month later she was sent to Washington for an official visit to the Military Intelligence Bureau, with Barnes noting that Genevieve, was wholly self-taught, and 'specially qualified for such work having made a special study thereof'. She hoped Parker would be happy with her taking on such 'a man-size job', as her life careered in a totally different direction from that expected ten years before. She wrote effusively to her mother-in-law, Elizabeth Hitt:[6]

> *'All this seems so funny to me; at times I have to laugh. It is all so foreign to my training, to my family's old-fashioned notions about what and where a woman's place in this world is, etc., yet none of these things seem to shock the family now. I suppose it is the war. I am afraid I will never be contented to sit down without something to do, even when this war is over, and we are all home again....*
>
> *This is a man's size job, but I seem to be getting away with it, and I am going to see it through. It does not seem to be affecting my health in any way, for everyone says I have never looked so well. I am getting a great deal out of it, discipline, concentration (for it takes concentration, and a lot of it, to do this work, with machines pounding away on every side of you and two or three men talking at once), the other fellow's point of view, and working side by side with the woman who has to work if she is to eat or wear any clothes.'*

Parker was amused and fully supportive of his wife's work and espoused to his fellow officers in France. 'Good work, old girl,' he wrote in June 1918, 'everyone here thinks it is splendid that you are able to handle your own office and many officers have said they wish their wives had the energy and ability to do something instead of loafing and worrying about their perfectly safe husbands.'

Parker and Genevieve had one daughter, Mary Lueise, who was four when her mother started full time work in Washington. It helped that she could afford household help, a servant and that her younger sister and mother lived close. The work was exhausting but she stuck with it until Armistice day when she voluntarily resigned to prevent other clerks from losing their jobs after the war. Though Genevieve never worked in codebreaking again, she worked for a few months in the Radical Section of the Bureau of Investigation for J. Edgar Hoover, and Mary Lueise later helped William Friedman at Arlington Hall during the Second World War. Genevieve died in obscurity in 1963 unable to talk about the important tasks she undertook, but Parker kindly wrote on her death certificate: 'retired code and cipher expert'.

* * *

Agnes Meyer Driscoll, on the other hand, made it into the National Security Agency's Hall of Fame, but not until 2000. Women in national security, code making and codebreaking, certainly had to wait a long time to be recognised. An historical marker was eventually placed outside her former home in 2017 honouring her achievements.

Agnes was born in Geneseo, Illinois on 24 July 1889. At the age of six her family moved to State Street, Westerville, Ohio as her father, Gustav Meyer, taught music at Otterbein College. She also attended classes there from 1907-1909. Her next seat of learning was The University of Ohio, Athens, where she majored in maths and physics and received a Bachelor of Arts degree in 1911. Agnes also studied music, statistics and foreign languages, attaining fluency in German, French, English, Latin and Japanese.

There were few options for her, an accomplished woman after graduation, but to become a schoolteacher. She moved 1,200 miles to Amarillo, Texas, first, as director of music at a military academy and then chair of mathematics at a local high school. In June 1918, however, she decided to sign up to help the war effort in Europe, when a sweeping decision was made to allow women to join the US Navy. Not only was she able to register but she was a Chief Yeoman (F), the highest rank possible for females at the time in the US Naval Reserve.

WOMEN IN CODEBREAKING

America had been at war fourteen months in a global conflict that started in Europe when the heir to the Austro-Hungarian throne, Archduke Ferdinand and his wife were assassinated in June 1914.

As political head of the Royal Navy, Churchill was ambitious to the point of considering himself a military strategist with bold plans to victory, but after a failed navy campaign in the Dardanelles in January 1916, he became the scapegoat in relation to the Battle of Gallipoli, dropped from war cabinet meetings and sacked by the Admiralty. At the time ministers declared the need for harmony and less conflict in personalities, which Churchill recognised as a problem, and his response was to resign from the government and depart for France, famously saying to the Prime Minister:

'I am an officer, and I place myself unreservedly at the disposal of the military authorities observing that my regiment is in France. With much respect and unaltered friendship, I bid you goodbye.'

As German submarines sank multiple allied ships in the Atlantic, the English Channel and the Irish sea, the US senate discussed arming US ships. But when news about Zimmermann's telegram was published on 24 February 1917, America's strained neutrality changed. Two days later, President Wilson told Congress that, 'arming US vessels would protect our ships and our people in their legitimate pursuits on the sea'. All Ambassadors were called home and ships could be armed to defend themselves. The New York State National Guard and Navy Militia were ordered into service, and the US Navy seized two German cruisers. As he spoke, news of a torpedo striking the Laconia began to trickle through. Thirty passengers died, many of them American, but this news did not influence reluctant congressmen to change their minds until 6 April. At 1.18pm in a tiny office in the White House, Woodrow Wilson signed the declaration of war. Congress had passed the statement earlier that week with a vote in the Senate of 90 to 6. This followed a seventeen-hour emotional debate by the House of Representatives in a final vote of 373-50. It was a dramatic turnabout for the President and America, who for over a hundred years had obeyed George Washington's advice to avoid an 'entangling alliance'.

British Prime Minister David Lloyd George commented to the press:

'America has at one bound become a world power.' Despite their decisive entry into serious conflict America attempted to recognise the people's determination to preserve neutrality as they faced relentless pressure from belligerents, including German submarines sinking US vessels in the Atlantic. Nonetheless, by the end of 1917, America had also declared war on Austria, conscripted ten million men for military service – with strict penalties for draft dodgers – and deployed troops to the Western Front, Flanders and northern France.

* * *

The word 'yeoman' is traced back to medieval England when attendants served noblemen or noblewomen. Now yeomen (and some yeowomen) performed administrative and clerical duties at a high-level, observing protocols, naval instructions, commissioned officer reports, naval messages, visitors, telephone calls and mail; comparable, perhaps, to today's high-ranking factotums or personal assistants. As well as office administration some became radio operators, photographers, radio-fingerprinting experts, torpedo assemblers or camouflage designers. Agnes was assigned to the Postal Cable and Censorship Office, in Washington, where she reviewed correspondence for evidence of espionage, and before long was transferred to the Code and Signal section of the Director of Naval Communications (DNC, Op-20). The department was responsible for developing codes and ciphers and operating signals for the navy. Like Friedman for the army, along with others, Agnes was introduced to the art of code making which, by deduction and with practice, was excellent training to find solutions for codebreaking. After the war, in November 1918, she opted to continue this work as a civilian for the US Navy for many years.

* * *

Intelligence in the US Navy in 1920 was a concept, with theoretical studies carried out during and after the war, but an organised system of intercepting, decrypting and analysis of derived intelligence did not exist. As with the Army, naval cryptologists only produced limited systems to protect their own communications. Agnes worked a year with Lieutenant Commander William Gresham, head of the Code and Signal Section, developing a device for the navy called CM (Communications Machine), a type of sliding alphabet technique. This was a standard cryptographic system, for which, in 1937, they were awarded $15,000 by Congress. Gresham had died but Agnes shared the prize with his widow.

There were several early attempts at patenting designs for such machines, each offering completely secure enciphering systems and Agnes was allotted to testing them. New systems were often insecure, and it was Agnes job to find out. They were called 'nut jobs'. Inventors would come and go, leaving their latest models for the department to test. Frequently, the prototypes were the same machines being considered by other countries and enemies, but Agnes was the intruder who exposed their faults and weaknesses. One businessman, Edward Hebern, claimed to have invented an invincible 'Electric Code Machine, the first cryptographic apparatus to be designed using the rotor principle.'

In 1921, he advertised an 'unbreakable' cipher in a marine publication, which Agnes, twenty years his younger, quickly solved. Encouraged by the result and looking for a reliable cipher for the future, her commanding officer sent Meyer's solution to Hebern. The inventor wasted no time and visited the Navy department, in Washington, filing his first rotor patent on the way.

The Navy was thrilled with the machine's capabilities. One naval communications director said, 'I remember we wanted to get some right-away, for the whole Navy.'

With that encouragement, Hebern – a quiet, even-tempered man of medium height, with blue twinkling eyes – secured loans and investors, and built a gleaming factory in Oakland, California. While he extolled the virtues of his grandiose plan, he also convinced Agnes Meyer, in 1923, to move to California.

However, the business plan and partnership went sour after a rare state investigation was conducted into Hebern's stock dealing, and only two machines were bought by the Navy out of the twelve originally proposed. The company went into bankruptcy

Edward Hebern, 1869–1952. (Courtesy of the NSA/National Cryptologic Museum)

and Agnes returned to the safety of her Navy job. Hebern did not give up, despite his tarnished reputation, and continued to pursue the system he patented while fighting International Business Machines and other bureaucratic red tape.[7] Two of his machines were later captured by the Japanese in the Second World War.

In the two years after the decryption of Hebern's advertised message, but before she moved to California, Agnes went to Riverbank Laboratories. There she briefly studied cryptology under William and Elizabeth Friedman and met Genevieve Young. She also spent five months with Herbert Yardley in New York, working on intercepted diplomatic correspondence from Japan.

Elizabeth saw Agnes as 'a person who thought only of furthering herself' and ridiculed her decision to work for Hebern, as William Friedman had also broken the cipher of this machine and gave it a

Agnes Meyer Driscoll on the roof of the Navy Building, Washington DC, late 1920, the same time the On-The-Roof Gang members trained there. (Courtesy of the NSA/National Cryptologic Museum)

negative report.[8] Friedman's pessimism also caused the Navy to lose interest, which aggravated Agnes, especially as she considered her naval codebreaking skills equal to his, in army signals. She also despised that he was always two or three pay grades ahead – a prime example of the sexist climate at the time.

By the time Agnes returned to her civilian navy department, she had married Michael Driscoll, a Washington lawyer for the Department of Commerce, but other changes had also taken place with the creation of the Research Desk, a cryptanalytic mission, in the Code and Signal Section. It was headed by Lieutenant Laurance Safford, who later became known as the Friedman of the Navy. Agnes was his cryptanalyst, assisted by two clerks. He organised methods of interception and analysis, while she provided the cryptanalytic and technical base of COMINT (Interception of enemy communications). For eighteen years Safford and Meyer worked together in establishing the Naval Intelligence department of OP-20-G, working primarily on Japanese naval and diplomatic communications.

Their first break exploited the Japanese Navy's operational code, the Red Book (not to be confused with a later Friedman/Rowlett Red Code and the German Red code exploited by British intelligence). In Agnes' office she had a 'real' Red Book after one was snatched by the Office of Naval Intelligence and copied. However, the Japanese used an additional cipher on top of this code to encrypt the code groups and recovery of these became her main challenge. Initially, relatively simple transposition or additive systems were used and there was some success but, after a few years, dozens of systems were being used with many keys. Unfortunately, due to a shortage of Japanese linguists in their department, few messages were translated.

* * *

In Army Signals, several women were hired by William Friedman, while Elizabeth, his wife, successfully etched a path through a male dominated world of her own. The Anti-Saloon League in 1919 (which coincidentally had its headquarters in Agnes Meyer's former family home, in Westerville, Ohio) succeeded, with the Temperance Movement, in pushing through the Eighteenth Amendment to the US Constitution. Its ratification prohibited *'the manufacture, sale, or transportation of intoxicating liquors within, the importation thereof into, or the exportation thereof from the United States and all territory subject to the jurisdiction thereof for beverage purposes....'* Religious groups at the forefront of this legislation believed all America's problems revolved around immorality and crime, and in the case of America's participation in a European war, unpatriotic citizenship. The language of the amendment called for enforcement and the National Prohibition Act was enacted.[9] Known as the Volsted Act, after Minnesota representative Andrew Volstead, chair of the House Judiciary Committee who championed the cause, the act took effect in 1920.

But neither the Eighteenth Amendment nor the Volsted Act was enforced with success. The problem for the prohibitionists was that consumption of alcohol was not outlawed, and millions of Americans were quite ready to drink distilled spirits illegally. This led to organised crime and bootlegging, a term that allegedly originated in the 19th century Midwest, when flasks of illicit liquor were concealed in traders' boot tops when visiting Native Americans. Around the country, illegal stills were built for 'Moonshine', distilled from corn, for those who desired to purchase and drink. Foreign distillers – under no manufacturing restrictions – also partnered with American gangsters seeing the opportunity to make a fast buck.

Elizabeth Friedman became the government's secret weapon for catching criminals when the Coast Guard approached her husband.[10]

Bootleggers: Alcohol being discarded down the sewer under orders of US law enforcement and Coast Guard officials. (Library of Congress LC-USZ62-123257)

WOMEN IN CODEBREAKING

However, he was too busy and passed the request to her; a common occurrence to which she was accustomed. Under law enforcement, the Department of Justice appointed her a 'special agent', which also meant she could work from home as by then the Friedmans had two children.

Known as rum-running messages, her clients as well as the Justice and Treasury Departments, were the Customs Bureau, the Coast Guard and other agencies. The gangsters' lucrative business involved elaborate shipping of contraband cargo from abroad – among which were millions

Elizebeth and William Friedman with their children, Barbara and John c.1930. (Courtesy of the George C. Marshall Foundation Library, F-582)

of bottles of medicinal whiskey. Ships in international waters, radioed coded messages to smaller vessels who took on the illicit hoards. But Elizebeth started breaking the crime syndicates' codes which resulted in successful prosecutions where, as a witness, she testified in court on numerous occasions. When Prohibition was finally repealed in 1933, she continued her work in law enforcement which sometimes involved notorious and dangerous criminals, and the need for protection. The codebreaker, lady law enforcer, was also a reporter's dream for headline news, with articles such a 'Ciphers Hold no Mysteries for her', and 'Local Matron Decodes Cryptic Messages for the Treasury Department'. But she was embarrassed knowing that her job of strict confidentiality was under threat along with progress made in cryptanalysis. The publicity also made her colleagues jealous and created further tensions in their close-knit intelligence community.

They understood secrets, codes and ciphers better than anyone in America but always among rivalry, jealousy and a claustrophobic interdependency to achieve results.The Friedmans and Meyer were at the centre (the Hitts by then were history). Meanwhile, George Fabyan's codebreaker incubator remained impressed with Agnes Meyer and he wrote to the navy to offer her a job at Riverbank, 'should the Navy decide to release her'. But instead, she continued training many male naval personnel in the art of cryptology for the rest of her career, while Elizebeth trained cryptologists for the Coast Guard.

Elizebeth Friedman – Headline news in Women's Features, June 1937. (Washington DC Evening Star)

Chapter 11

Signals, Operators, Poppies and WACs

Janice would have been astounded to learn she would one day be part of this important group of American women codebreakers. Sending and receiving messages, 'Signals' was predominantly the domain of men in the US Army and Navy, but by 1942 codes and ciphers were being taught by women professors. As the prominent cryptanalysts in America (and the UK) were men, it's unlikely that women would have been mentioned in Janice's training material. They were merely seen as 'helpers' and referred to as clerical staff, though they often undertook the same analytical tasks and produced the typed coursework.

* * *

Part of communication and relayed signals telegraphy history goes back to France and Claude Chappe. The grandson of a wealthy baron, his uncle was eighteenth-century astronomer Jean-Baptiste Chappe d'Auteroche, famous for his observations of the transit of Venus. Chappe the younger was privileged and destined to serve the church, an idea he abandoned during the French Revolution. Instead his uncle's book introduced him to telescopes and he and his four brothers went on to develop a practical system of semaphore relay stations. One brother was a member of the Legislative Assembly during the revolution and with his help they built a 120-mile line of fifteen stations to manually spell out wartime messages, 'dispatches'. Each station, referred to as an 'optical tower', stood on high ground and used a telescope to read messages from cross-arm structure panels, coded angles and rods mounted on a pole on top of a tower. In 1792 the first signalled messages were successfully sent from Paris to Lille. At first the invention was called the 'tachygraph', meaning 'fast writer', but Chappe preferred the word 'semaphore', derived from the Greek meaning 'sign-bearer'. The army favoured 'telegraph' – 'far writer'.[1]

Their invention eclipsed the beacon and smoke signal systems and eventually spanned all of France. It was the first practical telecommunications system of the industrial age until the 1850s when electric telegraphy took over.

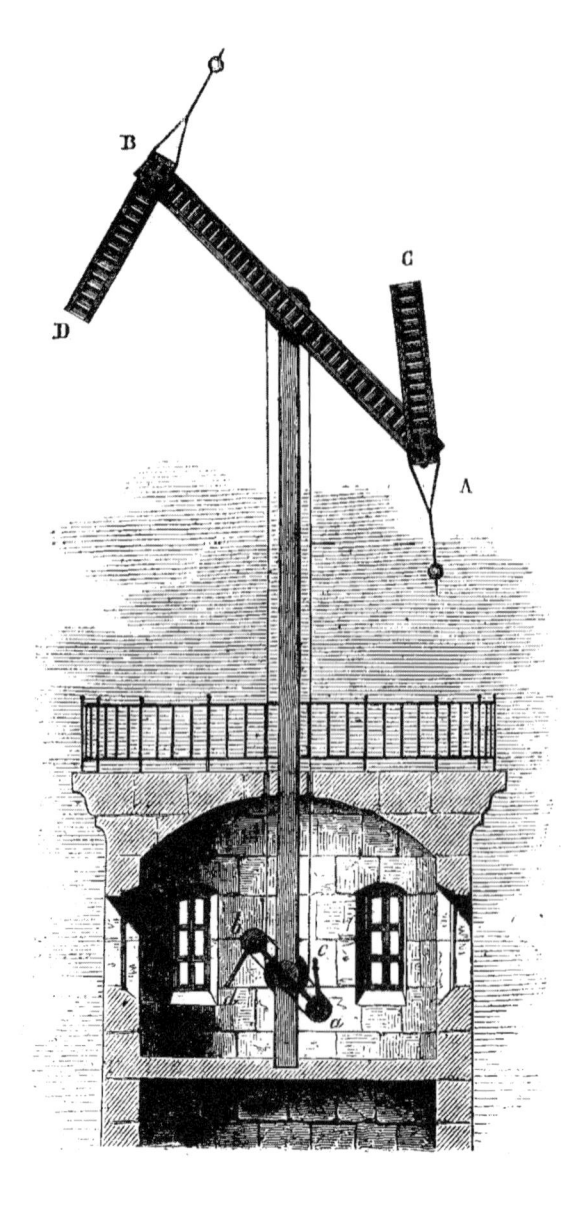

Telegraphe De Chappe
(Luis Figuier 1868).
(Public Domain)

SIGNALS, OPERATORS, POPPIES AND WACs

An alternative flag semaphore system used two flags in specific positions to indicate letters. The equipment was simple but unreliable in windy weather or days of bad visibility. When the weather co-operated the flag semaphore line could reach over a reasonably long distance. In America another manual system, 'wigwag', was developed by US Army, Major Albert J. Myer, a surgeon, using one-flag movements right or left (or by torch or kerosene lantern at night). This was waved back and forth in a binary code, similar to the actions of dots and dashes. The one flag system was considered more mobile than previous means of optical telegraphy and was used by both opponents in the Civil War.[2]

Electric telegraphy, in 1840, was a fledgling point-to-point text system for messages. Through dedicated wires and coded pulses of electric current, the system transmitted information over long distances and was most used in early telegraph messaging using symbolic codes. Far faster than letter writing, the first electric telecommunications system provided a speedy way of communication. Two or more telegraph offices, with some distance between them, were connected by a string of wires supported by wooden utility poles. It was popular until it too, was overtaken by superior systems.

There were many but the most successful fell into two categories. One consisted of needle telegraphs from British inventors William Cooke and Charles Wheatstone in 1837 and the other comprised amateur systems where a pulse activated a telegraph sounder, such as a click. The most famous of these was the invention by American portrait painter, Samuel Morse where he tapped out urgent messages using the dots and dashes alphabetic code on a switch called a telegraph key. Both systems used a single wire, though the Cooke and Wheatstone needle telegraph version tried five wires at first, only to discover they were too costly to install. Instead, they opted for a single wire and trained operators to use a code.

In 1840 the electric telegraph had replaced the optical telegraph in most countries, except France, and became the standard way to send urgent messages for a fee within their country. The exciting advent of submarine telegraphic cables came in 1854 and saw elevating communications to other countries. The impact was huge for families and businesses who benefitted tremendously from instantaneous contact, boosting trade and travel. The Morse code system was standard for all international signalling communication networks by 1865.[3]

* * *

Until the First World War, recruitment of women to the military was rare. Some served in the revolutionary American War of Independence (1775-1783) and in 1811, recommendations came for female nurses, but women did not officially serve until forty years later on the hospital ship USS *Red Rover*, when African American women were paid to serve as crew on the Mississippi River. Instead, a female who wanted to fight had to cunningly disguise herself as a man. During the Civil War (1861-1865), it is estimated that 400-750 disguised women served in the military, but this cannot be corroborated due to concealment of their sex.

In 1901, the Army Nurse Corps was formally established by US Congress and around 21,000 women served in the ANC and US Navy Nurse Corps during the First World War, when 10,000 registered nurses went overseas, many to the Western Front.

'Hello Girls', also served as part of these battlefield units, and were some of the first to go, not as nurses but telephone operators to keep officers connected to their troops. The formal name for this assigned group was the *Signals Corps Female Telephone Operators Unit*. Male soldiers had refused to be switchboard operators, calling it 'women's work', but General John J. Pershing thought women would be more reliable.

Over 7,000 women applied for a position but only 450 were accepted. Signal Corps and telephony training was at Camp Franklin in Maryland.[4] Parker Hitt, under Pershing, supervised the battlefield communications and was supportive of the women and their intellectual capabilities, for these bi-lingual women were no ordinary telephone operators. They worked in Paris and on the front lines, and when officers were often a hundred miles from their troops, they kept the lines of communication open.

In September 1918, Chief Operator Grace Banker from New Jersey, assembled with a group of women to the battlefield's muddy periphery to operate their telephone exchange in the Saint-Mihiel Salient. Pershing's first major command of the American Expeditionary Forces hoped to break through German lines to capture the fortified city of Metz.[5]

Marching a massive advancing army and equipment over battlefield quagmires, became a logistical problem, but the women with their gas masks and helmets, under frightening cannon and gunfire, kept their switchboards operational around the clock. Calling, listening, writing down messages, translating and sometimes decoding – even under

SIGNALS, OPERATORS, POPPIES AND WACs

'Hello Girls' operating switchboards in France. (Public Domain)

heavy fire they did not leave their posts. The attack was successful as the Germans retreated – a moment of pride for America – but the battle was not recognised by Supreme Allied Commander Ferdinand Foch, nor were the women recognised for their service. They were simply expected to blend back into everyday American life, without military discharge or commendation.

Most of the Army Nurse Corps was demobilised reducing their units to a carcass in 1920, but the group was ready in case of another war. Signals, Army Nurse Corps and Navy Nurse Corps received the equivalent of officer ranks and were permitted to wear army insignia on duty, but they didn't receive equivalent pay, nor were they considered part of the US Army or US Navy. Nurses played a huge role in conflict, but other military roles were non-existent (save for the telephone operators – a small experimental group). But attitudes were changing. With the firm actions of women voting and winning debates in Congress, the scene was set for the force of women to be recognised. Suffragists gained more followers; women wanted to be more a part of man's ruling world. Step by step this was being achieved and gradually, women like Genevieve

Hitt, Elizebeth Friedman and Agnes Meyer Driscoll created a path for the force of female intelligence, logic, hard work and efficiency. The female pen was replacing the male dominated aggressive warrior sword.

* * *

Helping the war effort, for most American women, was a voluntary must, but if America joined the Second World War the Women's Army Auxiliary Corps (WAAC) would need to be expanded. Chief of Staff General George Marshall was impressed by the British women's services and liked the idea of regenerating this US service for the Army. A female voice and force in military matters at the time was US Congresswoman, Edith Nourse Rogers from Massachusetts; the first woman elected to Congress in the House of Representatives, after her husband's death.[6]

Edith had visited England with her husband during the First World War, and while there volunteered at the Young Men's Christian Association (YMCA). The British nineteenth century organisation had spread its angel wings rapidly and, as the name suggests they aimed to practise Christian principles by developing 'body, mind and spirit'. The centres were predominantly run by volunteers and before long their help was needed in France to assist soldiers and civilians alike. Notable supporters and volunteers included Olave and Robert Baden-Powell and Clementine Churchill.[7] This seed propagated within Edith and she enrolled to become a 'Gray Lady' in France with the American Red Cross. Later, she served at Walter Reed Hospital in Washington, where her experience in Europe led her to a lifelong commitment to veterans, which for her included the little-celebrated groups of service women, including nurses and telephone operators.

She was fearless, as demonstrated in 1932 when she stared down a gunman in the gallery of the House of Representatives when he demanded the right to speak. She told him, 'You won't do anything.' Her experience with shell-shocked veterans at Walter Reed kicked in, and with eyes focused on his she persuaded the troubled young man to drop his pistol. Most other congressmen had fled, but the dangerous situation was dissolved by Edith and one other. The gunman was arrested.[8]

At the same time as Edith was building her dedication to the humanitarian aspects of war, another American woman, Moina Belle Michael, a schoolteacher from Good Hope, Georgia, conceived the idea of using poppies as a symbol of remembrance for those who served in the First World War. Today, it is a symbol in remembrance for two world wars, and loss of any life in war.

Moina Michael was born in 1869. She was the eldest daughter and second of seven children born to Alice Sherwood Wise and John Marion Michael, a veteran of the Confederate army. The family were rich cotton plantation owners but growing up Moina always wanted to help others and became a schoolteacher in 1885. After many years teaching, she travelled to Europe during the summer of 1914, but her exciting vacation was curtailed by the outbreak of war. At the time she was in Germany but able to leave and went to Rome. En route she was touched by other people's plight and helped 12,000 stranded travellers find a safe passage home to America. Boarding the British royal mail ship, the RMS *Carpathia* – famous for rescuing survivors of the *Titanic* – Moina eventually arrived in the United States, and home, Athens, Georgia. Four years later the RMS *Carpathia* was torpedoed and sunk by the German submarine *U-55*.

By 1917 Moina was a professor at the University of Georgia and took leave of absence when America entered the war. This time she travelled to New York to volunteer at the YWCA training centre for overseas workers. There she was able to relay her European experience to others, her love of the people and the scenery, but this also led to grim news reports conveying destruction of the people and places she loved. On 9 November 1918, while on duty at the annual YMCA Overseas Conference, she read John McCrae's poem in a tatty copy of the November edition of *Ladies' Home Journal*. It was given to her by a departing soldier. '*It seemed as though the silent voices again were vocal, whispering, in sighs of anxiety unto anguish …,*' on the back of envelope she scribbled the first lines of her own version.

'*And now the Torch and Poppy Red, we wear in honour of our Dead. Fear Not that ye have died for naught; We'll teach the lesson that ye wrought, In Flanders Fields.*'

The first lines of her poem, *We Shall Keep the Faith,* were inspired by John McCrae's words. He was a Canadian surgeon who died in Northern France. His poem *In Flanders Fields,* disturbed Moina enough to write her own thoughts and pledged to always wear red poppies in remembrance – a symbol of Flanders Fields. 'This was, for me, a full spiritual experience', she later wrote in her memoir.

THE SECRET LIFE OF AN AMERICAN CODEBREAKER

McCrae's well-known poem was written on 3 May 1915 for his friend Alexis Helmer's funeral who was killed at Ypres. The poem, originally called, *We Shall Not Sleep,* was later published in *Punch* on 8 December 1915. The idea of a silent breeze, stroking white crosses row on row in the sunset glow then, in the last stanza, poppies, *If ye break faith with us who die. We shall not sleep, though poppies grow,* reverberated through Moina. She showed her poem to a few gentlemen at the conference, who gave her $10 for her to buy red silk poppies from Wanamaker's store, which they wore, and the tradition was born.

America's action in the war led to a truce with Germany on 11 November 1918. Armistice Day. Moina returned home and to the University of Georgia, always wearing a red poppy on her collar. Before long she had earned the name 'Poppy Lady'. She pursued her career teaching veterans, beside a lifetime of philanthropy and service as one of Georgia's most famous women. Moina's enthusiasm and efforts were supported in France by Madame E. Guerin after she visited America in 1930.

Armistice Day continues to be marked on the eleventh hour, of the eleventh day of the eleventh month each year – Veterans Day in America, Remembrance Day in Europe. Services and parades are held to solemnly

> Oh! you who sleep in Flanders Fields,
> Sleep sweet – to rise anew!
> We caught the torch you threw
> And holding high, we keep the Faith
> With All who died.
>
> We cherish, too, the Poppy red
> That grows on fields where valor led;
> It seems to signal to the skies
> That blood of heroes never dies,
> But lends a lustre to the red
> Of the flower that blooms above the dead
> In Flanders Fields.
>
> And now the Torch and Poppy Red
> We wear in honor of our dead.
> Fear not that ye have died for naught;
> We'll teach the lesson that ye wrought
> In Flanders Fields.
>
> By Moina Michael, 1918

Above left: We Shall Keep the Faith by Moina Michael, 1918.

Above right: 'The Poppy Lady', Moina Belle Michael. (Public Domain, University of Georgia Rare Documents)

remind us of all the men and women's lives sacrificed, to celebrate the end of hostilities on the Western Front,[9] and to instil in future generations that events of war should never happen again. A US postage stamp, several roads in Georgia and a Liberty Ship are named in Moina Michael's honour.

* * *

Despite telephone operators and nurses serving on the front lines during the First World War, the idea of women in uniform was still controversial: Who will look after the household? Who will care for the children? Who will cook, who will clean, who will do the washing? The female employees and volunteers of the United States Armed Forces were mostly civilians, and as Edith Rogers had seen, they received no benefits – no housing, no food, no insurance or medical care, no pension, no legal protection, no compensation for their families in cases of death – in stark contrast to British Army women loaned to American Expeditionary Forces (AEF), who received at least some benefits in line with their responsibilities.

Though controversial, American military in 1941 expected to enrol 11,000 women and a law was proposed, but this languished for a while in the shadows of the Bureau of the Budget, after the quota was considered too low. However, events in Pearl Harbor soon changed the situation and when America officially entered the war in December, there was a sudden rush to resurrect the bill, though it was not signed into law until 15 May 1942. With the WAAC re-established to full military status, the myth that it was perilous for women's femininity, rendering them unmarriageable, was mostly deflated. With renewed support from General Marshall (having rejected an earlier proposal he then agreed women would be 'useful'), Edith's recommendations transformed the Women's Army Auxiliary Corp, modelled on the British ATS (Auxiliary Territorial Service). Prior to 1943, women's involvement in the military was fewer than 1,000 for the army and 700 for the navy; most were nurses.[10]

However, the terms 'immorality' and 'camp followers' were still uttered for prostitutes and infatuated female fans who chased certain types of soldier from one assignment to another. A massive slander campaign on the home front, hence, stalled recruitment. Soldiers vehemently opposed women in uniform, warning their sisters and

US Representative, Edith Rogers built her life around the humanitarian aspects of war. (Public Domain)

friends they would be labelled, if not prostitutes, then lesbians. Fierce local women of idle chit-chat whined and viciously harassed newcomers who were 'not welcome in their towns'. Most resented the attention WAACs received and the competition for employment, especially where women replaced their menfolk who had left for war. Complaints from disgruntled or discharged recruits also did not help, but eventually, all investigations indicated the rumours were unnecessary or untrue.

Intelligent girls rose above the mayhem. Jobs for women with brains, good morals and imagination were in abundance in Washington. They were needed for clerical and encoding work. Marshall also believed they were suited to telecommunications due to their fine motor skills and dexterity. Girls had a willingness to work boring and routine jobs and (perhaps like Pershing), he felt they made fewer mistakes than men.[11]

The new WAAC recruitment goal was for 25,000 women in the first year, but the Secretary of War, Henry L. Stimson, authorised a recruitment expansion to 150,000. As 'Auxiliaries', meaning not part of the regular army, the women were trained, given food, clothing, housing, medical care and pay, but they did not receive overseas pay, death benefits, medical help as veterans, retirement or disability pensions. Neither were they governed by army regulations if captured, meaning they were not protected by international conventions in respect of prisoner of war status.

SIGNALS, OPERATORS, POPPIES AND WACs

Edith Nourse Rogers' first graduating class was at Fort Des Moines, Iowa, August 1942, and the word 'Auxiliary' was also dropped cementing the importance of the women's role in the US Army – WAC, the Women's Army Corps had achieved full military significance.

'Silence Means Security', whispered one of the WAC's propaganda posters. The women were trained in three disciplines of confidentiality depending on their ability and efficiency: linguists, office clerks, postal clerks, typists, stenographers and switchboard operators. Others became mechanics and cooks or undertook other non-combative training. As Janice embarked on the mysterious cryptology course, many were also being recruited for other secret roles around the country including at Oakridge, Tennessee. Here 422 WACs supported scientists and administration in the Top Secret Manhattan Engineering District.[12]

African American women also served in the WAC, but segregation was much the same as American civilian life then, especially women's boarding houses in Washington DC, although specialty training schools were not segregated. The US Army's aim was to have a force of 10 per cent African American women – proportional to the US population of the time – but only 5.1 per cent enrolled.[13]

WAC Army Captain Frances Keegan Marquis was the first female to command the newly formed 149th WAC Post Headquarters Company for deployment overseas. Almost 200 volunteers sailed from Daytona, Florida as the first women's expeditionary force of the Second World War. Their mission was to serve with General Eisenhower at his campaign headquarters in Algeria, North Africa. The WACs had secretarial, linguistic and other specialist duties in administration, including postal duties and switchboard. Ernie Pyle, a roving correspondent during the Second World War, said of the 149th company that, 'When a WAC takes over a switchboard from a soldier, efficiency goes up about 1,000 percent.'

Captain Marquis had a hand-picked team of women and, as expeditionary forces, they had to remedy all manner of problems. Often this was finding equipment that had been delivered to the men's division, such as typewriters, cooking equipment and transport![14] She was popular with the press, being the first female officer in this role, but she was not always liked by some of her troops when it came to promotion, and rumourmongers accused her of favouritism rather than ability – some, much to their chagrin.

Chapter 12

WAVES

Other branches of US Military also expanded their bases. The Navy WAVES (United States Naval Women's Reserve – Women Accepted for Volunteer Emergency Service), SPARS (US Coast Guard Women's Reserve), US Marine Corps Women's Reserve and the civil WASP (Women Airforce Service Pilots), grew to emulate the main shore-based strengths of the earlier established British female services such as the Wrens (WRNS – Women's Royal Navy Service), the ATS (Auxiliary Territorial Service) and WAAF (Women's Auxiliary Air Force). There was great admiration for women in uniform. They always looked magnificent.

* * *

Janice discovered she was to join the WAVES, an illustrious group of uniformed women, called to war as non-nurse American recruits. Like the army in 1919, nurses who served answered to male US Navy officers. Now, twenty-three years later, Naval Reserve Lieutenant Commander Mildred H. McAfee was commissioned to lead women. The popular good-humoured president of Wellesley College had taken leave of absence for the position as director.

Prejudices of the male-led Army were also prevalent in the Navy. The idea that women would remain permanently in the service was absurd to US Navy chiefs. They believed the word 'emergency', meant only temporary, to the end of the war, when female service would cease. According to Virginia Gildersleeve's memoir – Dean of Barnard, one of the Seven Sisters colleges at the time and instrumental in founding the WAVES – the old guard of Admirals and the Chair of the Senate's Committee of Naval Affairs, had argued that 'admitting women into the Navy would break up homes and amount to a step backwards in civilisation'.[1]

WAVES

Despite resistance from conservative officers, the Office of Naval Intelligence started to recruit female college students as early as January 1942. In that sector women had already proven themselves having the required skills of diligence, logic and concentration to succeed and above all, the necessary attribute of confidentiality. Further demands for female participation in the US Navy also came from other sectors, including Margaret Chung, the first known American-born Chinese female physician, and the First Lady of the United States, Eleanor Roosevelt. They knew the programme was needed. On 30 July 1942, Public Law 689 was signed by President Franklin D. Roosevelt permitting women to serve in the Navy. The law passed with the substantial efforts of these women as part of the Navy's Women's Advisory Council. The WAVES were *in* the Navy, but most could only speculate if the women's service would survive after the war, as commissioned officers were told their service was only for the duration of the war – plus six months.

'It was an exciting time. One thing people ask is: "Why were we chosen?"' Janice recalled in her interview. 'But we never did find out why.'

'It was not hard to keep the secret from family and friends because this was war time, and nobody asked.' She was sure her family might have wondered as they knew she had special classes on Fridays, and probably they went to her public induction service.

'At some point I know my family was checked.'

Janice's father was too old to be drafted and nobody else in the family was in the Services, but she discovered afterwards the FBI had gone up and down the block, talking to neighbours where she lived, to uncover information about her and her family.

* * *

As Janice absorbed the secret cryptology course, a conference took place in Casablanca in January 1943, code named SYMBOL. The main participants were Winston Churchill, Charles de Gaulle, Henri Giraud and Franklin Roosevelt. They discussed future battles and likely outcomes such as the Italian campaign, a future cross channel invasion, a declaration of 'unconditional surrender' by the Axis Powers – Germany, Italy and Japan – and, following the Churchill/Roosevelt invasion of French controlled Algiers, unification between the French fighting forces of de Gaulle's France and North Africa, through Giraud.

THE SECRET LIFE OF AN AMERICAN CODEBREAKER

On 17 May 1943, replacing the October 1942 Holden Agreement,[2] BRUSA was signed after a month of discussions. The talks regarding the handling of intelligence took place under orders from Chiefs of Command, President Roosevelt and Prime Minister Churchill. The agreement was constructed for Britain and America to formally share a deeper level of information, including TOP SECRET ULTRA. Methods and analyses of Britain's war systems and strategies would be revealed, parallel with America's success on Japanese codes and codebreaking methods. Joint regulations for the handling and distribution of the intriguing, highly sensitive and confidential material was established. This led to the formalisation of strict security regulations, procedures and protocols for co-operation, as part of signals intelligence (SIGINT) and US National Security Agency, when three military officials, Colonel Alfred McCormack of USA Special Branch Military Intelligence, Colonel Telford Taylor of Military Intelligence and Colonel William Friedman, Army Signals Intelligence, visited Commander Edward Travis, head of British Royal Naval Intelligence, to implement the process.[3]

* * *

At the same time, RAF Wing Commander 'Jim' Rose, Analyst and Deputy Head of a GC&CS section who determined the military importance of 'intelligence received', visited Washington to select a dozen US personnel to work at Bletchley Park, many of them women. The extended codebreaking collaboration between America and Britain was beginning to gel. In total 480 American personnel would spend time at Bletchley Park.

Janice had taken the Navy course and passed the test in 1943. She could recognise letters of the alphabet that were most frequent, and those that appeared together – *s* and *t*; trios like *est, ing* and *ive*, and quads like *tion*. Terms such as 'route transposition', 'cipher alphabets' and 'poly-alphabetic substitution ciphers' were explained, where the Vignère Square was demonstrated (A poly-alphabetic system that uses a key and a double-entry table). She learned the names of ciphers and their functions, manual methods of codebreaking – non-additive maths and those where strips of paper were pulled through slatted cardboard like a slide rule to reveal a solution.[4]

WAVES

*Playfai*r was another system – using a *diagraph* invented by scientist Charles Wheatstone in 1854, which encrypts pairs of letters. The diagraph substitution cipher employed a table where one letter of the alphabet is omitted, and the remaining 25 letters are arranged in a 5 x 5 grid. Usually the J is omitted, but will share a spot with I, the letter preceding it. Messages are encoded by breaking the grid into 2-letter pieces. Repeated letters in the same piece are usually separated by an X.

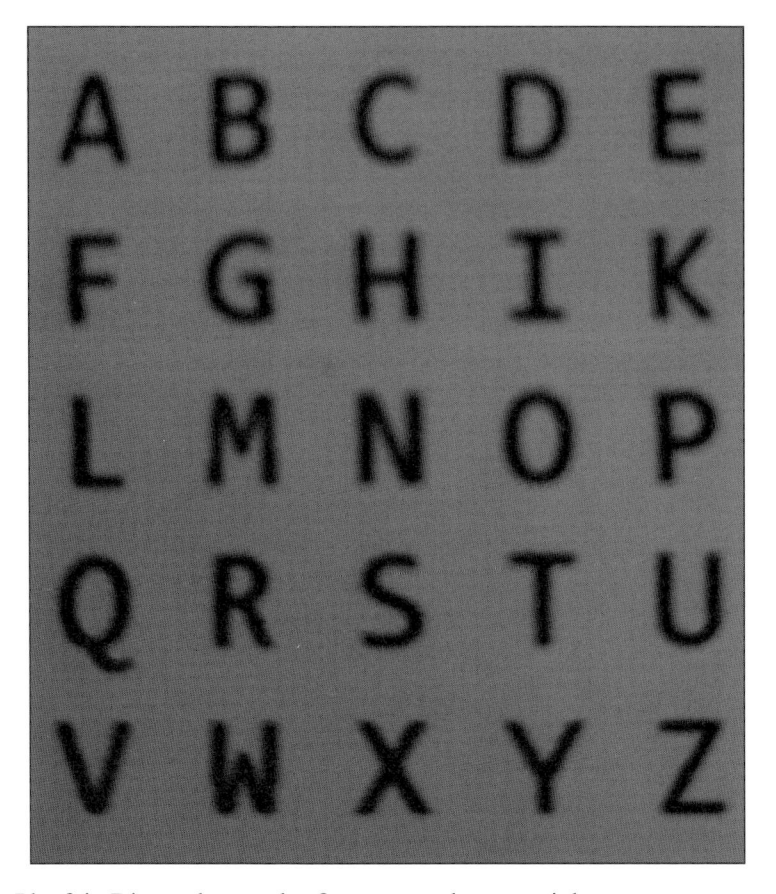

```
A B C D E
F G H I K
L M N O P
Q R S T U
V W X Y Z
```

The Playfair Diagraph was the first pen and paper cipher system to encrypt pairs of letters in cryptologic history. It carries the name of Wheatstone's friend Lord Playfair of St. Andrews, who promoted its use. At first the British Foreign Office rejected the secret system after agreeing it could indeed be taught to schoolboys, 'but you could never teach it to attachés!' It was eventually used in the Second Boer War, the First World War and the Second World War. The single letter substitution cipher of the Vignère Square was more complex. (Rumkin.com)

The message 'Hello one and all', might then read: HE / LX / LO / ON / EA / ND / AL / XL. If there is not an even number of letters in the message it was padded with an additional X. Letter pair positions were noted in the grid, while HE formed two corners of a rectangle. The two other letters in the corners of the rectangle were therefore C and K. Then H was slid to the E column. Directly under the E is K. Similarly, with E, it is slid back to the H column and the letter above is noted, C. Therefore, the first two letters of code are KC. LX becomes NV. If two letters were in the same row, they simply slide the letter one position to the right. LO became MP, EA – the E then rolls behind the graph to the same line and becomes an A with A becoming a B. A and L are in the same column and move down one letter for each etc., until the coded message reads KCNVMPPOABOCFQVN. Non letters are ignored and not encoded. Numbers must be spelled out. Punctuation is also ignored.[5]

* * *

In May of 1943, a Public Induction Service was held at Janice's training college. Navy, Navy WAVES, Army WACs and Marines; there were even women in the Coast Guard (SPARS). So many women were entering the services, nobody thought anything about her special group of WAVES, what they did or why they were there.

'After our group of eight or ten attended the Induction we graduated in June, and early July we were sent for eight weeks Naval indoctrination. The Navy had two schools for WAVES – Smith and Mount Holyoke, both in Massachusetts. I ended up at Mount Holyoke for four weeks as Seaman followed by four weeks as Midshipman. It was a quick wartime crash course so that we could be slipped into the system. We had lectures on naval history, ships, airplanes and everything. We had a drill twice a week and had to pass. I would say there were at least a hundred WAVES that summer at Mount Holyoke. We took exams and became Ensigns, just like that.' She snapped her fingers.

'About eighty had orders to Washington to General Communications, and all of us, who were Ensigns were cleared to handle TOP SECRET information.'

Janice Martin became an Ensign in the WAVES in the summer of 1943. (Janice Benario Archive)

Janice had rapidly become a Junior Commissioned Officer.

I WANT TO BE A NAVY WAVE
Marching song to the tune of 'I Want to be a Friend of Yours'
By Betty McClinchie
I want to be a Navy WAVE, mmm,
And a little bit more.
I want to be an Ensign, too, mmm,
And a little bit more.
I want to wear a suit of blue, mmm,
And a little bit more.
One blue stripe would be all right.
But oh, for a little bit more!

Chapter 13

Going to the Chapel

Officer Janice Martin was proud of her new position and her new uniform. Washington's Bureau of Naval Personnel issued a long list of Women's Reserve uniform regulations. The document was approved by two men, Randall Jacobs and Frank Knox, but one hopes women had some input. With some adaptations, the regulations emulated British Wrens.[1] The rules used standard US Navy phraseology and was strictly enforced by senior officers in all orders and discussions: personal pride in wearing the uniform with no other attire to be worn in public other than WAVES high grade issue uniform with insignia respective to their rank, corps or rating.

Only when taking part in exercise or if at home with less than three guests present could the women be out of uniform. If a WAVE became a bridesmaid or married, their commanding officer could authorise a bridesmaid's dress or wedding gown, or an attire other than that prescribed by the senior officer for the day, season or occasion. Women's uniform orders, in general, corresponded to those of men's uniform re locality, and the duty performed with variations for weather. Civilian clothes could not be worn with any part of the uniform except if the garment was not distinctly Naval in appearance, such as the lightweight water-repellent navy-blue raincoat/overcoat and Havelock (a matching rain hat designed to cover the main hat of the uniform, said to originate from an 1850s British General in India, Sir Henry Havelock, to protect his neck from the sun). An umbrella, considered non-military, was not to be carried.

WAVE officer's hats were navy blue with interchangeable white or grey cap covers, depending on the uniform of the day or season. The brimmed hat was constructed of high-grade cotton or wool. White uniform cap covers were either cotton Palm Beach cloth, tropical worsted or similar lightweight cloth. Grey uniform cap covers were to match the colour and fabric of the uniform. All hats were to be worn squarely on the head with brims curled up on each side and straight at the front and back. Hair was not to be seen under the front brim, nor over the jacket or coat collar. WAVES were permitted to wear make-up, but only enough to be presentable, or 'look human', as some described.

A host of other rules came into force such as women could only remove their navy-blue jacket when the prescribed navy-blue shirt, and the reserve blue tie – of rayon or silk – was tied under the collar and worn with the appropriate insignia of rank or rating. Skirts were flared with front pockets. A general grey Working Uniform could be worn with a white short-sleeved shirt and black tie; jackets could be removed indoors, but these had navy-blue plastic buttons, instead of the main uniform's gilt button. The black tie had to be worn with white shirts, long-sleeved or short-sleeved, with Service Dress White. Belted uniform shirt dresses were also provided. The black service shoes always had closed toes and heels, both for drill and dress shoes, but black pumps could be worn when not on parade. White service dress shoes were to be worn with Service Dress White. Heels up to 16/8ths (2 inches) were permitted, but suede, patent or novelty shoes were not. Beige stockings and black or white gloves were allowed.

Underwear was up to the women, but they had to ensure they possessed adequate and freshly laundered supplies. Cleanliness and neatness were of the utmost importance. No pins or jewellery of any form could be worn when in uniform, except for an inconspicuous wedding band, or authorised military decorations, medals and ribbons. Flowers were not to be worn or carried. Only a US Navy issue muffler of white silk, rayon or wool, was permissible for winter months. A Navy design black handbag with a shoulder strap was provided for bare necessities. This had a special cover which converted to a prim white purse in an instant. Under-slips were not to show below skirts and all stocking seams had to be straight, right side out. Only plain hose was permitted, no decorative motifs of any kind. Navy-blue cotton ankle socks were only to be worn with slacks, with a coverall or while exercising.

Exceptions were protective coverings for their job, such as smocks or coveralls and caps. Slacks could be worn with the prescribed matching jacket, but they were only to be worn while performing their job (the jacket could be removed while working). Articles of official clothing had to be marked and labelled with the WAVE's name written in legible indelible ink. Some women made clothes for themselves or had tailors provide certain uniform garments, but all had to follow the strict US Navy rules for fabric, pattern and specification. Everything was regularly inspected for care, cleanliness and fitting, but transfer or exchange of clothing was not permitted without authorisation from the commanding officer.

Such rules were not treated with scepticism or flippancy, but solid deference by all recruits and their leaders, especially following a period of bad press regarding females in the military. An attitude of appreciation and respect was paramount, but there was favouritism for the WAVE uniform. Their smart navy-blue was far popular than the WAC's uncomfortable khaki drab.

* * *

Ranked above Chief Warrant Officer and below Lieutenant, Ensign Janice Martin prepared to enter the secret world of the USA war rooms.

'We were assigned to an office in the Naval Communications Annex. It was there we received our individual orders. One girl from Radcliffe, two others from Goucher and I were assigned to this very secret office. We were instantly cleared at a higher level of secrecy for TOP SECRET ULTRA. Only our section, the highest commanders and Churchill knew about it.

Onc of the girls from Baltimore I knew was Jane Thornton Apostol. She was also from Goucher. The bus ride was long from Main Navy in the centre of Washington. When we arrived, the four of us were taken into an office and then, separately, into the chapel, we were told that if word got out, or if any one of us talked about our work, it would be considered treason. And, yes, treason meant you'd have to be shot.'

She paused for a second to contemplate that time.

'Then we were taken back to the office, where no one else could go except for around thirty-five people who were already in there.'

One imagines the strict rigidity the new recruits felt after receiving such a startling edict, and their reluctance after to look each other in the eye. There were two other WAVES from Goucher, but nothing could be said to anyone outside about who they were or what they did.

Janice had been sworn to secrecy at various times on this journey, during training at college and the WAVES induction course. Even so,

Arial view of the Navy Communications Annex, formerly Mount Vernon Seminary, a Collegiate High School for Girls 1917-1942. (National Archives NARA)

when entering Navy Intelligence another document was required, the United States Oath of Secrecy. It was compulsory for all military and civilian personnel to sign stating they would 'support and defend the Constitution of the United States, against all enemies, foreign and domestic'. They 'swore not to discuss their activities with anyone outside official duties for now and forever,' because 'to do so would result in prosecution under the Espionage Act of 1917.' The new recruits were photographed holding a sign with their name, rank and serial number. Their image was then mounted onto an official ID card permitting them entry to certain parts of the building.[2]

Her office at the Naval Communications Annex (NCA) was a requisitioned girls' school, on Massachusetts and Nebraska Avenues, next to the American University.

'The Navy had taken over the girls' school, and our office was in the former gym. The doors were locked and could not be opened without punching a code into a buzzer device. When the door opened all anyone could see was a large room divider with nothing on it. Nobody could see us or anything behind the screen; it was just a blank room divider.' The door code changed every week.

'Each of us had a wooden desk with three drawers on one side, and a wooden chair. There was no modern office furniture, just aging yellow pine, hard to touch and hard to sit on for eight hours – very austere. At the time it didn't frighten us, but it took a while for the situation to sink in and to realise how isolated we really were,' Janice added thoughtfully. 'In the NCA there was a cafeteria where you ate your meals, you knew the people around you. I knew other Goucher girls who joined the WAVES who weren't in our class. Some worked there, but you couldn't talk about anything to do with your job over lunch.

We passed the time of day with things like, what your mother was doing, new clothes, old clothes, things you were wearing, or other everyday things…, every date you had, where you had been, which movies you'd seen… and so on.

Of course, my parents made sure I had the morning paper while I was in DC, I wanted to be on top of events in Baltimore and global news. We could talk about anything, but absolutely nothing about our secret work.'

'Loose Lips, Sink Ships! It couldn't be drummed into us often enough. Our TOP SECRET ULTRA work was the most secret of all.'

'The Bombe Machines,' Janice recalled, 'were in the room below.'

Chapter 14

Battle of the Atlantic

Bombe machines found cipher solutions quickly when suggestions, 'cribs', were provided by human decoders. These hints became 'menus' for Bombe machines and if a menu was successful the cipher key was revealed and messages for the day could be decoded. Bombe machines did not decode messages; this was the job of decoders and other machine operators once the key was known. Janice worked on the results of deciphered and translated German Enigma messages and helped prepare TOP SECRET, categorised and analysed reports.

For their analysis, large maps adorned the walls to track movement of dangerous German U-boats. The collective aim was to guide supply convoys safely to their destination. These included the shipment of Allied troops across the Atlantic Ocean in both directions, and matériel for D-Day preparations.

'Wolfpacks – we *knew* where the German U-boats were,' said Janice. 'Allied convoys were marked by small red flags attached to each pin. Submarines and convoys were marked with moveable metal markers.'

Neutral countries' shipping was also tracked. Under strict security, intelligence from Janice's section was passed for further analysis to a higher authority where decisions were made from the data they supplied.

'Information from our office was compiled and a daily envelope passed to Admiral Ernest J. King, the Chief Naval Officer (CNO) in the Navy Department. We were the intelligence layer in the organisation directly beneath the Admiral's office – just one step from the top.'

Whether Janice's department also made recommendations, however, is unclear. During the Second World War Admiral Ernest Joseph King, Commander in Chief, United States Fleet and Chief of Naval Operations (COMINCH-CNO) directed the United States Navy's operations, planning and administration, and was the US Navy's member of the Joint Chiefs of Staff and the Allied Combined Chiefs of Staff. The Admiral participated in most important war conferences but had seen little previous action.

His naval career had been resurrected in 1939 by his friend, Admiral Harold 'Betty' Stark, who recognised King's talent for a certain style of command. He considered him wasted on the General Board – a group affectionately known as the elephant's graveyard – where senior personnel advised other senior officers before retirement. After Fleet Admiral William D. Leahy, King was the U.S. Navy's second most senior officer and the second Admiral to be promoted to five-star rank. One of his many quotes defined his rigor:

'The mark of a great ship-handler is never getting into situations that require great ship-handling.'[1]

King served as staff in the Atlantic Fleet during the First World War and was a frequent visitor to the British Royal Navy. At times, he saw action on board their ships, but his apparent Anglophobia grew from

Admiral Ernest Joseph King, Commander in Chief of United States Fleet and Chief of Naval Operations (COMINCH-CNO). (National Archives Public Domain)

his supposed bad experience. After that time, he became a captain and later led the US Naval Post Graduate School. He was appointed Commander in Chief of the Atlantic Fleet in 1940, Admiral in February 1941, Commander-in-Chief of the USA Fleet by December 1941 and CNO during 1942. He was considered the greatest Admiral of the 20th Century, but some military historians say he never commanded wartime ships or fleets at sea and that his 'unexplained' Anglophobia caused him to make bad decisions costing Allied lives.

One of these incidents, King's dissenters say, was his aversion to the British recommendation of land-based blackouts along the eastern seaboard. Commercial ships travelled without adequate convoy protection and back-lit vessels along the eastern coast were easy targets for German U-boats. His refusal to implement the blackout system led to disastrous shipping losses and loss of life. He also refused the offer of British convoy escorts when America had only a small number of vessels. Instead of escorts the US Navy and US Coast Guard performed routine anti-submarine patrols, but their regularity became known to German U-boat commanders who attacked in line with US schedules.

* * *

The Battle of the Atlantic was one of the longest military campaigns in the Second World War, starting September 1939 to May 1945. It was a tonnage war, a term coined by Germany's supreme commander Admiral Karl Dönitz. The U-boat commander's aim was to destroy as many supply ships as possible and starve war-torn Britain into submission.

The potential breakability of the German naval cipher was of little concern to Dönitz. He had seen the excellence of the German navy's code books and Enigma cipher system and was certain his U-boat tactics and orders were safe. He planned group attacks where the first U-boat to find a convoy would radio its position and quietly maintain covert contact with the target. U-boat HQ would centralise the information, including locations of enemy (Allied) vessels, then direct other submarines to the convoys' position for a combined attack. But during this time, 'pack' radio silence was maintained to divert and confuse the Allies, who were also listening. Dönitz and his German submarine officers believed the plan would work, leaving allied convoys and their supplies on the bottom of the ocean and choking Britain's imports.

Though Dönitz knew high-frequency transmission activity would break the vital rule of radio silence, 'the invisible arm', in his view coordination of U-boats outweighed the long-distance radio direction-finding skills of the enemy. He further thought the foe unable to solve coded sighting reports and, even if they could, there would be no time for countermeasures to his coded U-boat instructions. Their wolfpack strategy and the strength and invincibility of the Enigma messages would prevail. But he was wrong.[2]

Submarine Kapitänleutnant Fritz-Julius Lemp, under Dönitz's command, had claimed a quarry of victims since 9 March 1941, including several merchant ships in the Atlantic. Now his U-boat shadowed the westward-heading convoy OB318 and Lemp transmitted a sighting report. It was a signal that was intercepted by the British. Efficient direction-finding had located the enemy transmitter and the convoy was advised to alter its course. Dönitz, however, ordered the U-boat to maintain contact and attack if possible. The next day the allied convoy was attacked again and the hunt escalated to capture the notorious *U-110*.

HMS *Aubretia*, a convoy escort ship, traced the 252-foot *U-110* using sonar (ASDICS),[3] and with destroyer HMS *Broadway*, dropped depth charges attacking the submarine. Affected by the explosions, the new Atlantic Type IXB U-boat was forced to surface and as it emerged, HMS *Broadway* prepared to ram, but instead fired two depth charges underneath the craft to stop it from scuttling. Navy orders were given to refrain from destroying the submarine but instead board the craft, take the crew prisoner and recover their code books. A battle raged, and under gunfire from HMS *Broadway* and HMS *Bulldog*, a British B-class destroyer, Kapitänleutnant Lemp eventually gave orders to abandon ship and set the craft to self-destruct. HMS *Bulldog* closed in for the kill and for what turned out to be their most important task.

As *U-110*'s crew surrendered and boarded the navy tender alongside, 28-year-old Lemp saw the submarine was not sinking and attempted to swim back to destroy the German records and systems. Now a deadly gun battle ensued, and fifteen men were killed through drowning or gun fire, including Lemp. In the end thirty-two German Navy personnel were captured. But along with them came the main prize of German Enigma cipher keys, daily schedules, lists of daily rotor-arm settings and an Enigma Machine.

The next day, under Churchill's orders, the submarine was quietly sunk while being towed to Iceland. The capture of *U-boat 110* on 9 May 1941 was kept quiet, and the Enigma machine and code books were surreptitiously taken to GC&CS at Bletchley Park. Codebreaker, Alan Turing, now had the bounty he needed for more efficient codebreaking. Soon further 'captures' or 'pinches' were made, and Bletchley's message processing centre was able to decrypt and analyse German Navy Enigma messages at a much faster pace.

Though confidential talks had taken place with US military during their visit to Britain, February 1941, Churchill kept the demise of *U-110* and the codebreaking prize a closely guarded secret. For many months, the event remained highly classified under TOP SECRET ULTRA and President Roosevelt was not aware of the capture until informed by Winston Churchill in January 1942; even then he was told the codebooks came from a weather ship. The seizing of *U-110* and its treasure, later named Operation Primrose, was one of the best-kept secrets of the war, and for decades after.

However, other intelligence was divulged, and senior officials from Bletchley Park were dispatched to Washington to aid in the exchange of codebreaking systems. Churchill's correspondence to President Roosevelt referred to his secret source as 'Boniface', a cover name for a non-existent spy and the covert Bletchley operation. In exchange America agreed to provide information on their Army Signals success on attacking Japanese ciphers; a much-needed fix for Churchill in February 1942 after the fall of Singapore.

* * *

After losing its stellar submarine *U-110*, Germany continued attacks on merchant shipping in another era they called their *Happy Time*. There were two such periods. The first *Happy Time* was during the early phase of the Battle of the Atlantic from July 1940 after the Fall of France. U-boat crews referred to *Die Glückliche Zeit (Happy Time)* when German submarines successfully attacked British shipping in the Atlantic. Over 280 Allied ships were sunk off the north-west approaches of Ireland with losses of nearly 1.5 million tons of merchant shipping and many lives.

BATTLE OF THE ATLANTIC

This lasted until October, though some historians stretch to April 1941 after Allied hits on German targets caused prominent U-boats and their commanders to be lost, two of whom were Günther Prien and Joachim Schepke in March 1941.

The first 'happy time' grew from British shipping's lack of radar and technology to detect enemy submarines during night-time surface attacks. ASDIC could only detect submerged German U-boats. High Frequency and Direction Finding was needed. Known as HF/DF, the science was developed in 1926 by a Scot, Robert Watson-Watt, as a system for locating thunderstorms and lightning. He worked for the UK Met Office, but this wasn't developed for intelligence until the late 1930s. In the early days of war, the advantageous detection qualities of HF/DF became apparent for air combat, and rival manufacturers fought to meet the high demands for units. RAF Fighter Command planes were first to be fitted with the advance information scheme as part of the Dowding System, a ground-controlled interception network across United Kingdom airspace. The units helped win the air fight in the Battle of Britain, but it wasn't until 1942 that smaller HF/DF (known colloquially as 'Huff-Duff') units became available as common fixtures on Royal Navy ships, and Robert Watson-Watt was one of the first advisors to visit America, after Pearl Harbor.

Attacks on the Eastern Seaboard

Operation *Paukenschlag*, literally translated as Operation Bang (or Operation Drumbeat), was considered the second *Happy* or *Golden Time* for German submariners. From January 1942, Germany attacked the North American coast. To many this period is known as 'America's Second Pearl Harbor', with blame squarely laid at Admiral King's feet for failing to act earlier, and the convoy system where a shortage of suitable escort vessels (combat destroyers) left merchant ships vulnerable. Though some say that lone merchant ships might have been more successful in delivering their cargos, if a tempting hunt for a group of vessels – a prime tonnage target for hungry German Wolfpacks – didn't exist.

Germany considered that America's defence was weak and disorganised, as five long-range U-boats prepared an extended journey with maximum supplies and weaponry, to inflict great damage on their foe. Each submarine carried sealed directives only to be opened after passing 20°W. The primary target was the Eastern Sea Frontier, a US Naval area stretching from Canada to St. Augustine Florida, with a 200-mile buffer from the coastline, though for this mission only Maine to North Carolina was targeted.

'Weak and disorganised' was an understatement. Rear Admiral Adolphus Andrews was lacking any kind of modern fleet with only seven coast guard cutters, four converted yachts, three 1919-vintage patrol boats, two gunboats from 1905 and four wooden submarine chasers. He had approximately 100 aircraft, but these were only useful for short range flights and training. There was a larger aircraft, but in traditional US Navy and Army Air Force conflict, this was not under his control. Nonetheless, the USAAF plane was not equipped for anti-submarine work.[4]

As early as 18 December 1941, the U-boat pack of five Type IX submarines departed Lorient in France and made way through the Bay of Biscay.

Meanwhile, Allied Signals Intelligence, British wireless listeners known as 'Y', were on twenty-four-hour watch to pick up Morse code messages for all shipping. Operators waited patiently with headphones, a pad of paper and a pencil, ready to spring into action as soon as a signal started broadcasting. Often, they worked on the same radio band, day in, day out, and became familiar with the sender's signals, though they were unable to detect them. Secretly 'Y' operators intercepted and expertly captured the enemy's Morse code message. Military services recruited mostly women as listeners in Britain, Navy Wrens, Army ATS and Air Force WAAFs. Some trained at Greenwich or Wimbledon in South London, or Beaumanor Hall in Leicestershire, while others worked at remote costal stations. Young male radio enthusiasts were also recruited as part of the Royal Observer Corps and listened from home. Others worked from outstations around the world.

On HMS *Flowerdown*, a land-based facility in England, near Winchester (not a ship at all), a Wren noted the end of a submarine message – she was accustomed to the sender's style of sign-off message – and ripped off the sheet to pass directly to her supervisor, who hovered behind ready to relay the message by teleprinter or motorcycle dispatch rider to the government war station at Bletchley Park.

After the message was registered, decoded and analysed it was reported to Charles Rodger Noel Winn's Submarine Tracking Room at the OIC. The submarine's position was plotted on a chart. Winn sent a coded early warning cable to the Royal Canadian Navy (the enemy could listen too – hence the coding); with a small amount of evidence, he concluded the location of the target and sent a detailed warning to Admiral King, citing 'a heavy concentration of U-boats off the North American Seaboard'. Not only were the five U-boats on their way, but other packs too, a total of twenty-one U-boats. The intelligence was to be relayed to US combined area commanders, but despite the need for urgent action, nothing was done.

Due to the British experience of moving troops around in convoys via the east coast of America (the 18th Division), they had recommended that obvious standard routes be avoided where possible, that navigational markers, lighthouses and other benefits to the enemy be eliminated and that a strict costal blackout be imposed on all villages, towns and cities. Moreover, air and sea forces should patrol by day to restrict U-boat flexibility. None of the recommendations were followed. On 18 December, coastal shipping used their usual routes and navigational lights. Communities on the coast did not wish to 'consider' turning off their tourist illuminations as it was 'bad for business'. There were no orders, only requests, which nobody heeded.

Why was America so unprepared on the East Coast? Roosevelt had loaned fifty obsolete First World War destroyers to Britain in return for foreign bases, but this was almost irrelevant since the turning circle of such large ships to repel submarines was futile. Their firepower, however, for a surface attack would have been a significant deterrent. Nevertheless, anti-submarine vessels were still not high on the list of priorities in the new US naval construction programme. Meanwhile, freighters and tankers were sunk in coastal waters, and any destroyers that were available remained in port. At the time of the first attacks twenty-five Atlantic Convoy Escort Command Destroyers were recalled to the US East Coast, including seven in New York Harbor.[5]

On 14 January, when *U-123* sank the Norwegian Tanker *Norness* close to Long Island, no warships were employed, allowing the same U-boat to sink the British tanker *Coimbra* off Sandy Hook, New Jersey, the following night.

Admiral Andrews was warned two days before that three or four U-boats were about to commence an attack on coastal shipping, but he refused to institute a convoy system saying it would only provide the U-boats with more targets. By this time there were thirteen destroyers in New York Harbor, but all were idle and *U-123* spent the next few nights hitting easy targets such as navigation lights. At times *U-123* was operating in such shallow waters it would not have been able to conceal itself.

The original five U-boats of Operation *Paukenschlag* (Drumbeat) were having a field day, or should we say 'night'? They cruised the eastern coast by day submerged and surfaced at night to attack the merchant vessels silhouetted against the nearby lights of tourist seaside towns and cities. Twenty-three vessels were sunk including the US freighter *Norvana* at Cape Hatteras in North Carolina; there were no survivors. As the early pack of U-boats headed back to Europe more were dispatched, and more Allied vessels were sunk. The U-boat commanders were competing on tonnage. Over 120 allied vessels were lost.

On 24 March 1942, the Royal Navy provided anti-submarine trawlers and ten Corvettes to defend the East Coast. Admiral King finally arranged for adequate resources to establish day and night vigilance from Rhode Island to Key West, Florida, and became more aggressive with fleet destroyer attacks in the Atlantic. Gradually the decision to float convoys and implement a coastal blackout in towns was made, and by 1 April the tables started to turn when Andrews restricted ships to daylight sailing between safe anchorages. This resulted in an immediate reduction in Allied losses as vessels travelled in full convoys along the East coast.

The Allied convoy system was also effective in the Gulf of Mexico, proving that ignoring early protection advice was a big mistake. By August 1942, the U-boat hazard was better controlled and contained by America and the allies, but still a threat. The advances in Signals Intelligence work in England had proved successful, but more was needed to stay on top. Vast quantities of enciphered enemy messages had to be intercepted, deciphered, translated and analysed to track further Wolfpack attacks and other threats. A multitude of other war instruments needed to be expanded – Radar, sonar, high frequency direction finding, more vessels, more aircraft, more aircraft carriers, more matériel, more men and more women to carry out future operations.[6]

* * *

BATTLE OF THE ATLANTIC

As American citizens mobilised for war in 1942, there was concern that, as in London, American cities would be bombed. If Europe fell to the Germans, America would be next. Conflict with Japan also helped galvanize this fear. Men and women signed up for the army, navy and air force, and American Boy Scouts were asked to support air-raid wardens.

One of their duties was to assist in enforcing blackout rules. Only emergency vehicles were permitted after dark. Charles, a teenage scout, was assigned to cruise a usually busy street in one of the affected cities. He was to warn anyone infringing the law if he saw a light, contacting the offenders through an emergency phone number. It was exhilarating to be alone and traveling by moonlight, where the only danger was a snagged tyre in a streetcar track.

His first encounter was a lit cigarette. In the shadows of a well-known hotel, he could see the outline of a sailor pressed up against a girl along the front wall. Confronting the man, Charles said: 'Sir, I need you to put out your cigarette. We have a trial air raid going on and there are to be no outside lights, or cigarettes.' The man swore, while his date removed the cigarette from his mouth and rubbed it out against the wall, reprimanding him: 'You know better than that, Jimmy. Let's go to my place; you can smoke there.' They left.

Some of the windows in the hotel showed lights too, so Charles asked the front desk clerk if he could knock on doors to ask the occupants to turn off their lights. The clerk said he'd rather call them. With room plan in hand, the clerk and scout went into the street to work out which rooms offended. Charles was permitted to call from the hotel lobby desk. One room didn't answer, so they went up in the elevator to knock on the door. Charles shouted to ask the occupant to turn out the light. The door was never opened but the light went out.

The scouts were also introduced to different types of poison gas. Charles said he attended four nights of classes in the basement of a church which sponsored his troop. There he learned a little about Phosgene, Lewisite and Mustard gas. The class was taught by an army officer from the Chemical Warfare group, at Fort Macpherson. Charles' father had been gassed by Germans in 1918, and as a result spent a year in a Veteran's lung hospital in Albuquerque. Excited to hear of Charles' course, he volunteered to be a guest speaker, but that didn't happen. Neither was Charles' city bombed or gassed. Trial air raids were abandoned after a year.[7]

* * *

THE SECRET LIFE OF AN AMERICAN CODEBREAKER

Churchill's most secret source – TOP SECRET ULTRA – was fully in operation on both sides of the Atlantic by 1943 and in Janice's department, OP-20-G. Admiral King's central control and his submarine tracking room were on the third floor of Main Navy on Washington's Mall, close to the Lincoln Memorial, facing Constitution Avenue, but Janice's satellite day-to-day work of this secret section was in the converted girl's school on Nebraska Avenue.

'We didn't have a department name, just a number: OP-20-GI-(2A). Op referred to Operations, 20 was the 20th division of Naval Communications, G Section Intelligence, and 2(A) represented the Atlantic.'

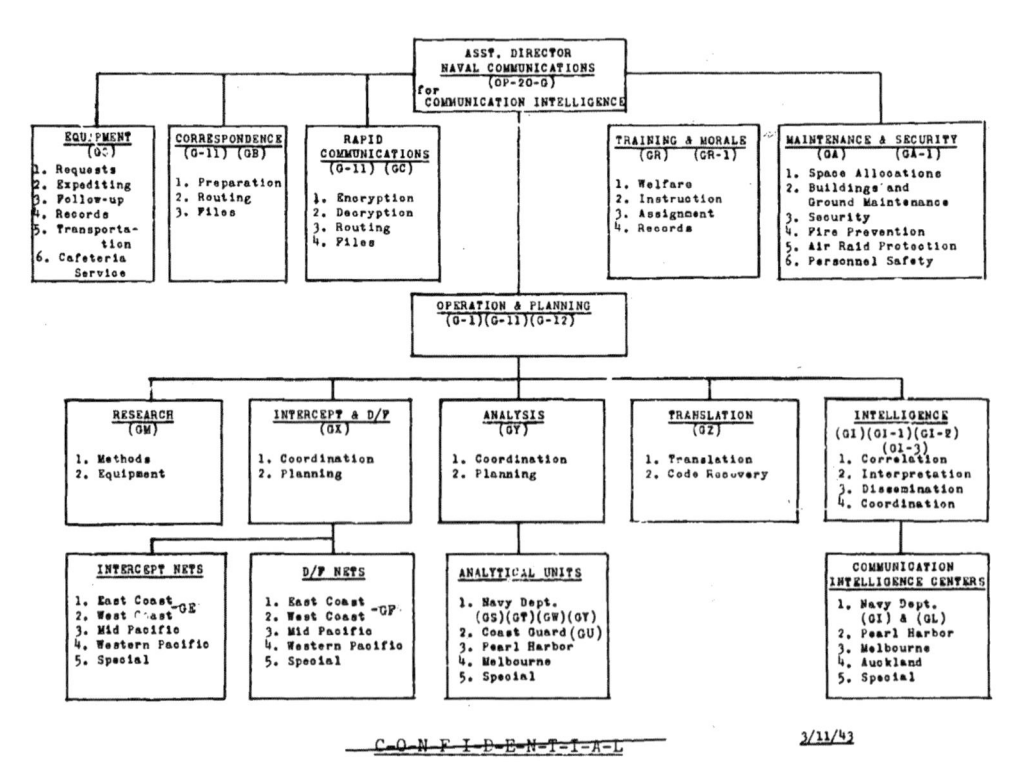

US Naval Communication Intelligence Organization, November 1944. (Courtesy of the NSA/National Cryptologic Museum)

BATTLE OF THE ATLANTIC

OP-20-GI-2(A) Additional names: Erminnie Bartlemez (extreme left), Marjorie Boynton (front, with blonde hair, looking to her right), Constance McCready Rush (front, 3rd from left), Knight McMahan (front, center left with hat at his feet), Bernard Roeder, commander of the unit holding his hat, Willard van Orman Quine, standing behind William Lindsay, (seated). Janice is behind the lady in the white dress. (Courtesy of the NSA/National Cryptologic Museum)

'The intelligence information we prepared was from the German High Command, orders to the submarines and back; it went straight to Admiral King's offices as TOP SECRET ULTRA. The daily envelope was collected by a serviceman armed with a gun. He had a leather pouch with a padlock. He came, knocked on the door and we knew what he wanted – we had prepared and double sealed the envelope. This had to be handed over to the man, who signed for it, put it in his pouch next to his gun, and walked out. He was a naval officer. He then got into his car and drove the report down to Main Navy, where it went right up to Admiral King and the United States Submarine Tracking Room. That envelope could go nowhere else.'[8]

Janice did not know the name Enigma; not until many years later was its identity widespread as the cipher source of most intercepted German messages.

Before Janice became a WAVE, a Royal Navy proposal had been ratified at an Allied Atlantic Conference. Now Western Approaches escorts in the Atlantic, northwest of Britain, reorganised to release destroyers for anti-submarine warfare. Five Anglo-Canadian groups protected vulnerable merchant convoys in the North Atlantic and five US groups covered the mid-Atlantic. Known as Hunter Killer units,[9] by now the new militarised escorts chased the lifelines of German U-boats. These massive submarines, type XIV, refuelled the smaller but dangerous VII and IX U-boats and their crews. The big feeders were called *Die Milchküh* (milk cows) and, with the combination of strong signals intelligence and effective force, the Allies' work was almost done by October.

The Kriegsmarine lost twenty-five U-boats to Allied naval vessels and aircraft that month, plus eighteen in November. Dönitz recognised defeat in the Atlantic and, it is said, he lost interest and went elsewhere for easier pickings. Over 240 U-boats in 1943 were either forced to scuttle or were sunk under the formidable presence of allied destroyers, frigates, US Coast Guard cutters, corvettes and sloops, as well as several air squadrons.[10] But compared to the 11,800,000 tonnage of merchant ships sunk by Germany, 1941-1942, this, so to speak, was a drop in the ocean.[11]

Chapter 15

Working in Nooks and Crannies
and other strange places

The divisions between US Naval Intelligence and US Signals Intelligence existed before the Second World War, but late in 1940, FDR gave approval for government officials from the army and the navy to share American cryptanalytic systems with Britain the following spring. The heads of department were involved in the discussions, including William Friedman of SIS, and after ten days, a meeting was agreed. However, Lieutenant Commander Laurance Safford, who ran the then small naval section of OP-20-G, vehemently threatened to cancel the exchange, after first accepting the idea. The politics in his department and against SIS refuted co-operation with the British, but still he demanded the US Navy have access to all British achievements![1]

Sinkov, Rosen, Currier and Weeks had attended, the first exchange of information and techniques, in February 1941 as earlier described. However, it was more than a year before other American delegations were sent to England. In the meantime, plans to expand operations in Washington went ahead.[2] London's secret relocation idea had permeated, and similar moves were made to emulate necessary facilities for an expanded naval intelligence, OP-20-G and SIS. Nevertheless, unlike GC&CS, the army and navy sections continued to operate separately, due to their insurmountable disagreements and divisions.

On 1 February 1942, Safford was replaced by Commander John R. Redman and twelve days later a reorganisation took place, including the cryptography and security sections of OP-20-G. From that time on efforts were made to keep OP-20-G strictly an effective Radio Intelligence organisation. Other re-organisations took place during that year, but a proposal to move the overcrowded departments from Main Navy to another building, was not made until August 1942.

The Old Munitions Building

Like the British Admiralty and the War Office in London, both the US Navy and the US Army were central to the city of Washington DC. In 1918, the Main Navy and Munitions departments moved into temporarily constructed buildings along what is now Constitution Avenue – between Foggy Bottom and the National Mall, then known as B street. Under the collective direction of the Navy's Bureau of Yards and Docks and the United States Department of War, the buildings were made of fire-resistant concrete, rather than wood, with large metal-framed windows which ultimately led them to survive many more years. By 1940 they resembled worn multi-storied warehouses, where each building's several limbs displayed corridors of workspace that stretched over a vast expanse to the back end of each floor. The buildings were linked on upper levels by a bridge enclosure over the central roadway.

The ground floor of both buildings was a hive of activity, often with delivery boys on bikes flying through well-used and battered doors with mail and telegrams. The main floors above had clunking office machinery for sorting, collating and filing, plus wooden desks and chairs in large, but quieter, open plan areas. Massive windows gave ample light and opened in multiple sections to provide fresh city air, depending on the season. Almost everybody smoked. The collection was known as the Munitions Building, the heart of America's military. However, only a few small rooms were allocated for the day-to-day business of US Army and Navy codebreaking.

The US Navy had formally established a cryptology element to their operation in July 1922. This was known as the Communications Security Section (CSS) or DNC OP-20-G, part of the Office of the Director of Naval Communications. This would later be the site of Admiral Ernest King's office, but prior to that, in 1928, an operators' school for enlisted Navy and Marine Corps interceptors was established at Main Navy on the roof of the Munitions Building, as much for privacy as for lack of space. The original operators' classroom was specially constructed with eight intercept positions. Their instructor was Chief Radioman Harry Kidder, who taught himself to recognise and intercept Japanese radio communications while serving in the Philippines. His first graduates were known as the 'On the Roof Gang'. By 1935, the unit was renamed the Communications Security Group (CSG), but OP-20-G was more common.

The Army, then under acting chief of Staff George C. Marshall, moved to the Munitions Building in 1939 along with the army Signals Intelligence Service – interceptors and cryptanalysts – but by the following year, most departments hoped to move out of the old overcrowded and cockroach infested offices.

Naval Communications Annex

When the decision was made to move OP-20-G, numerous sites were considered but not until December 1942 was it decided to requisition the land and buildings of the Mount Vernon Seminary. Five miles from Main Navy, at Massachusetts and Nebraska Avenues, possession took place on 15 January 1943.

The building was once a private non-sectarian school for girls, founded by Elizabeth Somers in 1868. She taught the daughters of prominent statesmen from her home at 204 F Street NW, which became known as the 'Family and Day School for Young Ladies'. On 5 November 1917, the girls' boarding school, now Mount Vernon Seminary, relocated to a new building on Nebraska Avenue. The modern facility had the capacity to house 130 resident students, but by 1928 its dormitory and classroom campus had doubled in size to nearly forty acres.

Fourteen years later, the US Navy department made a compulsory purchase, and granted the seminary 'just compensation for the property in the interest of the war effort'. The girls' school moved to Foxhall Road and later became part of George Washington University.

The expansion of the navy department, from a central city building to a quieter establishment, emulated that of Bletchley Park. In 1938 the British government wanted to quickly find a secure place for growth away from their London War Office and the Admiralty, without drawing attention to new construction. That's when the once grand but deteriorating Victorian mansion on a country estate 50 miles from the centre of the city was adapted to accommodate increasing staff levels. Elmer's School adjacent to Bletchley Park was also requisitioned for specific training courses. Bletchley had reasonable rail connections from the north and south of the country, as well as to London and Oxford and Cambridge Universities. More importantly, however, was the main telecommunications switching station nearby at Fenny Stratford.

By 1941 Bletchley Park in Buckinghamshire, was humming with activity, though some in Washington thought GC&CS was 'in London'.

In America, the Naval Communications Annex was Janice's office. The large Victorian-style red-brick school had been converted and architectural remodelling plans used every nook and cranny. The elegant structure, on well-to-do Nebraska Avenue, had deep slated roofs, multiple rooms and hidden circular stairwells cascading to various entrances. As one person wrote: 'A maze of narrow corridors appeared like a medieval castle with secret passageways, ripped from the pages of a mystery novel.'

Among large mansions and foreign embassies, the sprawling edifice with magnificent views of hills and rivers from the uppermost windows often held new visitors in awe.

The Navy's codebreaking operation rapidly expanded from a few hundred people to over a thousand. Much of the school's personality remained in the hurried transition, but Janice's office as part of converted gym, was split into sections, including a cafeteria. Marines guarded the doors that were securely locked after each cryptologist and cryptanalyst shift change. Apart from visiting the restroom or the cafeteria, Janice was not permitted to move from one section to another. Only when she went to her accommodation did she see a change of scenery.

Arlington Hall

The US Army were six months ahead of the Navy when they requisitioned Arlington Hall for Signals Intelligence, another old building, with four administrative floors. Again, this move was similar to Bletchley's and was once a school. The private post-secondary women's educational institution was founded in 1927 and by 1941 had moved to the hundred-acre site. Like Mount Vernon Seminary, the Arlington Hall Junior College for Women was only five miles from central government, but south, across the Potomac River, in Virginia.

Fortuitously for the army, the school was failing in all respects due to the Depression and impending war, but it had attempted to pull itself out of the doldrums by offering hotel-style resort accommodation. The estate was settled on a former swamp and pastureland, along an old streetcar line connecting Washington to Falls Church. The grounds included riding paddocks, a hunting course and a golf course, a tea house, and various small cottages. The site was noticed by a group of Army Intelligence officials looking for another location. It was perfect; not too far from Washington and far enough from the city to keep staff and secret agents hidden. There had been previous talk of SIS being housed in the Pentagon, but the new construction was still just that, under construction, and space was limited – top brass military would also be breathing down their necks. So, in a proposal that was swiftly handled by the War Department, $650,000 was paid to the school (less than they wanted) and the students and other occupants were evicted.

Soon the army moved in with tools and small amounts of weapons, but mostly filing cabinets of intercepted messages, desks and chairs, in a procession of vans. Fences were erected and guardrooms built. The activities of Arlington Hall were not to be mentioned outside the gates, but then in true government fashion, a press release was accidentally issued, when an abundance of pamphlets circulated to persuade young women to join the WAC. The message was exciting, and almost presented Arlington's facilities as a hotel spa. In a parody of 'Mr. Smith Goes to Washington', a popular and controversial Frank Capra film that premiered in 1939, the leaflet offered bathtubs and showers, 'tempting, nutritious dishes', career opportunities and 'smartly tailored dress uniforms'. Included were photographs and illustrated scenes of serenity, cherry blossom in bloom, the Washington Monument and the building's elegant façade displaying the Stars and Stripes.[3] What more was to be had for the girl with the Star-Spangled heart?

It was all part of the army recruitment drive nationwide. But instead of principals and professors from prestigious women's colleges, young handsome army officers approached local teacher-training institutions encouraging, 'a move to Washington to help the war effort'. The strategy, probably designed by a man, was considered the best route to charm women and trick them into thinking they might find a future husband. This may or may not have been effective. Intelligent women didn't necessarily fall for artificial plots, but some did meet and marry. Ultimately, the goal for US Army Intelligence was to recruit trustworthy, discreet females. They were vetted and when approved they took a long train journey to the nation's capital; a reverse scene from Britain's cities to the countryside and Bletchley Park three years earlier.

Some recruit's homes were three or four-hours from Washington. Their annual pay could be in the region of $1600 – more than teaching and the prospect was exciting, even if a little mysterious. Some families had fallen on hard times in the Depression, and now with black market prices hitting the roof – butter, coal, cotton textiles, to name a few – they could at least send money home. They couldn't talk about their new position, but all were keen to help the war effort. War Stamps issued by the Treasury – an initiative from the First World War – were printed for people to purchase, as a form of saving, to help fund the war. These were often as low as 10 cents and collections could be redeemed for Treasury Certificates or War Bonds.

Many women were selected for the inner intelligence circles of Arlington Hall Station. But others were allocated to different places such as Vint Hill Farms in Virginia and Two Rock Ranch (TRR) in Sonoma County, California. Both locations were on land acquired by the War Department in 1942, where camouflaged, converted ranch houses and outbuildings were used as operational listening stations to intercept messages, as well as administration and cryptography training centres. At TRR, officers and enlisted personnel were billeted in tents at first, and water supplies were disguised by a haystack. False furrows were also created to add to the story, covering their tracks, so to speak. Both were facilities for Signals Intelligence Service (SIS). Vint Hill Farms, close to Arlington Hall was also used as a refitting station for signal units returning from combat prior to redeployment overseas.[4]

Listeners were not codebreakers. To some this position was unimportant; they were viewed as telephone or radio operators. Their intercept work, therefore, was safe. However, en masse, they were crucial in collecting 'depth'; enemy messages to decode. Listeners were the first step in the chain after an enciphered message was transmitted. Specific training was given in the navy and army and when proficient, recruits were often posted to other obscure places, such as huts or other questionable outstations, some perched dangerously on cliff tops or in a desert shack. In Britain, Royal Observers were often in their bedroom in their parent's house; ATS Listeners were in a stable!

Another odd place for female recruits to be posted was the Ballistics Laboratory at Aberdeen Proving Ground, Maryland. Among eminent scientists and engineers, women would say they were secretaries and clerks – which ostensibly was true, but they worked beside these people on highly classified weapons and instruments. Edwin P. Hubble was one. He played an important role in advanced equipment used in exterior ballistics, where one of his most outstanding developments was the high-speed clock camera, which made it possible to study characteristics of bombs and low velocity projectiles in flight.[5]

College heads of maths and astronomy departments were encouraged in a heated frenzy, to accommodate 'the secret war course', expand their teaching staff and churn out more female maths majors. The Ballistics Laboratory asked for the entire class of fourteen, so did other engineering laboratories, and the US Bureau of Ships asked for as many as could be trained as quickly as possible for engineering assistants. The pay in engineering and cryptography was between $1,970 and $2,400 for the first to apply.[6]

Factories, munitions, clerical work – America had never seen such full employment – unemployment was almost zero per cent by 1943 (from 7.7 per cent at the beginning of the war). Everything anybody did was for the war. America needed labour; America needed immigrants. Thousands of Mexican people were also recruited to the workforce under the Bracero programme to help US farms and factories remain productive.[7] *Bracero* means 'labour' in Spanish.

A 'Women at work' initiative emphasised defence and factory work, with various other employment opportunities. The Magazine War Guide recommended that all publications participate and, as in England, the government made promotional 'sign-up-to help-the war' films. Rose Will Monroe was one of the real-life aircraft assembly plant workers who appeared as herself beside Hollywood star Walter Pigeon. Soon after, another real life 'Rosie', Rosie Hicker, was reported in the press as having driven a record number of rivets, with her partner, into the wing of a Grumman TBF Avenger torpedo bomber. Both women became legendary and prompted the *Saturday Evening Post* to publish in its Memorial Day issue, 29 May 1943, the now familiar image of *Rosie the Riveter* by Norman Rockwell.[8]

In reality, life was uncomfortable for both army and navy recruits most of the time. Sleeping accommodation was primitive, in barracks with paper thin walls, shoddily built as a compound for hundreds of crammed-together women. To heat their rooms, they had to find and shovel coal into cast-iron potbelly stoves. Some WACs slept in the converted stables of a nearby Army Post. Often, they had less than glamourous positions such as security duty, where they sat all day guarding doors and, according to a new civilian codebreaker, Wilma Berryman, some were assigned to Arlington Hall's machine room which was one of 'the smelliest jobs you could ever have'.[9] Wilma had joined William Friedman's group in 1939 in an allotment of government funds for his cryptanalytic section.

Better accommodation at Arlington Farms was just a fifteen-minute bus ride from the fenced-in compound of Arlington Hall. The ten freshly built dormitories were designed only to last for the duration of the war, and each was named for a different state. Idaho Hall was one. They each housed 700 recruits. The two-story buildings of thin prefabricated walls had single or double private rooms lining numerous corridors. Their small room included a bed, a desk, a mirror, an ash tray, two pillows, a chair, a small wastebasket and a window. The bathroom and showers were communal along the hallway, next to a kitchenette and laundry room with ironing facilities, or women could choose to send their clothes to be laundered. One luxury was that maids cleaned their rooms. Women ate in the cafeteria or there was a lobby where they could sit and drink tea, dance or play cards. There were phone booths, snack bars, pianos to play and areas resembling 'dating booths'. A degree of socialising went on with soldiers or sailors – after all the 'girls' were adults – but a front desk reception clerk would always be present to monitor each residence. All were safe and most behaved appropriately.[10]

The area close to the Pentagon and Washington was fast becoming known as 'Girl Town' or '28 Acres of Girls'. As well as military services, the Civil Service Commission had to cope with a defence build-up of thousands of civilians, mostly women, arriving in Washington for war work; so much so that the population had swelled by more than 200,000. The Arlington Farms complex, known as a 'duration residence for women', was quickly built to house 7,000 female workers. The press tended to write condescendingly about the residents as bright-eyed, bushy-tailed and fresh-faced Americans who poured into the capital 'from remote sleepy towns or the confused cities of other states'. Civilian women were known as government girls, often abbreviated to g-girls.

* * *

Janice boarded four miles from her wartime workplace near the centre of Washington. She chose to live in a rented room, rather than WAVE accommodation, and paid for relative privacy. However, she soon discovered that transport facilities from Dupont Circle were not efficient; she either caught a streetcar or walked. She didn't own a car. 'I walked an awful lot; had to.'

She remembered the long periods of enforced exercise since street cars either didn't go to the cross section on Nebraska and Massachusetts Avenues, or the timetable had finished for the day. Her shifts, or 'watches', seemed complicated too.

'The hard thing was that we worked varied shifts at the NCA. At the beginning I learned I had Monday off. Another girl had Tuesday, somebody Wednesday and one Thursday. We worked one week from 8 until 4 o'clock. I got off on Sunday at 4 o'clock, had Monday off and did not go back to work until 4 o'clock on Tuesday. So, there were forty-eight hours when I could go home 40 miles to Baltimore and be back to work in DC on Tuesday. Then I worked from 4 o'clock in the afternoon until midnight, and so on for Wednesday, Thursday, Friday, Saturday and Sunday when I left at midnight, but had to return by midnight on Monday. The break then was just twenty-four hours – we never had enough sleep on that watch.'

The twenty-four-hour shifts mirrored those at Bletchley Park, and recruits soon adjusted to the pattern, though perhaps not lack of sleep.

WAVES who opted to live in the hastily built barrack-style quarters did not have transportation problems as they lived across the street from the Naval Communications Annex in McLean Gardens. Twenty per cent of the accommodation was allocated to OP-20-G and arrangements were made for Hot Shoppes Inc. to manage retail, cafeteria and mess halls. As recruitment increased, more living quarters were added expanding the development from twelve barracks, to fifteen, but with an 'improved interior design',[11] a beauty parlour and auditorium – which included a swimming pool – considered good for WAVES' morale.

Janice always had her mail addressed to her lodgings, never to the Naval Communications Annex. 'My boarding house address was the only place I gave. There were many women's boarding houses around and that's where I chose to live, in the centre of Washington on Dupont Circle. Mine, however, cost more than my pay. I don't remember how much exactly, but I thought it was a lot of money. I was the only person

WAVES crossing the street from their purpose-built apartments to go to work. (Washington DC Department of Transportation)

in uniform. As an Ensign officer I was initially given $21 a month to live on, $5.25 cents per week.'

The equivalent compared well to the Bletchley employees for similar work, around £3.13s.6d (£3.75). Janice continued: 'My father must have helped initially, but when I received increased Ensign pay, he insisted I have a Savings Bond. I was getting more money than I'd ever had before.'

The US Navy codebreaking office treated the women differently from men in terms of pay. As an indication a November 1941 memo proposed salaries of $1,440 per year for female clerks, typists and stenographers, while men with the same jobs made $1,620.

Chapter 16

Handling Top Secret Intelligence

As at Bletchley Park and other stations a mix of enlisted military personnel and civilians were sworn into the secret work of codebreaking. With cards and pencils, sheets of paper, sometimes graph paper, all worked intently on the individual tasks for which they were trained. In a low murmur of fans and rustling paper an industrial silence ensued while German, Japanese and other codes and ciphers were broken at the Naval Annex and Arlington Hall. As Bletchley Park had become in England, these two locations combined, had become the largest message centre in America.

Most intercepted messages were received by teleprinter. Often they had to be stripped of their initial superencipherment using a reverse deciphering method to reveal the root enciphered message. In all cases the key to the codes had to be found. Information at the beginning and the end, a familiar word or phrase, helped unearth the solution for all intercepts to be decoded, translated and read for a day. German and Japanese messages were key, but Japanese was more of a challenge due to the Rōmaji and Kana language and characters, although Bletchley Park had already excelled in this, based on the work of John Tiltman. He advocated, contrary to the School of Oriental and Asian/African Studies, that learning enough Japanese for codebreaking purposes would only take six months, not two years, as codebreakers didn't need to speak the language. They just had to be familiar with its characteristics and patterns.

Some considered the work boring, but schoolteachers were well matched with logic and diligence. In most cases, women were chosen over men. Higher-level PhD graduates were often unconnected to real-world situations and those from a lesser background, perhaps with different thought patterns, often had more cunning and fight to find the solution. But one thing is certain, codebreaking required patience, literacy and numeracy, creativity and attention to detail, a clear mind, a good memory and above all, enough bravery to leap at a pretty good guess.

New recruits often found themselves at first sorting a web of messages to recognise familiar coded call sign digits, called a 'starter' (or a 'crib' in England), before moving on to other codes, which would eventually mean something to someone further down the line, but the job now was to notice specific patterns that led to common words. With each competency attained the next level was always in sight. The same process was used for German and Japanese codes, with additional recognition training for Japanese symbols and translation, specifically in military jargon. To the newly initiated this seemed complicated, but with practice their industrious results were frequent and useful, even if they couldn't read messages in their entirety. Unfruitful messages were never discarded but filed for future reference, clues perhaps to future enemy strategies. Though they did not realise initially, codebreakers often influenced the war's outcome.

The Naval intelligence Janice processed came via the Enigma cipher machine. Britain's secret codebreaking operation had speedily advanced their methods to read many of the intercepted German enemy messages, which gave confidence that Hitler could be tackled and beaten, but it was difficult to keep up with multiple intercepts in a timely manner. Breaking codes daily was the goal, but faster accurate methods were needed to stay ahead.

Simply put the Greek word Enigma means 'puzzle'. Earlier versions were used by banks and other commercial businesses to protect telegrams containing business secrets, but the Enigma machine, invented by Arthur Scherbius from Frankfurt, had its first public airing in the 1920s at the Congress of the International Postal Union in Bern, Switzerland. Unfortunately for Scherbius, however, the international audience for whom it was intended showed little interest. Instead, they considered it an expensive piece of 'puzzling equipment', much to his dismay.

Scherbius was well-known in the field of inventions, especially asynchronous motors, but during the First World War he succumbed to the pull of cryptography despite the science being underdeveloped in the German language. His first cryptographic invention aimed to code messages via telegraph. Previously, thick codebooks were printed for private firms, containing thousands of commercial codes. They represented business and personal phrases such as, 'Do not exceed the limit', which may have translated to JIWUL. The point was to save money on cable fees, but there was often an element of secrecy to be construed. The message titles always included the word 'code' which brought them under the influence of cryptology. His code words were often from other languages and made up, but they were always pronounceable. Cable rates were higher for unpronounceable words and numbers. Scherbius aimed to maintain economy while making non-secret messages secret with his new cipher machine.

After modifications and improvements, by 1924 the German post office – *Deutsche Reichpost* – had tested the machine and exchanged greetings with delegates of that year's Congress of the International Postal Union. As a result, Germany's government and Naval Command in Berlin decided to consider the Scherbius' invention to adapt for military use. Gradually, the original commercial model was phased out and a new and smaller Model C was produced, but Arthur Scherbius died in 1929 and never saw the impact his machine had in world conflict.[1]

Enigma's advantage was that it was portable and could be carried around the battlefield. The system was perfect for short concise messages. The internal mechanism was made of three rotors, each with twenty-six electrical contacts around the outer edge, representing each letter of the alphabet. To encode a message the German operator set the rotors in a pre-determined order and position using the current issue of his printed codebook: The Settings.

He then typed each letter of his message into the machine. By pressing a letter key an electric pulse went through to a rotor and lit up a different letter on a lamp-board. The operator noted the enciphered letter for each letter of the message typed into the machne. Each time he pressed a key the rotor moved one space, so that if he pressed the same letter, a different enciphered letter would appear in the lamp-board. When all the message letters were enciphered, the operator sent the message via wireless, or radio, in Morse code. This would then be deciphered by the recipient using their own Enigma machine and identical settings from the same issue of codebook. The clever movement of the rotors at each key stroke meant the letter and ciphers were constantly scrambled. The German navy then added a plug board which scrambled the messages further for super security, which they thought was unsolvable. But that was not so.

The Enigma machine, with added plug board, used by German forces to encrypt their messages. (Crown Copyright 2021. By kind permission Director GCHQ)

Other Listeners also picked up the Morse code enciphered messages. The first step in discovering enemy secrets was to intercept their messages sent via radio; literally, to eavesdrop and register the information. It was essential to obtain many, many messages as 'depth' of information was crucial to cracking a cipher. To do this, rows of ATS women in Beaumanor

Hall, England, and other outstations sat, with headphones and pencils, ready to intercept radio message signals through rows of radio receivers. But these ladies never spoke to anyone on the line, they only listened. The radio operators at Vint Hill Farms in Virginia and Two Rock Ranch (TRR) in Sonoma County, California emulated the highly trained British ATS recruits of the Royal Corp of Signals in the same arrangement of three eight-hour shifts per day, seven days a week.

From 1939, Beaumanor had been one of the grandest intercept training stations of the war. It was a palatial house with disguised stables and cellars, and in the bomb-proof outbuildings196 radio sets and around 1,300 operators were installed to intercept enemy messages. The War Office Y Group was known as WOYG. But Listening sections were generally known as the 'Y', a shortened form of wireless station.

British Army Signals go back to 'C' Telegraph Troop, the first to provide field army communications by means of visual signalling, mounted orderlies and telegraph. By 1871 the troop had expanded to five officers overseeing 245 other ranks and first saw action in 1871 during the Anglo-Zulu war. In 1884, the troop was amalgamated with other companies to become the Telegraph Battalion, Royal Engineers, which in turn became the Royal Engineers Signal Service in 1908, encompassing Postal and Telegraph divisions and the Field Force to provide communications during the First World War. About the same time wireless sets and motorcycle dispatch riders were introduced, though interception of electronic messages was possible from around 1900.[2]

Prior to this, records indicate that organised intelligence was pivotal throughout the Napoleonic Wars (1803-1815), and that had Napoleon kept up with modern processes he might not have been defeated at the Battle of Waterloo. He found intelligence unreliable and inaccurate and chose to base his strategies on in-depth studies of domestic newspapers, diplomatic publications, maps and earlier documents of military theatres of war. Most of the time he was successful, but his methods contrasted with Britain, Austria, Prussia and Russia, who acted quickly on new intelligence-gathering methods. This included the formation of large complex networks of corresponding agents, plus codebreakers and cryptanalysts. Thus, British codebreakers, such as linguist Sir George Scovell, cracked the Great Paris Cipher (disparagingly called *le petit chiffre*) to provide access to Napoleon's military intelligence.[3]

In 1810, Portugal had created a Military Telegraph Corps, but Germany and France did not have telegraph troops until the mid-late nineteenth century, and signals were conveyed manually and visually as the electric telegraph had not been invented. Prussia established a troop in 1830. The US Army Signals Corps (USASC) continued with aerial telegraphy ('wig-wag') during and beyond the Civil War, until 1867 when the electric telegraph became their responsibility, alongside visual signalling. In 1870 the USASC mandated a national weather service in Congress commanded by Major James Meyer, which reached international acclaim, and in 1907 an Aeronautical Division was formed under the US Office of the Chief Signal Officer.

During the time of London's Admiralty OIC and the Royal Engineers Signal Service, we see that Parker Hitt in 1911 and, the army Signal School at Fort Leavenworth in Kansas probably received intercepts from another department within their base. In competition, by 1912, Russia had moved rapidly with telegraph parks of new technology, within their sapper brigades. These were operated in co-ordination with field level units of the Russian Army Signal Corps, where engineers installed 193 telegraphs and 333 cable lines.

Meanwhile, Germany amassed several sizeable telegraph battalions and a prestigious Cavalry Telegraph School. When the First World War began, additional signals elements were established from the nine telegraph battalions and eight fortress signals companies for transport troops. In 1915, in a change to trench warfare, all German telegraph units were renamed *Armee-Fernsprechabteilungen*, army signals units. In trench warfare cable communications were often cut by the continual barrage of enemy fire, which resulted in re-establishing carrier pigeons and signal dogs, as well as interim sections of optical signals.[4]

* * *

Sometimes highly trained Listeners were transferred overseas too early, which irritated Gordon Welchman at GC&CS. His two-pronged rationale was that *'The mere number is not nearly so important for production of intelligence as the quality of the operators, and that high quality can only be achieved by experience...recruits from an ordinary training school are of little use until they have had special training. Entrusting a frequency to an operator who is not up to the necessary standard, entails missed traffic and corrupt texts. This means a loss of intelligence if the traffic is broken, and it may mean failure to break codes. Only too often a message is passed which would have given a good chance of breaking a key, but the vital portion has either been missed or is corrupt.'*[5]

The Listeners in America usually picked up messages via plain language radio traffic (R/T) or Enigma messages via Morse code, wireless traffic (W/T). When on listening duty (called a 'watch'), they spent four hours twiddling knobs on their receivers, up and down, to find a frequency.[6] Some Listeners called themselves 'twiddlers', and as soon as a message began, a flurry of activity would start as operators grabbed a pencil to write on the special pad. He or she noted the time, the frequency and signal strength, the addressee and the sender. Next, the Morse message was replicated into the small rectangles in the grid on the intercept form. They had to write clear and certain letters; guesses were not permitted. It was better to indicate an omission rather than speculate. When the message was complete it was ripped off the pad and held high, ready for the supervisor to collect. The message would then be relayed to the codebreakers.

The Decoders looked for the part of the message which resembled thirteen-digits. This 'crib' could appear as 'xxgjueysmidhybzxx', in a long line of other random letters. They were searching for the word *Wetterbericht*, German for 'weather report'. The 'kisses' at either end could delineate the beginning and end of phrases. Common words, once interpreted, could be used in the Bombe menus and most other messages for that day could be read, until the code changed at midnight. Other easy prompts from German operators ended with phrases such as *Heil Hitler* or *Nieder mit die Englander* ('Down with the English'). Working out 'cribs' and 'kisses' was time consuming but imperative. Janice's colleagues in another room worked on these too.

During the Battle of the Atlantic when First Sea Lord Sir Dudley Pound announced that the breaking of the Enigma *Shark* codes was drying up in the first quarter of 1943 – indicating that Germany had changed its enciphering system – he thought it unlikely Britain would obtain more than two to three pairs of breaks per month but felt the situation could improve after three months.'[7] He was too pessimistic since Bletchley's Hut 8 remembered there was a second key that had been placed in a drawer. The *U-559* had been hunted down in the Mediterranean and seized in October 1942 where codebooks and an Enigma machine were recovered. The second book had seemed unimportant at the time, but now new information indicated this was a new Short Signals key, showing that the new Enigma cipher had an additional rotor.

From March to June 1943 the U-boat cipher was aggressively attacked and a further ninety *Shark* keys were solved. But in July, a fourth rotor was added, Enigma model M4. Again, Hut 8 was not deterred and reconstructed the wiring within a few days. They also confirmed the rotor selection for the machine was made on the first day of each month, a regularity that simplified the Allied codebreakers' tasks once more.

At this time, the BRUSA Agreement, streamlined communications between the intelligence departments of Washington and Bletchley Park. America assisted with *Shark* and with their first success 'extremely gracious and hearty congratulations', came from Bletchley Park's Hut 6. Later America reported the British said, 'they undoubtedly knew far more than we did.'[8] However, some US Bombe machines were underutilised, and Britain asked Washington to work on three-rotor codes to attack German Army and Air Force ciphers under their direction. With lines of secure communication and new technology, the 1943 accord provided an improved American operation that mirrored Bletchley Park's codebreaking procedures. Germany's obsession with weather forecasts also helped in providing the Allies with cribs for the rest of the war. Together they quickly and efficiently exploited the 'cribs' and 'kisses' to overcome the so-called 'dark period' using *U-559* codebooks. The new M4 cipher was still called *Shark*, but the German Navy called it *Triton*.

Meanwhile, the pride and self-importance of Agnes Meyer Driscoll did little to endear her to British codebreaking – in fact instead of moving with new ideas and faster technologies she created a huge rift. Britain was appalled by the amateur operation of the US Navy's overall intelligence operation, and not just because of her. From 1941, Britain shared reports that were ignored – and quite possibly never received – by the people for whom they were meant. But in return America felt Britain withheld information on Enigma. Both situations had an element of truth. American codebreaking was dysfunctional,[9] and Britain held back considering that their success should be utilised only for defensive and diversionary tactics – protecting convoys – rather than offensive

HANDLING TOP SECRET INTELLIGENCE

strategies. America was considered too aggressive and inclined to attack, which would place Top Secret Ultra in jeopardy. Their British codebreaking factory had to be kept secret at all costs.

* * *

OP-20-G's mission was to intercept, decrypt and analyse naval communications from Japanese, German and Italian navies, but Janice was only involved with German Naval communications. All she knew was that important information – provided by human decoding, reports and machine menus, was fed into the machines to quickly find the daily key to the cipher. It was crucial for all intercepted messages to be decoded, deciphered, translated and read as fast as possible. The mysterious machines, however, did not automatically decipher all messages, that was the manual job of decoders and message analysts.

Janice worked closely with the plotting and tracking rooms at OP-20-G where command centres flagged radar and enemy radio transmitter positions. In this way Allied forces protected many vessels and troops in the Atlantic, information and their positions expertly pinpointed on a map. Location and direction of enemy craft in the air, land or sea were carefully recorded to provide a clear visual of the aggressor and potential victims.

As convoys escaped and battles with submarines at sea subsided, the supply of short signals waned, which indicated again that something different was afoot. The codebreakers returned to the drawing board once more to solve a new cipher. Another rotor had been introduced to the Enigma machine. Now a billion more hurdles had been created instead of just a few million. Meanwhile, German Wolfpacks were still a threat to vulnerable merchant ships in the Atlantic.

Chapter 17

Bombe Machines, German Codebreaking and ULTRA

Lieutenant Joseph Eachus of the US Naval Reserve was destined to visit Bletchley. He held a doctorate in mathematics from the University of Illinois and had completed a navy correspondence course in cryptology. After the attack on Pearl Harbor he was sent to a large room at Main Navy and, on his first day, he thought everyone was nuts: a man practised speaking Japanese to himself, one was sending Morse code to his own monitor, and another tried to call a second phone on his desk, via Alaska!

At that point he was too new to be part of the first exploratory party of Americans to Bletchley Park in February 1941, but later, it was felt he could be spared to work there. His brief was to study British cryptanalysts' methods and assist in codebreaking, after which he would relay the British methods back to OP-20-G. Eachus was the first to work in Britain for several months before colleagues arrived for longer assignments and, as the only American, he struck up a friendly relationship with the GC&CS Commander's secretary, Barbara Abernethy, whom he later married.

Under the BRUSA Agreement a contingent of US Intelligence personnel reached Bletchley Park in 1943 with extra supplies. Rationing in Britain meant more food and clothes from America would be helpful. From 1942 until the end of the war, more than 600 Stateside recruits would spend periods of time at Bletchley Park and its outstations. Three units of US Army personnel were sent to learn and assist on the British Bombe. US Signals Security Detachments, 6811th, 6812th, and 6813th also managed intercepts and cryptanalysis. Their intensive training was conducted by British cryptanalysts including John Herivel and Helene Lovie Taylor for Hut Six – SIXTA. Detachment 6812th consisted of 200 men and was stationed at *HMS Pembroke V*, a building in Eastcote, near Ruislip and west of London. Under Colonel Mortimer Stewart, a former IBM employee, their brief was to help operate twelve Bombe machines manufactured by the British Tabulating Company. They called their area of high security the *United States,* naming each machine for an American city. The men were seen to be rather forward, especially when they arrived in 1943 and one lieutenant is reported to have said: 'These Bombe rooms contain marvellous machines, and many attractive ladies!'

Despite a penchant for females, American servicemen were efficient. They quickly learned machine operation and other elements of Bletchley's most secret methods. America's role in attacking Germany's naval Enigma was beginning to equal Great Britain's. In return the US sent information to Bletchley on Japanese ciphers where William Friedman's established knowledge of PURPLE was key.

Joseph Eachus worked alongside British codebreakers, absorbing and reporting on GC&CS codes and cipher systems, but when other Americans arrived, he returned to Washington for a brief visit in the spring of 1943. There he discovered his division of OP-20-G had moved to the new Naval Communications Annex, and was now called OP-20-GY(A); Y for cryptanalysts (or Y for Wireless Listeners, as at Bletchley), A for Atlantic.[1] His absence noted other changes too. Hundreds of women were pouring into Union Station, employed as new government workers. Posters and flags adorned the forecourt adamant in their message that their war would be won. There was even a canteen for servicemen and servicewomen. Janice would be assigned to the NCA a few weeks later.

Eachus' work centred around what was called 'the back room', which in fact was three rooms on the ground floor of the building. All were individually secret and secure, where staff in one room knew nothing about the work in others, though they could take a pretty good guess. One housed the cipher machines and communication tele-typewriters to receive intercepted messages from the outpost Y stations, GC&CS and the US Navy's U-boat plot. The second room consisted of four women for each shift or 'watch', to sort intercepts – both from U-boats and U-boat command. The cryptanalysts worked in the third room. Their leader was Howard Engstrom, a Yale University mathematician. Between them they anticipated cribs using the standard phrases and words, though sometimes it was not always easy to dig anything out of a message. Decoders were often discouraged, but if something was found their elation often led to overtime as they speedily applied the new lead to many other messages.

One of the signs on the wall, found in the codebreakers' training materials, encouraged lateral thinking on a difficult problem from a line in British poet Thomas Gray's 1750, *Elegy Written in a Country Courtyard:*

> *The ploughman homeward plods his weary way. The ploughman plods homeward his weary way. The ploughman plods his weary way homeward. The ploughman his weary way plods. The ploughman his weary way plods homeward. His weary way the ploughman homeward plods. His weary way homeward the ploughman plods. His weary way the ploughman plods homeward. Homeward the ploughman plods his weary way. Homeward his weary way the ploughman plods.*[2]

The missive was designed to remind decoders to look at things from many ways, read between the lines. Sometimes the most bizarre thought could be correct. There were days also when the enemy helped. It was much easier for them to say the same thing the same way every day.

Allied decoders, however, also had to be aware of how they conveyed or re-transmitted enemy messages to other departments – for example to Main Navy or the Admiralty. Thus, other signs reminded them to add another layer of encryption. One said: 'Parallel texts lost a battle.' Meaning if a message was sent in both cipher and, at some other point, in clear text, it would be easy (for the enemy) to intercept, compare and find their secret code. Therefore, most messages coming into Allied decoder areas in a process labelled 'protective security', were skilfully paraphrased and re-encoded via SIGABA in the US or Typex in the UK.

Janice's paraphrased reports of message intercepts and map plotting were sent to Main Navy: 'Nobody could come into our office except high-ranking officers from the Navy Department downtown. We prepared the material and every morning at 7.30, the person on the 12-8am shift fixed a large yellow envelope with the messages processed during the night. We had research people who studied submarines and they put in a report too. At the top in big red letters we always wrote 'TOP SECRET ULTRA'. That meant the large yellow envelope could go nowhere except to those cleared to handle ULTRA documents, intercepted information from German High Command, orders to their submarines and back.

We worked alone. Again, and again we heard: "Loose Lips, Sink Ships." It was the most popular of the many phrases, emphatically used to remind us all to keep our mouths well and truly shut.'

Supervisors handed out individual work. There was no discussion, they knew what was needed.

'There were about thirty-five people on my watch – all Naval personnel. The senior watch consisted of male Naval Reserves and a commander. The Junior Naval division was a mixture of men and women, and the shipping desk consisted of all women – WAVES. Each day a man came. He was a naval officer, armed with a gun and a padlocked leather pouch. When he knocked on our door, we knew he wanted our yellow envelope, the one we had already prepared and sealed. We signed the envelope over to him; he put it in the pouch close to his gun and left.

As a high-ranking messenger, he had a huge responsibility to maintain the secrecy, making sure messages arrived safely and reached the correct person. He walked out of the building, got into his car and immediately drove to the main Navy Department on Pennsylvania Avenue where it went straight to Admiral King and the United States Submarine Tracking Room. No other place could that envelope go.'

The work we did was highly confidential on TOP SECRET ULTRA. There were codebreaking machines called Bombes and Bombe Operators below us, but I was not down there. Nobody ever did say anything, at least not until several years later.'

Codebreaking Machines

Alan Turing has become a mythical figure in British codebreaking, but if it wasn't for the Polish codebreakers who, via French agents, shared their faster codebreaking knowledge with British Intelligence he may not have held such status. The main cryptographic analysts who joined the Polish Staff's Cipher Bureau in Warsaw were Jerzy Różycki, Henryk Zygalski and Marian Rejewski. In 1927 they concentrated on breaking the Enigma cipher and eventually reconstructed the internal workings of the machine, identifying the indicator system used by the German Army. Zygalski worked on a manual crib and decoding technique using twenty-six perforated paper sheets. These contained the alphabet duplicated horizontally and vertically in a matrix of 26 x 26, each sheet representing the 676 possible starting positions of the middle and left (slow-moving) Enigma rotors.

When the sheets were stacked in a certain order and placed over a light box, the small pinholes revealed a starting position of daily wheel or ring settings used on the machine. This was a successful aid to their codebreaking for many years. Meanwhile, German forces increased their Enigma communications thinking their system safe, but most were being intercepted, read and transcribed.

However, in 1936, there was perhaps an inkling of doubt, as significant changes to Enigma machines were made. New safeguards were employed, and codes were tougher to break, which meant the Poles needed new methods to hack into the German system. But by 1937 the likelihood of a German invasion in Poland had increased and their operation was under threat. When the German invasion of Czechoslovakia took place in 1938, the Poles tried to pass their knowledge to France and Britain. Poland, they felt, would be next. The German military had also introduced an additional wheel to Enigma in December 1938 which saw the Polish team struggle. The German operator had a limited choice of configurations, but with an additional rotor his choice increased. The problem for Britain was later magnified when Germany boosted the number of plug-board connections to ten elevating encryption possibilities to 159,000,000,000,000,000,000![3]

After two tri-lateral meetings in 1939 including the three Polish codebreakers, French and British intelligence representatives agreed in July to exchange information on their codebreaking secrets. British representatives over the two meetings were Alastair Denniston, John Tiltman[4], Hugh Foss and Dilly Knox, plus Hugh Sinclair Chief of MI6 and Humphrey Sandwith. Tensions between Poland and Germany had reached breaking point and after war was declared by Britain and France, all evidence of Polish codebreaking was destroyed and their staff evacuated from their secret headquarters in the Pyry Forest south of Warsaw. But ten days later, French intelligence, delivered a replica Enigma machine to Colonel Stewart Graham Menzies of MI6 in London, 'a gift from the Poles'.[5]

The information gained from the young Poles at the beginning of the war, meant Britain could start dissecting the cipher machine. Both

BOMBE MACHINES, GERMAN CODEBREAKING AND ULTRA

Knox and Foss worked to replicate and further improve the manual and mechanical solutions to Enigma, but it was Turing who fully embraced the task and developed a successful combination search machine which ultimately was able to quickly discover the daily keys to the Enigma cipher.

'Nobody else seemed interested,' Turing is reported to have said, as he persevered with the mechanics and combinations of the machine. His idea was to build a large imitation of Enigma, in fact several Enigma machines. It was destined to become the largest and one of the fastest machines to break a cipher leading to message-reading on a massive scale. Another two years would pass, however, before America was tasked to develop the third iteration of this highly secret weapon.

Turing used the advances of the Polish codebreakers and Marian Rejewski's mathematical permutation theory. This was designed to help solve the connection problem between the typing keyboard and the entry drum inside the machine.[6] Both Knox and Turing tried this, but after several attempts and no result, a secretary known as Mrs. B.B. suggested a more logical approach to the wiring, simply to follow the QWERTY keyboard A to Q, B to W and so on, but that was considered a ridiculous idea, the connections had to be scrambled to be secure. But her idea worked! (And was later confirmed by the Poles.) When the Germans came to solder the machine's wiring by hand it was too risky for it to be confused and, therefore, they used a regular keyboard as Mrs. B predicted. Knox had struggled for months, but this simple step was one of the greatest achievements in cryptographic history.

This and Turing's deeper analysis of the Polish work yielded successful results as he fully grasped the mathematical mechanics of rotors and functions behind the complicated Enigma and its adversary, the Polish Bomba. Progress steadily increased in building a replica code book, but for faster results acquisition of a current and complete book of decryption tables was needed. These were eventually forthcoming, through 'pinches', as described in U-boat counterattacks and by 1940 Turing had designed a bigger and faster code breaking version which he called 'The Bombe'.

If Turing is hailed as the Bombe hero in Britain, it is Joseph Desch for America, who progressed and built a new Bombe version at NCR (National Cash Registers), 1942-1943. With ideas of his own and

The UK Bombe machine which helped speed up codebreaking at Bletchley Park and Eastcote. (By kind permission Director GCHQ)

blueprints from England he followed Turing's design. But credit for the first Bomba machine will always go to Poland and the codebreakers there who developed the first device enabling faster codebreaking.

* * *

As Churchill began to share secret information with President Roosevelt and his aides, under the approval and guidance of Bletchley Park's Edward Travis and John Tiltman, Turing provided information to Joseph Desch at NCR in Dayton, Ohio, in April 1942. By summer a version of Bletchley Park's Bombe was underway for US Navy use. America then followed Britain's lead in extensive recruitment and training of women to provide an efficient force of WAVES ready to operate the new American machines.

BOMBE MACHINES, GERMAN CODEBREAKING AND ULTRA

The NCR Navy Bombe was larger and heavier than the UK version with design-updates reducing the time to achieve a successful 'Stop'. In America it was called a 'hit' and the products from these were called 'stories'. Now in its third life, the original Bomba was faster and more efficient than all previous designs.

Joseph Desch, an electrical engineer, was Research Director at NCR. Born in Dayton, Ohio in 1907 to a German family descended from blacksmiths and wagon builders, he pursued a career in radio testing for General Motors after university. This led to teleprinter communications research for Telecom Laboratories, a process lab in Frigidaire, then NCR to innovate for their Electrical Research Laboratory. The team's brief was to expand on pioneering ideas regarding the use of thyratrons (gas filled tubes), fast-firing vacuum tubes (thermionic tubes) and circuitry in counting devices, all with the idea of developing high-speed processors to enhance NCR's mechanical machines.[7] The laboratory was also awarded several 'warfare' contracts by the National Defence Research Committee (an agency of the US federal government later known as the Office of Scientific Research and Development). In their research, the lab and Desch were influenced by others in the same field, one of whom was the British scientist, Welshman Dr C.E. Wynn-Williams.[8]

Wynn-Williams (1903-1979) was noted for research on electronic instrumentation used in nuclear physics, plus his work in the development of modern computers. Like many scientists of the time he was a wireless enthusiast. He entered Trinity College Cambridge in 1925 and continued his short electric waves research at the university's Cavendish Laboratory. This was under the supervision of New Zealander Sir Ernest Rutherford, an expert in the exploration of nuclear physics, which included radio activity and the nuclear atom. In 1932 Wynn-Williams published details of his thyratron-based scale-of-two counter, which allowed particles to be counted at much higher rates than before. This opened new avenues for research and was widely copied in Europe and America. By 1935 he was appointed assistant lecturer at Imperial College, London and, as war loomed, he was recruited with other scientists to develop the discipline of RADAR at the Telecommunications Research Establishment, Malvern (later known as the Royal Radar Establishment).

As Britain shared its secrets with America, other avenues were sought for faster codebreaking. Wynn-Williams was already on the scene for rapid science and his theories were explored not only by Desch, but by

Bill Tutte and Tommy Flowers in England. In the US, however, rather than trying to reinvent another wheel, Desch stayed with Turing's design to develop a much improved and vastly successful high-speed Bombe for the US Navy. Tutte and Flowers in the Newmanry at Bletchley Park, on the other hand, worked on another type of codebreaking machine altogether.

* * *

Desch's lab became the US Naval Computing Machine Laboratory in 1942, where, rather like Room 40 and Bletchley Park, the unofficial name of Building 26, seemed to stick. The 96-acre NCR site had grown in Ohio's farmlands when Dayton became a mobilisation point for American attacks on Canadian and British troops during the War of 1812. The conflict brought banks, business and factories, and growth continued through the Civil War. During 1884, NCR's founder, John Patterson and his brother, acquired many acres and property to create a country training compound. Patterson pioneered modern sales tactics and their Sugar Camp complex served as a summer retreat for sales trainees of cash registers, accounting and adding machines and, strangely, ornate fairground calliopes.

In the Second World War, Janice was not part of the Bombe culture but was aware other WAVES were posted to different parts of the country. Over several weeks between 1942 and 1943, 600 in their uniforms boarded trains, often at midnight, to begin a 500-mile journey 'west'. That's all they knew. Janice only heard stories and was happy not to go. The crowded carriages were part of an ordinary troop train – dirty and lacking comfortable sleeping compartments. Some women hoped for California, but Dayton's Union Station was not at all what they expected.

As they mustered for roll call, each clutched a shoulder bag and small suitcase holding everything they needed. The following chilly bus journey was short and before long they were driving through the old-style gates of Sugar Camp, their billet for the next few weeks. They could be forgiven for thinking they were at a Girl Scout camp, as the serenity of NCR's 31-acre compound consisted of pleasant, elevated land featuring maple trees and rustic cabins. Four women were assigned to each two-bedroomed cabin, but with additional recruits arriving in April and May 1943, small folding beds were squeezed in to accommodate two extra. Now there were six women per cabin. There was a bathroom between the two rooms. Initially there was no food service, so WAVES went to Dayton. Tomato soup and grilled cheese sandwiches were often a café favourite. An official ceremony had taken place when they arrived and the Stars and Stripes was raised, but all they needed was sleep. The new Navy recruits, after initial training in Washington, then queued for linens and pillows and separated to find their cabins, but still nobody told them about the task they would soon perform.

Major companies such as Ford, IBM, Kodak and General Motors helped with the war effort and co-operated with government needs in supplying war matériel. Universities such as MIT and Harvard also developed new systems and within this framework NCR was proud to contribute. The WAVES became a talking point for the town and good publicity for the company. An NCR photographer captured not only their arrival but also their daily activities, swimming, walking, eating and having fun – but never their work.

The cover story was, 'WAVES will take courses in the operation of special accounting machines', though the general public would have wondered why it took so long to learn such a task. NCR's campus resembled a mini city with its own wells and electric power plant. It even had its own movie theatre. The women working in Building 26 laboured seven days a week, in another three-tiered 24-hour shift system. Every day, in all weathers, in readiness for their 'watch', more than a hundred WAVES mustered in Sugar Camp's courtyard, to march four abreast to Dayton. The spectacle was always punctual, and locals felt they could safely set their watches by it.

In tight security armed Marine guards lived in and patrolled Building 26. WAVES sat at large tables in vast former cash-register training rooms. Each had about twelve people and a supervisor and every day they were instructed to sit at the same table, the same seat, and grab the same long flex that hung from the ceiling. Using solder, wire and small mechanical parts nestled in a dish in front of them, they constructed small wheels made of Bakelite, brass and copper. After initial training, with diagrams, they created small baskets of interlocking wires that attached to each wheel.[9] There was no room for mistakes. The colourful wires had to match the diagrams, with each wrapping around a prong on the wheel and fastened on the tip by a blob of melted solder. When the weld cooled the joint had to be tugged to ensure it was secure. The work was intense, but as proficiency increased, many likened the task to lacemaking. Some women had worked on telephone switchboards before and the switch and disc mechanisms seemed familiar. They were not told what the wiring and the wheels were for, but simple guesswork suggested they were for an important machine.

Joseph Desch became familiar with the women and their work, and all enjoyed the surroundings of Sugar Camp which included a luxury Olympic-size swimming pool. Desch was liked and respected for his brilliance and would often take his meals with WAVES in the new cafeteria. The inventor was involved in all aspects of this secret project, and the women tried not to speculate. However, it wasn't difficult to work out their section numbers went from zero to twenty-five, and

US Navy Bombe machine at NCR, based on earlier Polish and British designs. (Courtesy of the NSA/National Cryptologic Museum)

BOMBE MACHINES, GERMAN CODEBREAKING AND ULTRA

that the sum of twenty-six digits represented the alphabet. Security was tight as, while people around them were loyal to America, there was still a lingering group of Bund, Nazi sympathisers, with rumours of German spies kidnapping the women if they discovered the work of Building 26. The floor above employed a team of men secretly constructing apparatus in a form none had seen before, but everybody kept quiet. All had to remember the secret nature of their work every minute.

* * *

The workings of Adam and Eve, as America called their first naval Bombe machines, were carefully assembled in Dayton by a top secret research group of engineers and mathematicians, many of whom had trained at Bletchley Park, Eastcote [10] in northwest London, Knockholt or Hall Place in Bexley, Kent, either as senior administration, Bombe operators in American bays, or as part of the Signals Security Detachment.[11] Alfred Friendly was one of several US Army integrees at Bletchley Park, who after the war remained in Europe as press aide to Averell Harriman, overseer of the Marshall Plan. He later became editor of the *Washington Post*.[12]

Al Friendly, a journalist and US Army Integree at Bletchley Park, became a longtime friend of Jean Campbell-Harris, who later became Mayor of Cambridge and a representative in the House of Lords, where she was enobled as the Right Honourable Baroness Trumpington. (Press Partners)

THE SECRET LIFE OF AN AMERICAN CODEBREAKER

The US Army Bombe was larger and physically different from the British and US Navy Bombes, after a contract was signed with Bell Laboratories on 30 September 1942. This version was designed to find the key to 3-rotor traffic, not four. It was known as '003' or 'Madame X'. It did not have drums representing Enigma rotors but telephone type relays, which provided distinct advantages over manually switching out drums by simply pushing a button.

The secret US research group included Marshall Hall, a mathematician at Yale University, and Donald Menzel the eminent astronomer from Harvard, who had learned to read Morse code at a young age and became an Eagle Scout specialising in cryptanalysis. His multi-talents took him to Harvard and while there he was asked to join US Naval Intelligence as a lieutenant commander, leading an intelligence division. His later studies included the effect of the sun's aurora and emissions on the propagation of radio-waves.[13]

Similar US Army Bombe developed by Bell Laboratories. (Courtesy of the NSA/National Cryptologic Museum)

Hall, like Bill Tutte at Bletchley, was rather an expert in combinatorics (an area of maths with many applications ranging from logic to statistical physics or evolutionary biology, to computer science) and group algebraic structure theory. He spent a year at Cambridge University before the war and six months at Bletchley Park in 1944, where he used his expertise in Japanese codes as a representative of OP-20-G. His short time there possibly reflected some of the friction that could be found at Bletchley, where pockets of 'them' and 'us' feelings existed.

The Washington bombe research group divided their time between Bletchley Park, Washington and Dayton. The group also included John Howard an engineer from MIT.[14] Probably the same John C. Howard Jr.[15] of US Army 6812th Signals Security Detachment, in the American bombe operators bay who, in 1943, trained at RAF Eastcote. Howard was in charge of the refining process for the new machines, and with him was a group of women proficient in higher maths.

Bombe Machines – Operational

While Janice was finishing her course on cryptology, new recruits were scoring high on boot-camp maths aptitude tests. One was a young woman called Louise Pearsall. Prior to this she had no maths-related opportunities in her career since maths was just not expected of women – it was the domain of men. Now recruits with the skill and desire to excel in this area, suddenly found themselves in a position to undertake an important role. The bombe project offered work in statistics and probability and was often seen as 'work they had been searching for all their lives'. Louise, 22, from Elgin, Illinois, had aspired to become an actuary in insurance, calculating risks using statistical projections. However, the dean at Elgin Academy, and other potential employers, reminded her that actuarial maths – referred to by many after the war as 'Rocket Science' – was a man's field. Nevertheless, she went to the University of Iowa, where she was the only woman in her calculus class. But after two years she left due to the family's finances, and the view of her father who thought employment in the actuary field would never be available to Louise.

Instead, she took the opportunity to join the WAVES, and after basic training as an 'ordinary seaman' – the same as Janice – she was assigned to specialised training in Wisconsin where she took classes in physics, Morse code and radio operation. However, she failed to graduate due to an audio-dyslexia which made it hard for her to master the ability to receive Morse. As a result, she was re-routed from the requirements of a radio operator to the codebreaking project of Enigma.[16]

In March 1943, Louise was assigned to Washington and the Naval Communications Annex, under the leadership of John Howard. It was her job to sit at a desk and manually simulate what the Bombe machine would ultimately produce faster. The testing was necessary to produce a flawless Bombe machine and her main task was to test Enigma key settings. This involved manually figuring out various permutations such as if 'X' became 'M' and 'T' became 'P', what was the mathematical formula that would take the letters through all possible sequence permutations. The work was intense and absorbing. These were 'Menus' – instructions for Bombe machine operations, including the newer versions in Dayton.

Desch worked hard to perfect the first two-experimental prototypes – Adam and Eve – under great verbal pressure from his superior, Commander Ralph Meader, described as 'Tongue lashings', by Desch's daughter, Deborah Anderson.[17] The commander was known for his bullying tactics and pushed Desch into action by making him believe he'd be responsible for countless American deaths if he didn't come up with a high-speed Bombe soon. Ultimately, hundreds of high-speed machines were built to break Enigma ciphers within hours of a new code being used by Germany. But it wasn't just the engineering and maths, the naval team also had to understand the nature of the messages and German U-boat commander jargon.

* * *

The American code breakers in Washington worked closely with Bletchley's Hut 8, swapping intercepts and cribs and constructing Bombe menus for the new American machines. They communicated secretly by two radio and cable systems via British Security Co-ordination, in New York's Rockefeller Center. Secrecy was maintained using a Combined Cipher Machine (CCM), a combination of British Typex, with a receiving adapter at Bletchley to decipher the American Electric Cipher Machine (ECM), or SIGABA in a reverse system with an adapter, for America to receive messages.

BOMBE MACHINES, GERMAN CODEBREAKING AND ULTRA

One day Louise, four other women and a handful of male colleagues relocated to Sugar Camp and NCR. Their mission was to test the machines and ensure they worked perfectly. Each bombe machine was 10 feet long, 2 feet wide and 7 feet tall, the size of two large wardrobes, towering over operators. They weighed more than two tons and had hundreds of moving parts including the wheels and wires assembled by women on the floor below. Overall, the components were 'sourced from over 12,000 suppliers', noted one memo.[18] Some parts were unavailable in America and had to be made, such as diodes (the thermionic 'gas' tubes), high-speed commutators (a reverse switch attachment to ensure the correct flow of electrical current) and carbon brushes to lubricate or clean the wheels. The slightest fragment of copper or dust caused malfunction. It was an amazing feat at times to keep the Bombes running.

As in England several staff were needed twenty-four hours, every day. A log for 3 May 1943 shows the first two experimental tests were under way, but innumerable failures were noted – incorrect wiring, shorting of electrical current and copper particles on the wheels, were just some of the obstacles.[19] The summer heat and humidity in Dayton, a river town in the mid-west, was also a problem.

As Janice prepared for Washington, Bombe menus in Dayton were being tested and machines whirred into action. Multiple wheels with colourful wires spun swiftly to eliminate millions of 'negative' code combinations and reduced the amount of time to achieve a 'Hit', a 'Stop', or a 'positive cipher' – the crucial moment when the code could be broken. But every day there were many false hits before the correct combination was found. Each run could take twenty minutes, provided there were no breakdowns, and the machines produced tremendous heat. The operators, mostly WAVES, found they were sitting one minute and then jumping up to fix a problem the next. The best was to sit patiently and wait for a successful run – rotating wheels and spindles, more oil or solder, fix a loose or broken wire connection; set alternative permutations of Bombe menu input, set the commutators, stand up, sit down, wait – repeat. Every Bombe operator got to know the intricacies of their machine.

* * *

By September, the third generation of 100 Bombes was ready for delivery to Washington. The consignment entailed secrecy and a certain amount of reverence deserving, almost, a 'royal' train to transport the machines and their operators to the sturdy floors of the 'laboratory building' at the Naval Communications Annex. Dayton's railroad spur ran just behind Building 26 and as each machine in its own crate was loaded onto a flatbed trailer, Louise Pearsall and John Howard waited for the first shipment to be dispatched. Their passenger carriages were uncomfortable for the long overnight journey to Washington, and the flatbed trailers were not that secure, but who else would be interested in the machines?

After several minutes of waiting, John Howard, left the carriage to investigate the delay. Eventually he returned to his seat as the train got underway. Grimly, he told Louise that a group of men had been detained under suspicion of sabotage. Was this connected? Was this Bund? How did they know? Only Howard and Pearsall knew the reason for the train's delay. They vowed that top secret missions had to be better protected.

* * *

Alighting at DC, military men and women were separated. Men went to Main Navy and women to a central facility at the Washington Navy Yard.[20] The machines were securely transferred to the NCA. To Louise's surprise, sailors in the processing line at the navy port jeered and made rude or snide comments. She had no idea why, but later learned their poor rhetoric was due to rumours of female misbehaviour in Dayton – WAVES in general.

The Navy pruned out women who were considered a security risk – with notable ejections by Commander Meader. Two women were caught making love with each other in the grounds of Sugar Camp, and another woman took to constantly wearing her WAVE raincoat; she was pregnant. The women, however, were able to protect each other and the baby was born, but eventually they were all discharged under the sexist standards of the day and labelled 'Lost girls' or 'Women with a bad reputation'.

An enlisted WAVE on 20 August 1943 was transferred back to central processing in Washington because she had gone to the compound dispensary in Dayton with heavy menstrual bleeding. An examination showed 'an incomplete abortion' six weeks prior, before entering the navy. Another arrived with menstrual bleeding and abdominal cramps where her records also showed an 'induced abortion before entering the service'. In 1942 when regulations were established for WAVES, officials worried that the no-pregnancy rule would create problems in prompting enlisted women to have illegal abortions. They were right.[21]

The NCR Bombes were so high security, that more women were expelled from Dayton than anywhere else, causing all women returning to Washington to be doused with a terrible and unwarranted reputation. Louise however, stood her ground and pushed through the processing line.

After six months in Washington, Dayton trainees taught younger girls how to run and maintain the Bombe machines – some aged only 18. There were some security breaches and inefficiencies, but mostly because many did not know why their work was so important. One supervisor on the Bombe deck recalled a time when a correct rotor solution printout was accidentally thrown out. John Howard had to provide an explanation to prevent a recurrence of unnecessary delays.

> *'Eventually we got the answer and then realised that the wheel order had already been run and should've been a jackpot. Well, it had obviously been thrown in the burn bag by mistake. So, John got permission from his superiors to tell the girls something to give them some sense of how important the work was. We shut down operations for about ten minutes and he got up on a chair in the middle of the operations area. He didn't tell them specifically what they were doing, but said they were attacking an enemy cipher and it was a very important job.... And that's all they knew.'*
>
> It truly was a matter of life or death![22]

People who prepared Bombe Menus were called 'cribbers' and those Washington codebreakers produced were sometimes sent by pneumatic tube – resembling Bletchley's spit and suck machine – to the Bombe Deck. Speed was of the essence. This was the area below where Janice worked and took up the whole floor. The vast area with high ceilings, was split into three rooms, each zone was then divided into bays where four black Bombe machines were located, 120 machines overall. Each supervisor had an assistant plus four operators. When they arrived on duty, they signed a logbook and immediately got to work setting their machine from the Bombe menu – moving the commutator wheels, rotating to the start position. Each wheel weighed nearly 2lb and had to be carefully fixed so that it didn't fly off and break a limb! With flashing lights, spinning cogs, wheels and wires the machines were hot and always needed more ventilation to keep the motors cool. At best they were noisy, but during the heat of summer the rooms were stifling, and windows were opened to prevent operators from passing out. The clatter could be heard on Nebraska Avenue.

They waited for the machine's calculations to confirm a 'hit' and the printout verifying the settings, was, hopefully, the solution to intercepted Enigma messages for the day. The sheet was then passed manually through the M-9, replica of the Enigma machine, with four rotating wheels alternately switching up a notch each time a letter key was compressed. If German plain text could be read, the precise settings – the cipher key – was then turned over to typists in another room. A group of 'hits' were called 'stories'. The typists used special machines to read many more messages. With the precise settings for the day, they reset their machines. SIGABA, was the American version of the British Typex machines used at Bletchley Park. Each coded message would be typed in and the plain German text would appear. The decoded message strips would then be adhered to the back of the original message for translators in the next room, who would pass to another department for analysis and categorising. Often these were revealing and sad to the operator, if she spoke German, but codebreakers tried not to dwell on the lives they couldn't save.

After the recovery of a key, decoded messages and strips of typed German plain text were carried in baskets by junior staff to translators in Janice's map-room. Two translators were always on duty, ready to convert the text into handwritten English. Typists would then type the message and hand it to the senior watch officer, who then passed it to the intelligence section. The translated reports were often grim, but then everything in war is grim. One U-boat commander advised a U-boat submariner that all his family had been killed in an allied air raid. U-boats sunk reported loss of life, more vessels sunk, no survivors. Their messages relayed victories and defeats – it was gruelling and distressing work.

BOMBE MACHINES, GERMAN CODEBREAKING AND ULTRA

The intelligence Janice helped compile as TOP SECRET ULTRA reports came from enemy signals intercepted via various sources and outstations. Fortunately for the Allies, Admiral Karl Dönitz still needed contact with his U-boat fleets during submarine radio silence, which meant signals continued between his headquarters in Lorient, France, and wolfpacks in the Atlantic. Distance also meant messages went over high frequency radio, which provided more opportunity for Allied interception.

The Axis powers also communicated with each other via Enigma messages, especially blockade-running, as they attempted to exchange and replenish supplies to and from Japan. Special keys and other ciphers were used, but these messages were also intercepted. The sea journeys using ships and submarines filled with supplies to fuel their war effort were often long and harrowing. One sub destroyed by a US submarine, carried German technicians and several Japanese personnel as well as plans for high-speed submarines, torpedoes, German anti-submarine countermeasures and radar equipment, plus the influenza virus. Codebreakers could read distressing but useful diplomatic messages from Tokyo to Berlin:

> *'…our inability to utilise them owing to the loss of the ill-fated ship is truly unfortunate and will have a great effect throughout the Imperial Japanese Army and Navy.'*

Others, from Tokyo, took four months to arrive on the west coast of Europe. They carried 80 tons of rubber, 2 tons of gold bullion and 228 tons of tin, alloys molybdenum and tungsten for tanks and weapons, opium and quinine. The submarine went down, causing Berlin's embassy to notify Tokyo: *'The disaster which has befallen these liaison submarines one after another, at a time when they were playing such an important role in transportation between Japan and Germany, is indeed an extremely regrettable loss to both countries.'*[23]

Janice worked with her Goucher friend Jane Thornton. She was glad to have someone to confide in, though they couldn't talk about their work outside their section. Every day behind the screen in their vast room they used flags, pins and co-ordinates to display information from intercepts on 12-feet-wide wall maps of the Atlantic, then compiled preliminary intelligence reports on German U-boat locations, U-boat

Commands, positions of allied vessels and convoys. Other Goucher women worked on 'neutral shipping' at another desk, including Jaqueline B. Jenkins-Nye. The co-ordinates were important not only for diverting convoys but if a foreign ship went off course, it was possible they were secretly supplying U-boats.

Their overnight intelligence report included intercept translations, suggestions for gaps in information, co-ordinates, U-boats sunk, crew levels, fuel capacity, cargo etc., all stamped 'TOP SECRET ULTRA', in magenta ink at the top of each page, before being placed in the large, double-sealed, yellow envelope and delivered to Admiral King by the naval officer with the gun.

Cryptanalysts 'in the back room', and men and women of OP-20-GY(A)'s submarine tracking room relied heavily on Enigma solutions for regular reports of all vessels in the Atlantic. It was mutually agreed between the teams on both sides of the Atlantic that interception work would be divided fairly. Janice worked with British counterparts when intelligence needed confirmation, such as daily German weather reports intercepted via Bletchley for the Bay of Biscay or other areas in the Atlantic, but she confirmed the transatlantic teams never used their real names.

American codebreakers with British counterparts in England communicated via the Rockefeller secure message system CCM and ECM. Their counterparts were anonymous but Ensign Fran Steen, a WAVE, remembered one was called 'Pretty Weather' and another man went by the name 'Virgin Sturgeon'. America says that only 15 per cent of messages were solved by the British, the remaining by OP-20-G, but Britain claims the opposite. What is true is that, most importantly, everyone came together to defeat Hitler. Some codebreakers who saw the whole picture had nervous breakdowns, Joseph Desch's daughter said, 'He had nightmares about men dying for years.' [24]

* * *

It was imperative for enemy messages being relayed to other Allied military chiefs, via radio or teleprinter, to be paraphrased and re-enciphered, to prevent the enemy from realising their messages had been intercepted and read. It was a specific skill, and this was part of Ultra's success. It was crucial to keep the mass of information, and how it was mined, secret.

BOMBE MACHINES, GERMAN CODEBREAKING AND ULTRA

Data from OP-20-GI-2(A), meantime, was filed and categorised for future use, in the same way as the Admiralty's OIC and GC&CS at Bletchley Park. Each intercept was duplicated in the characteristic purple ink on a spirit duplicating machine, cross-referenced in at least two, and up to eight, categories, then stored using 5x8-inch index cards in open topped file boxes. The master file was chronological with the whole system branching into a manual search engine. Extended cards held individual U-boat and ship positions, map co-ordinates, assignments, new equipment, weather, personal nuances, status reports, etc. The information was also transferred to IBM punch cards for faster processing. In England this was known as the (IBM) Hollerith system.

'The Library' (OP-20-G-L) traditionally was women's work and here many of the new recruits, filing clerks, were disappointed not to be in other mixed intelligence environments, but tight friendships flourished against the backdrop of millions of enemy messages. The women saw everything from new communications via teleprinter, the indexing, the file cards that categorised every word in the message, and the analysis. Each woman was cautious and protective of the data, used in future strategies. There was talk in the department but gossip outside their office walls was never a problem. The cards and files primarily served translators, watch officers and high-ranking officials to answer questions and fill in gaps on message intercepts, past and present, aiding in strategy for all military forces. Data was also retrieved by codebreakers for suggestions on cribs.

By mid-1943 Britain and America had such a good handle on German naval signals that they rarely failed to solve a key. They had enough high-speed bombes to try many different options and from August that year naval Enigma was read rapidly, without major interruption for the rest of the war.

* * *

By 1944, WAVES had replaced most men in intelligence gathering. Captain Henri H. Smith-Hutton, who headed Combat Intelligence at the time, concluded: 'The plotting room was better run because men were not as smart as the carefully selected WAVES.' [25]

And what of the yellow envelope that Janice's department prepared? The main Submarine Tracking (or plotting) Room, where the envelope went, was on the third floor of the seventh wing of Main Navy. The room was also known as F-21 and led to another secret room that was always securely locked. The hidden part of this thirty-man Combat Intelligence Section (CIS) of Admiral Ernest J. King, Commander in Chief of the USA Fleet, handled all TOP SECRET ULTRA intelligence reports. King, as chief of naval operations was also in charge of a larger Office of Naval Intelligence which dealt with long-range and strategic issues. The CIS divisions were known as F-2 for the Commander, F-21 and F-22 for the Atlantic and Pacific branches.

Commander Kenneth A. Knowles, the NCA's counterpart at Main Navy, was part of F-21. He'd given up his naval career due to near-sightedness, but when America entered the war he was recalled. Then, in May 1943, King created the Tenth Fleet (which despite the name, had no ships) as a land-based administrative body to direct an anti-submarine war. Knowles' unit was designated as intelligence staff for this and the US Fleet. The Submarine Tracking, or Plotting Room, was the only way to enter the Secret Room, known as F-211. Three people worked inside with Knowles and a relief officer had spare keys. Only Lieutenant John E. Parsons and his two male assistants were permitted. At times, higher personnel with special clearance, were authorised. The intelligence reports of intercepted enemy messages were assessed and using one of the gigantic wall maps of the Atlantic, submarines would be plotted on the map using a bigram for the U-boat name or number and the captain's name. Other coloured tabs would note the *Milchküh*, a minelayer, a cargo carrier or vessel designated for combat. All U-boat areas were charted and studied in detail, with information derived from intercepts.

Commander Kenneth A. Knowles, Head of the Submarine Tracking Room. (US Navy/National Cryptologic Museum)

BOMBE MACHINES, GERMAN CODEBREAKING AND ULTRA

Intelligence information from Admiral King was reported to London's Admiralty OIC, at the highest level to shape strategy, but as head of the Atlantic combat intelligence, Knowles was probably the main consumer. TOP SECRET ULTRA information on U-boats and U-boat tanker identification enabled the Allies to take decisive action in defence and attack, to ensure safe delivery of convoys.

* * *

While American codebreakers kept the intelligence secret safe, only a handful knew that British codebreakers visited Main Navy and the NCA in the nation's capital. Updated telephone lists for Bletchley departments noted when their heads of staff were 'absent', in a semi-official roll call tracking personnel. If absent it was noted, for example: 'Welchman – gone to Washington'. The lists held at the British National Archives show that on 1 June 1944: 'Mr. H.R. Foss (O.C.) is at present in Washington on liaison duties with OP-20-G, TOP SECRET ULTRA.' (Some documents are also stamped 'Most Secret', or just 'Top Secret', depending on the level of classification.) That December, Foss worked full-time with US Navy Cryptography on Japanese ciphers. An ardent sandal-wearer, he was known by his Washington colleagues as 'Lend Lease Jesus', a nod toward Lend Lease passed in March 1941, and his footwear.

Chapter 18

Japanese Codebreaking

Janice's involvement with Japanese codes was zero. She knew there probably was a division doing just what she was doing for the Pacific Theatre of war, but in her words, 'I had nothing to do with that, only German and the Battle of the Atlantic.' But this book would not be complete if the achievements made in Japanese codebreaking were not mentioned.

During and after the First World War, governments decrypted as many of each other's diplomatic messages as they could, but in peacetime traffic reduced. Meanwhile, Japanese codes and ciphers became America's main focus and then a bargaining chip to discover Britain's developments on breaking German codes. America had lagged behind on intelligence derived from Germany and its allies, but the reality of U-boat perils in the Atlantic made this an important issue. Britain had also begun to look to America for Japanese codebreaking expansion, as GC&CS emphasis was predominantly on German codes, despite its multiple territories and interests in the Far East. British Intelligence knew that America listened more intently to Japanese traffic to protect their Pacific interests.

America was not a warring nation, preferring most times to find a peaceful way to reach a solution, while securing their own needs. Their navy was not strong and their air force almost non-existent, but relentless attacks and infiltration by the Imperial Japanese Army across South-East Asia was a problem. In a way, America was involved from the start, where on-going spats between the two countries, questioned Japan's belligerence in China and the Far East, as they seized land rich in raw materials – rubber and oil – and other mining commodities that Japan's topography did not produce.

After two and a half centuries of isolation, Japan continued its mission to modernise its ancient culture. Britain and America were once friends with Japan from 1902 to 1921, when they had actively supported

JAPANESE CODEBREAKING

Western nations after their embassies were besieged 1899-1901 during the Boxer Rebellion, a violent anti-foreign people's Chinese uprising[1]. But in this new tableau, Japan sought to use its influence over China to claim land and resources in southern Manchuria, while fighting Russia who also coveted the territory.

Japan won decisive battles, but it was costly to both sides in terms of manpower and resources, and they turned to President Theodore Roosevelt for help. But Roosevelt worried that they did not wish to negotiate a peace deal, and that Japanese military strength would impact the United States' interests in Asia. Instead in 1905, the President acted as intermediary to bringing the Russo-Japanese war to a negotiated conclusion. At Portsmouth, New Hampshire, delegates agreed an immediate ceasefire, recognising Japan's claim to Korea, evacuation of Russian forces from Manchuria (a Chinese territory leased to Russia since 1898 by the Qing dynasty) and turning over the Southern Manchuria Railway and mining concessions to Japan. Russia retained the Chinese Eastern Railway together with the right to station a Russian army for protection.[2] Consequently, the area became a buffer zone between Japan and Russia.

In 1911 there was a renewed ratification of the partnership between Britain and Japan, and during the First World War, they sent ships to the Mediterranean to protect British convoys. The Washington Conference took place November 1921 – February 1922 where America, Britain, Japan, France and Italy, established peace in a Five Power Pact. Britain and America would not build fortifications east of Singapore or west of Hawaii, and a ratio of ships for America, Britain and Japan was agreed at 5:5:3 (which, as we know, angered the Japanese as this was engineered via Yardley's Black Chamber a decade later). America wanted Britain to relinquish its agreement with Japan, saying all powers should be equal to preserve Chinese integrity. (Many have since wondered if a continuation of the alliance would have made any difference to the Second World War.) America secretly felt the conflict with Japan over China would increase, as well as trade conflicts in the colonies, and continued to covertly intercept Tokyo's communications through COMINT, which was easy to do.

Peace was kept until 1931 after another rise of Chinese nationalism under Chiang Kai-shek. This led to a staged occupation at Mukden by the Japanese Army on the pretext of protecting Japan's investments. During this time of Imperial Japanese Grand Manoeuvres, OP-20-G's analysis (the critical cryptanalysis of Agnes Driscoll and her team), indicated Japan knew of America's naval operations and planning, specifically War Plan Orange which strategised US Pacific Fleet operations close to Japanese home islands. The IJN then issued a new cipher with daily changing keys for the Red Book code. Agnes Driscoll was able to break in and, with stalwart traffic analysis from the US Naval team on Guam, she established her place in US Naval Cryptology history.

Driscoll did not stop there. In December 1930 a new Japanese code entailed 85,000 code groups that were then re-enciphered. OP-20-G called this the Blue Book but recovering both the code groups and the cipher was difficult as this had to be done simultaneously, without prior cribs and translations. However, with insight she ascertained the different categories of groupings by comparing similar patterns in earlier codes. It was also one of the first times she utilised the IBM tabulating machine to track her theories.

After the Mukden incident, America was called again and Henry Stimson, the United States Secretary of State, negotiated a truce in the three-week dispute. However, by February 1932 the Japanese regime, aided by Chiang Kai-shek's general weakness in dealing with Chinese unrest, proclaimed Manchukuo an independent state under the puppet Emperor Pu Yi, the last of the Qing emperors.[3]

The League of Nations appointed the Earl of Lytton, a British politician and colonial administrator, to investigate and after six weeks his commission found both parties guilty: the Chinese for anti-Japanese propaganda and refusal to compromise, and Japan as the aggressor. Japan rejected the report in September 1932 and resigned from the League of Nations, removing itself from the international body's sanctions and destroying all hope of reconciliation between the two nations.

In 1935 Japan insisted on naval parity with the US and when this was refused the Japanese delegation walked out of the London Naval Conference. Friction continued over Japan's positioning of troops and China's sovereignty, until in 1937 the rift resulted in all-out war.[4] Meanwhile, the British Empire feared for its Far Eastern territories and the USA stood their ground on taking positive action to persuade Japan to withdraw troops and make peace with China.

When war broke out in Europe in 1939, Japan felt betrayed by Germany who sided with Russia in the Molotov-Ribbentrop Pact, a Treaty of Non-aggression, when in 1936, Japan had signed the

JAPANESE CODEBREAKING

Anti-Comintern Pact with Germany in an anti-communist pact to stave off subversive activity. The Japanese government tried to improve relations with Britain and America, but the US remained firm in its peace policy with China. Japan then threatened to station troops in North Indochina to procure oil from the Dutch East Indies which led America to impose sanctions. As Europe suffered rapid German victories, the Japanese government fell, and a new militant government came to power that joined Germany and Italy in the military defensive Tripartite Pact of September 1940.

Japan hoped the alliance would neutralise the Russian threat in Northern China, and that Germany would be victorious over Britain leaving South-east Asian territories undefended. Meanwhile, Germany anticipated a Japanese attack on British soil to divert British forces to the Far East, leaving their European borders unprotected. It was a game of cat and mouse, but by 1941 it was clear that Britain wasn't going to collapse, and Germany attacked the USSR instead. Now Japan was once again in a vulnerable position with Russia. The USA and Japan had also reached another confrontational stage when America provided financial aid to China and continued Japanese economic sanctions, limiting materials. With Japanese opinion inflamed, ideas of peace were destroyed as they invaded and occupied wider territories to plunder alternative resources. Janice Martin noticed in the press that US dealings with Japan were deteriorating. Britain had also severed trade with Japan and froze her assets abroad. Churchill warned that war on Japan would be declared 'within the hour' if Japan declared war on the United States. He also stated that a powerful force was on hand to serve in Asia. On 30 November, reports indicated that General Hideki Tojo, the new prime minister, had not replied to America's proposals to improve relations. Instead, he had used violent language and threats 'to purge the Anglo-American influence from the Far East'. American intelligence listened for message clues, but at the time they didn't realise Japanese signals had been silenced for several days.

* * *

The Enigma machine, used in German military fields for short tactical messages, was known to William Friedman – mostly through the paper produced in 1928 by GC&CS's Hugh Foss and because the machine was available on the commercial market. Others in his team thought Japan probably used Enigma as a basis for their new system, but Friedman disagreed. Enigma was only suitable for short message reproduction. For more detailed messages, to and from diplomats and ambassadors in different countries, it was likely a more sophisticated enciphering machine was used.

Friedman's small group of codebreakers, including Rowlett, Sinkov and Kullback, were ready for expansion. Funding was never massive, but FDR's 'New Deal' provided funds for women to undertake government work in Washington. The plan also hoped to spur private business to take the same leap of faith regarding women. Discrimination still existed, but women had a distinct advantage when applying as they easily passed a standard civil service examination, the same exam as men. Friedman also liked to work with intelligent women, as noted by his own marriage to Elizebeth.

Women such as Wilma Berryman were hired before the Second World War when she moved from West Virginia with her husband to Washington for work. She had a maths degree and trained as a high school teacher, but during the Depression only first-grade positions were available. She read about Elizebeth Friedman's codebreaking achievements in *The Evening Star,* and this intensified her interest in a future role for herself. After enquiries she found the US Navy had an officers' correspondence course for civilian enthusiasts to learn from home. After several months she completed the course, and William Friedman came across her name on a civil service list of test evaluations. This chance led her to being employed in his Italian codes and ciphers department, where colleagues asked each morning, 'How's Benito today?'

Friedman's operation, under US Army superior, Major General Joseph Mauborgne, was a 'find things out for yourself" place, where newcomers were asked, 'What four things would Captain Hitt consider essential to cryptanalytic success?' and, 'What two places in a message provide the best chance of a successful attack, using assumptions?' (Respectively, the beginning and the end, using perseverance, careful methods of analysis, intuition and luck.)[5] Wilma loved it, and so did other female recruits.

The team was small and laboured to physically duplicate the inner workings of a new Japanese machine. This was something that had been done before with Enigma and they themselves had built a replica of RED and broken that Japanese cipher in 1936 (called RED due to the colour of the folder bindings and not to be confused with the German Cipher the British called 'Red'). They were able to read diplomatic traffic between Tokyo and its embassies around the world – Berlin, Rome, Lisbon, Madrid, Stockholm, Istanbul, Ankara, Berne and Washington DC – but in 1938 RED revealed a new cipher machine under construction and promptly dried up as Japanese diplomats moved to a new system. They called it their 'secrets-writer'. With little knowledge of the new machine and its unreadable cipher, Friedman's US Army team named this PURPLE, and collaborated with the US Navy to look for solutions.

The new cipher appeared far more complicated. One change in cipher systems was that cable companies no longer insisted on pronounceable codes. 'Sixes' representing vowels and 'twenties' representing consonants, were no longer needed. However, in the interests of 'cryptographic continuity', new systems often maintained elements of old and Friedman and Rowlett leaned on the supposition that 26 digits would still be used but the 'sixes' might not be vowels; they could be any letter.

The European war with Germany had begun by the time Friedman reasoned that PURPLE must consist of selector relay switches, the 'stepping switch' found in automatic telephone exchanges. The team thought they would solve the cipher quickly from the cipher patterns, using combined lateral thinking, concentration, a pen and paper and a desktop calculator with nine rows of keys and ten columns wide, to help expand their theories. 'Repetition…, repetition.' Friedman always insisted patterns were not called 'repeats'. As strips of intercepted meaningless letters were set before them, everyone knew that if all messages from a single day were compared 'something' usually would be found.

The complexity of ciphers can be revealed in layer after layer of alphabets and number settings, but to produce this manually would take an eternity, so, for speed Friedman's team used early IBM business tabulating machines (Hollerith based) to compute the billions (trillions) of complex options. Their objective was to produce a detailed mathematical model of the Japanese machine cipher. Working in total secrecy for twenty-four hours in room 341/6 in the Munitions Building, Friedman's team waded through sheets of mathematical intricacies while tackling the opaque and alien nature of the Japanese language that few

Americans understood. It was a snail's pace, and this eventually took a toll on Friedman's health. However, over time patterns steadily emerged and advances were made.

Codebreakers had their own methods to combat frustration. Rowlett went to bed early and woke in the middle of the night inspired. Friedman found solutions while he shaved, but Genevieve Grotjan Feinstein, sat patiently for hours, contemplating lines of letters. Friedman taught his students that if you scrutinise a cipher long enough from different angles, patterns ultimately form, as wheels and rotors eventually repeat a pattern. Friedman also taught mathematical ways of underlying behaviour not only in language but also in each letter. A simple example is E, if this is the most frequent letter used in plain text and you code this letter to Z, then Z would become the most frequent letter in the message. The first thing a cryptanalyst did, therefore, was to make a frequency count. He also agreed a foreign cipher can be broken without understanding the language, but you must know how the letters in the language behave. Such as in English S and T often appear together, but in Japanese Y is almost always followed by O or U. Gradually the team mastered the romanisation Latin script of Japanese, referred to as 'rōmaji', but still the solution eluded them.

Friedman was sceptical that codebreakers had to excel in crossword puzzles. These are fun and can be difficult, especially cryptic versions. However, the clues help you find the answer, whereas ciphers are designed to never find the answer, unless you know the key. This presents a subtle and important difference in how codes are broken. With codes and ciphers, one must be prepared to work for months or years – and then be prepared to fail – and often one must be a master *codemaker* for other peoples' codes to make sense.

***

As a civilian, Mary Louise Prather entered the government at a basic level in 1938. She was 25 and used her stenography skills in concealing or unravelling messages for cryptography and traffic analysis for Friedman and Rowlett. It was important for her to be precise. Her secret duties included logging intercepted enciphered diplomatic messages correctly, preparing decrypted messages for distribution and running complicated and temperamental office machinery – Hollerith/IBM keypunchers, punch card sorters, modified tabulators and spirit duplicators. Before long she was promoted to Administrative Assistant and Personnel Officer for the General Cryptographic branch, working with Rowlett in B Branch to replicate PURPLE, where conjecture reigned, and hunches were feverishly followed down a path that everyone hoped was not a dead end.

Gradually, the machine's puzzling design took shape. Now they searched for three long messages, all sent the same day, which were found and all they needed was a crib. Mary, in her meticulous way, remembered a successfully read intercept from another code system for the same date, and suggested this might be the answer. She duplicated the crib and the messages several times for the team to work on. Nobody had any idea what exactly they were looking for, but all worked individually to find an elusive clue. Then in the afternoon of 20 September 1940, a shy Genevieve Grotjan appeared grinning before Rowlett with a sheaf of papers. She had something to show him. 'We could see from her attitude that she must have discovered something extraordinary,' he said.[6]

Genevieve laid her worksheets on the table and with a pencil began to indicate where she had already marked two letters that appeared together on separate lines. One from the intercepted message above, one from the crib below. On a second worksheet she pointed out another coincidence in the same pattern which confirmed what the team was looking for. She then indicated a third and a fourth repetition, confirming the theory. She had broken the 'twenties', all thanks to Mary Prather who found the original crib.

Rowlett and Leo Rosen were the first to test this on the replica machine they had toiled over for so long. Having set up the indicator Rowlett started typing and the first three or four number groups came out perfectly the other side revealing Japanese plain text. This was confirmed by a message from the previous intercept that had been solved correctly. But the machine stopped. Mystified at first, Rosen realised a condenser over the relay points was needed for the master relay. The necessary component was acquired, and the machine worked perfectly.

The Friedman/Rowlett replica engaged two of the most advanced typewriters of the time, connected by a complex battery of relays and plug boards creating an impossible electrical puzzle. The message was typed in one side and, sure enough, the PURPLE text appeared the other. If Friedman's solution was correct then this replica would work in reverse, deciphering the intercepted signals. The team had accomplished the impossible, to their amazement and immense pleasure – the PURPLE cipher was broken. It was a colossal achievement. Some say other countries assisted, but this is not proven.

Reports from code systems broken at Bletchley were called ULTRA, or TOP SECRET ULTRA, but the codes for the Imperial Japanese Navy were known by American intelligence as MAGIC. These included reports from PURPLE, delivered by hand to the most senior personnel in the USA government, including the President and his Chiefs of Staff. The term MAGIC stuck when the US Army's Chief of Signals, Officer Major General Joseph Mauborgne, called the successful code breaking team 'magicians'.

In 1943 Mary Prather was recommended, by Friedman, to receive credit, 'for the careful keeping of records and the index of all messages'

The Friedman/Rowlett replica engaged two of the most advanced typewriters of the time and the PURPLE cipher was broken - a colossal achievement. Shown here, still together, in a crate during remodeling at the NSA 2021. (Courtesy of the NSA/National Cryptologic Museum)

JAPANESE CODEBREAKING

and 'it was as a result of her painstaking attention to detail that a paraphrased message was found which formed a very important link in the (Japanese) solution'. The memorandum dated 27 September 1943[7] to Colonel Corderman, recommended other Army SIS for the Legion of Merit or Medal for Merit Awards including Rowlett, Genevieve Grotjan, Robert Ferner, Albert Small and Samuel Snyder. Friedman further said:

> *'An immediate result of the solution was the possibility of constructing a machine to duplicate what the Japanese machine was doing. This was accomplished without the benefit of any information whatsoever in the way of captured or pilfered drawings, blueprints, etc., but solely from an understanding of the cryptographic principles underlying the system, so that the machine could be constructed. He then went on to confirm the major share of the credit for construction of the first and later models of PURPLE was due to Mr. Leo Rosen and Mr. Frank B. Rowlett.'*

Mary Prather finally received the Meritorious Civilian Service Award in 1969, after becoming Chief of the Stenographic Section and Chief of Soviet Information in the 1960s.

Japanese diplomatic secret messages were successfully read, but Friedman was hospitalised due, it is thought, to a nervous breakdown attributed to the mental strain of PURPLE. While in hospital the secret exchange to Bletchley Park took place in February 1941 with Sinkov, Rosen, Currier and Weeks. The success of PURPLE was Friedman's last foray in codebreaking. Suffering from total exhaustion he spent the first three months of that year in Walter Reed Hospital. His legacy, however, lives on as one of the greatest codebreakers of all time and of the pre-computer age.[8]

* * *

In April 1941, Genevieve Grotjan was given a raise. Over 180 codebreakers worked for the army downtown, enabling both the British and the United States to read diplomatic traffic between Tokyo and other Japanese embassies. But Germany, Italy and Japan were unaware of America's success on PURPLE when, on 27 September, they agreed a defensive military alliance in Berlin, known as the Tripartite or Berlin Pact, and their cross-communications opened a diplomatic box of treasure for the allies. However, this changed in December 1941 when all Japanese embassies, except Washington, were ordered to destroy all codebooks and cipher machines. Had they become suspicious, or was this part of their plan? Unfortunately, Washington did not realise this due to complete radio silence, and that two Japanese task forces, with aircraft carriers had left harbour to sail east on 25 November. The clock set to ambush the US Navy was ticking.

'PEARL HARBOR BOMBED; USA IS AT WAR!'

The shocking attack by the Imperial Japanese Air Force, on 7 December, left the country in no doubt they were now in the war, and a hornet's nest exploded with questions as to why America was not prepared. Was it the diplomatic department's fault or the navy's? They argued diplomatic messages did not carry military information. Was it the army's fault? They were proficient at reading Japanese messages. Did anyone, Roosevelt or Churchill, know an attack was a possibility? Washington's intelligence analysis was at its peak trying to establish the warning signs and who had missed a crucial message. At Bletchley Park an urgent cry went out for more Japanese linguists and an accelerated training programme was put in place to bolster Japanese Signals Intelligence.

Each intelligence agency blamed others for not intercepting or analysing the messages correctly, sometimes simply because they thought the other one was doing it. The disagreements between US intelligence widened, and like badly behaved children the government and military chiefs were forced to amicably find a way to work together. Finally, an agreement was reached where SIS (US Army) operators would listen and intercept messages on odd numbered days and Op-20-G (US Navy) would listen on even. It seemed ridiculous, but both sections then had a shot at systematically breaking important ciphers efficiently. The dispute was reminiscent of the Army and Navy in Britain after the First World War which, after collaboration of forces, became the largest intelligence factory of its time. Could American intelligence departments bury their differences and work together in a similar way?

* * *

JAPANESE CODEBREAKING

By 1942, an agreeable division of duties was in place between Bletchley Park and the US Navy where they worked together on most Japanese Naval codes as well as German Enigma in relation to Atlantic U-boat attacks. Developments on the new US Bombe machines were eagerly awaited, meantime, British Bombes were used to speed up the joint effort in breaking German Enigma.

The US Army (SIS) took responsibility for PURPLE, intercepting and reading the higher codes of diplomats in Japanese embassies. Meanwhile, the Japanese Military Attaché code was broken at Bletchley Park in 1942 under John Tiltman.[9]

Japanese code systems were complicated and part of this was due to not enough messages being intercepted to provide a 'depth' of intelligence, a necessary remedy required by John Tiltman from British intelligence. He had a reputation as one of the nicest men in codebreaking. A prominent tall, dark and handsome Scot from GC&CS, he served with the King's Own Scottish Borderers during the First World War. He was wounded in France and received the Military Cross for bravery, then seconded to MI1 (Army Intelligence). After a Russian Language course, he was stationed at the Indian Army Headquarters in Simla from 1921-1929 where he served as Cryptanalyst. There his job was to plough through a backlog of translation work, but he didn't mind. His later term for this was 'depth'. His team tackled intercepted messages and broke ciphers, then analysed, translated and redirected information in a system that became known as Traffic Analysis. All Russian diplomatic cipher traffic was read from Moscow to Kabul, Afghanistan to Uzbekistan and Turkestan.

Tiltman's excellent translation and decoding skills were so successful, the War Office had posted him to GC&CS for a year, but he stayed for more than a decade as a War Office civilian at Bletchley Park, during the Second World War. His systems and knowledge of cryptology led him to become one of the finest cryptanalysts in the world and of all time. He considered himself fortunate to have a varied experience of different languages and branches of Signals Intelligence, with many skills that few others had.

Progress was slow on major Japanese Army codes at Arlington Hall though knowledge gleaned from British Navy codebreakers indicated these were enciphered similarly to the Japanese Naval Code JN-25, which utilised an additive book code. As a regular visitor to Washington, he offered tried and tested ways to overcome difficult problems, and recommended the tasks be broken into bite size pieces to concentrate on one small area at a time. This would establish at least a route to crack the address. A message on its own might appear insignificant and reveal nothing, but a series of messages over time would lead to a pattern and broader representation of the adversary's plan.

Some Japanese traffic was missed due to the lack of Listeners, but also because messages from the field were transmitted on low frequencies making it difficult for the Allies to pick up signals. However, as the Imperial Japanese Army raided territories further from their base they were forced to transmit on higher frequencies, which aided the Allies. The IJA units also regularly reported useful information to their commanders, such as the number of casualties, the need for reinforcements and any other situation beneficial to their strategy.

Increased traffic (depth) reached Arlington Hall by 1943 and was better organised for Army codes using the systems Tiltman suggested. The innumerable Japanese codes were mind boggling, challenging and too many to detail, but eventually a WAVE officer, Ensign Janet Burchell, became responsible for traveling from the Naval Communications Annex across the Potomac for formal weekly meetings at Arlington Hall, to coordinate and exchange information.

The position required her to be aware of all code and cipher systems, captured materials and prisoner interrogations useful for their work, while the central library, OP-20-G-L, gathered all original message information and intelligence reports, to categorise and collate for future reference and strategy. This led Burchell to become the central go-to person when help was needed on a tricky intercept or cipher. Even though Janice didn't overtly process intelligence from Japanese intercepts, it is likely she knew of Ensign Janet Burchell, an important link between the Navy and the Army for both military, commercial and diplomatic codes of the German, Italian and Japanese High Commands.

As well as the Japanese Naval Codes in multiple numbers JN-11 (derived from JN-40), JN-20, JN-25, JN-39 (replaced by JN-40). JN-147, JN-152, JN-167 to name a few, there were Japanese Army Water Transport Codes and Japanese Dockyard codes. The Japanese Army had its own navy (after the Second World War this became the JMSDF – Japan Maritime Self-Defense Force) and was used when moving Japanese troops around the Pacific. They were some of the most important Army codes to tackle.

JAPANESE CODEBREAKING

One was '2468' or JEK. It seemed impregnable with tiers of maths each having a complicated route to follow. But with excessive efforts from Solomon Kullback's team at Arlington Hall (branch B-II) 2468 was finally broken on 6 April 1943. Abe Sinkov took the credit, but it was US Army Sergeant Joe Richard who noticed the code system changed every three weeks, which meant intercepts could be arranged via IBM/Hollerith tabulators by group and time period. Another person, British, born in India – Wilfrid Noyce from British Intelligence and the Wireless Experimental Centre in Simla, Delhi – realised the first letter of the third group of each message was not random, and that other groups were paired in 'doublets'. It was teamwork on a global scale. Noyce, whose family was from Liverpool, was head boy at Charterhouse and went to King's College, Cambridge before the war. In 1953, he was one of the first English mountaineers to scale Mount Everest.[10]

Bletchley Park relayed Noyce's message in April 1943 to Arlington Hall mentioning the peculiar aspect. In the second code group of each message, the first digit did not seem random. A second telegram from Australia confirmed this, where any digit in the first position of the third group shared a relationship with the corresponding digit of the second group: if the latter was 0, then the other would be 2, 4 or 9. When the team made sense of this, they went on to ascertain that two four-digit groups were buried somewhere that held the indicator, these would then reveal the vital section being used in the additive code book. Sometimes it was a hopeless search, but each new message that might hold the key was leapt upon. In close collaboration and many all-night sessions, they 'just squeaked by!' as Frank W. Lewis, the master cryptic crossword compiler lamented.[11] 'An account of these aspects would put any mere "spy thriller" to shame.'

As codebreakers barred themselves in on 7 April to study the controlling numbers, they established that if two-number pairs, say 11 or 77, appeared in a certain place, another pair appeared elsewhere, suggesting the groups were interdependent, but lined up in a pattern. Their work revealed the Japanese Water Transport Code used three additive books. The full indicator pattern or prompt was BPPS/RRCC. (Book, Page number, Sum/Row and Column). But the huge challenge was these indicator groups were between two early code groups in the middle of a message. Not at the beginning or the end. It was an intertwined system that only stealth and experience could unravel.

Colonel Preston Corderman was delighted with his team. Now they could decode the regular word *maru* to recover additives using their discovery. Soon they had the layout of the Japanese Army, and when the Japanese Eighth Army split at Rabaul, on the volcanic island of East Britain, and sent identical messages enciphered with the same additive but different rows and columns, the codebreakers were able to compare and pinpoint additives. These were called cross dupes. It was of vital importance for the Allies to prevent the supply of Japanese reinforcements, therefore, breaking the Water Transport code was just as important as breaking Enigma and other intelligence triumphs.

SIS Codebreakers at Arlington Hall. (US Army/National Cryptologic Museum)

JAPANESE CODEBREAKING

Japanese Diplomatic codes and ciphers were also important. RED and ORANGE were broken before the Second World War by Agnes Driscoll and Rowlett, but both eventually dried up, when PURPLE was introduced. Thanks to the US breach of this cipher, it was 'high pay off' or 'cream of the crop'. Full Diplomatic reports on strategy and policy were far more useful than Enigma's notelets.

Vice Admiral Hiroaki Abe, representative to an Axis military council, unknowingly provided substantial information regarding German deployments 'essential for allied military decisions in the European Theatre of war'.[12]

The Allies were starting to win, but OP-20-G couldn't make a silly mistake by revealing to the Japanese they could read their messages.

* * *

When Agnes Driscoll helped break the ORANGE machine cipher, OP-20-G projected the future lay in machines, but she preferred to stick with the timeworn habit of using paper ciphers and codes, causing consternation in the cryptology department. Anticipating her intransigence, the navy allocated work on another analogue version of ORANGE to one of her associates, Lieutenant Jack Holtwick. His assignment considered possible future modifications, however, the only US replica to derive from this specialised work in 1940, was codenamed CORAL, but cipher machines, books and manual ciphers of Kana and Rōmaji, continued to be broken.

After a car accident there had been a marked change in Agnes' personality resulting in stubbornness and irrational arguments. Eventually, she was sidelined by US Navy Intelligence and diverted from Japanese codes to work on German Naval systems and Enigma. The move, however, was not happy and signalled the end of her cryptanalytic success (though later the navy attributed the initial breakthrough of the then 'new' general-purpose code, JN25, to her). Agnes was in her early fifties, considered old by the Second World War and past her prime, and much like 'any profession that emphasises intellectual agility and extreme concentration' she had reached a time where she was outmatched and worn out. But Agnes carried on.

Transparency was not part of their lives, nor was it evident in department heads' decisions. Safford's reasons for suddenly changing his mind about the exchange of information in 1941, in retrospect, shows that Agnes Driscoll's move to German codes was perhaps to form the basis of a US Naval Enigma division of their own, under her direction, operating secretly and independently of Britain. Both Safford and Driscoll assumed little good would come from British systems, and Driscoll believed she could exploit German naval traffic – convincing Safford, perhaps, not to join the mutual trade of intelligence systems and their product.[13]

Her arrogance, born from more than two decades of success, perhaps clouded her view of German Enigma's scope. In the Atlantic, at the time, the US Navy did not have much in the way of intercept capability and therefore lacked the necessary depth of German traffic to exploit. America was ignorant of most German cryptographic systems and appeared not to have a naval Enigma machine. Driscoll assumed her department's cryptanalytic attack on Enigma would be simple – perhaps basing her ideas on easier commercial Enigma messages, of which she was familiar. US efforts to capture crypto-material could not be relied upon, and breakthroughs from operator mistakes were not expected – no 'depth', no experience. Though her department increased to fourteen after Pearl Harbor, she only had a staff of five initially. Instead, she built on a 'catalogue' idea,[14] where a known code word would be accompanied by other associated encrypted words, similar to a tetragraph, to provide a match and a possible route to a solution.

In August 1941, Agnes told Bletchley's Commander Denniston when he visited OP-20-G, that she was not interested in British help – her catalogue would do the job. It was the only way to exploit Enigma in her opinion and only a few dozen people were needed to solve the daily keys. Denniston, who was incredulous and probably stifled a laugh, kindly explained that her approach had already been tested and discarded since the method did not produce enough hits to recover the daily Enigma settings. What she hadn't known was that, between the US group trip to Britain in February and his US visit, GC&CS had broken the military Enigma in May. Nothing was mentioned before since the system of sharing information and methods was yet to be agreed.

The British success in this was due entirely to the work of several hundred people, not just a few, and the fast, analytical, Bombe machines.

JAPANESE CODEBREAKING

REF ID:A275386

10th September, 1941.

Dear Mr. Friedmann,

After a week's wait in Montreal I had a safe passage home and am just beginning now to describe my visit to my colleagues who are all extremely interested. It will be some days before I can get square with the work and start to pass to you some of the information you required.

I am extremely sorry that the arrival of Stevens from Singapore has been delayed so long but I feel it may give your staff an opportunity of a close study of the material they already have and I am sanguine of your success when the extra material and background reaches you.

I hope soon to receive from you a full description of your new method of attack on the Fuji cyphers. Our people have had a fair amount of success and I feel they will appreciate this new line.

I hope soon to hear of further progress made by Dr. Kullback's party.

Will you please give my greetings to Mrs. Friedmann and my thanks to her and to you for your many kindnesses during my stay in Washington.

Yours ever sincerely
A.G. Denniston

F. Friedmann, Esq.

Approved for Release by NSA on 07-15-2014 pursuant to E.O. 13526

Commander Alastair Denniston's September 1941 letter to William Friedman confirming his safe return to England after his visit to Washington DC. The letter also confirms the planned arrival of Tiltman's representative Major Geoffrey Stevens (Essex Regiment) of the Far East Combined Bureau (Hong Kong), to US SIS at Arlington Hall. (Courtesy of the NSA/National Cryptologic Museum)

It was astounding news for her, and she conceded she had not fully grasped the intricacies of Enigma. Denniston promised to provide helpful information, and reported back to GC&CS, with irony, that 'she was the best they had'.[15] Fortunately, he had a better relationship with William Friedman.

* * *

Early in 1942 Wilma Berryman moved army sections to tackle address codes, joining newcomer Ann Zeilinger Caracristi. The addresses (or headers) had started revealing clues. When a Japanese message was enciphered, a radio man attached details of the recipients (*chiya*), the sender (*hatsu*) and the delivery location or 'address' (*ate*). This was usually short and obvious and often led to a solution. The approach seemed mundane, but each step provided details of Japanese forces and their position.

The encrypted communication appeared as a line of numbers and, line by line, the two women plunged intensely into the task using their imagination, certain reference materials, good humour and determination to succeed. A 'chaining' method was also used, involving the lengthy process of subtracting one code group from another, in the hope that two code groups might have been enciphered with the same additive.[16]

Further help came when an aircraft was shot down over India and the British captured a Japanese codebook and set of additive sheets. These provided number groups for codebreakers, reconstructed templates on a number-by-number basis. This was a form of book-building as it was known in Britain and book-breaking in the United States. Britain sent copies of the sheets by Diplomatic Bag to Arlington Hall in January 1943, which helped the department move forward another step. Japanese unit ID numbers in the south Pacific were also useful.

With minute details, Wilma remembered a Navy crib resembled one of hers and, following her hunch, carried on matching the two levels of lines. She asked a male colleague – Al Small – what he thought and for both, it was a eureka moment. The captured sheets from Britain gave her the underlying code group, and the WAVES Navy crib gave her the possible meaning. If then, the deciphered group was 8970 and she knew from the captured blank that the code group for this was 1720, she could figure out the additive code was 7250. The Navy crib deciphered this as '*mo*'.

REF ID:A275384

22nd July, 1942.

My dear Friedman,

    I am taking advantage of Kulback's return to send you a few lines of greeting. I am sure his visit is of great service to both of us. Speaking for the Diplomatic Sections only, he now knows what all of us are doing and has seen weak points in the liaison in the case of the French and South American, and will, I hope, take steps on his return to clear up any misunderstandings. I consider that in Japanese, German and Italian we are now walking in step, and I hope soon to see the other subjects equally efficient.

    It will then be the time for you to come over and put the final touches on what I hope will be a record in international cooperation.

    I hope to have Colonel Hayes down at my home for the weekend and to introduce him to my golf course, which is known in these parts as a goat track, as it entails a certain amount of mountaineering.

    Please give my sincere greetings to Mrs. Freidman.

Yours ever sincerely

A.G. Denniston

Approved for Release by NSA on 07-15-2014 pursuant to E.O. 13526

Denniston's July 1942 letter to William Friedman confirming Solomon Kullback's return to Washington DC after his visit to Bletchley Park. 'Speaking for the Diplomatic Sections only, he now knows what all of us are doing....' (Courtesy of the NSA/National Cryptologic Museum)

Her colleague was ecstatic: 'You've got it! You've got it', he cried. Incredulous, Wilma thought she had falsely forced the result, but she hadn't. Her solution was Arlington Hall's first break into the Japanese Army's address system, and it had only taken three months. Bletchley Park, the NCA and Arlington Hall all worked together to uncover Japanese military address codes.

The laborious practice of mining for messages started in February 1943, around the same time the decision was made to move Agnes Driscoll away from German codes (seen as incompatible to the Allied Enigma problem) – along with three other women – Mrs Clark, Mrs Talley and Mrs Hamilton. Agnes had led the technique before on Japanese Navy codes, with her small team. The process had taken years.

Arlington Hall didn't have years, and Ann Caracristi also rose to the challenge. Reports kept the Pentagon, other sections and military apprised and by 15 March 1943, more army address codes had emerged. Every minute achievement was noted and eventually, by collecting all consecutive numbers, the Japanese codebook was recreated. Other small details crucial to the cipher were sum checks that aimed to prevent mistakes and garble; 0987, for example, was only three digits for the code word, with the last digit controlling the first three, in a process of reverse or 'false' maths: 0+9+8=7 (9+8=17 but you don't carry the 1). By the summer of 1943 other explanations were recovered revealing the code group meanings of Hiroshima, Singapore and Tokyo.[17] They worked hard. The solution was all that mattered. Days off were enjoyable, but work was always in mind, snatching any tangential thought that might provide an answer.

Another section at Arlington Hall tackled Japanese commercial codes. African American women worked with banks and businessmen's enciphered messages, to expose the names of large Japanese companies conducting business with Hitler. Mitsubishi and Dai Nippon were two. The contribution they made was huge, but due to the enforced segregation rules they were not permitted to mix with white women in other departments, despite their parallel roles. The war was already pushing social boundaries and underprivileged, and privileged, black women wanted their due parity with privileged whites.

All branches needed new employees en masse. It wasn't unusual for a bulk order of 200 clerks to be made, with no stipulation as to age, education level or experience. Eventually this changed and guidelines were given, but because new techniques evolved, recruiters had difficulty keeping up with the new skills needed.[18] It was a challenge as the Navy and other federal agencies including the new OSS, the FBI, munitions factories and other private war related entities were all hiring at unprecedented rates, at the same time. The private sector paid well, better than the Army or Navy, but both paid more than a teaching post. In this mindset the Civil Service Commission, funded by the government, turned its attention to hiring schoolteachers from the South. In the days of segregation, this was not a popular move, but the Army was made to abide by the rules of the commission and required Signals to recruit from the Fourth Civil Service District,[19] which included Maryland, West Virginia, Virginia and North Carolina.

The white women never knew the US Army's secret commercial codes section employed all African American people. The head, William Coffee, was a black man who studied English in Knoxville, Tennessee. He was born in 1917 and started his public service career with the Civilian Conservation Corps in 1937. Soon after 1940 he started work for the army's Signals Intelligence Service at Arlington Hall. Though hired on a janitor's pay he was promoted to the position of messenger and after further promotion found himself in charge of hiring a group of black cryptologists. His success in forming and directing the group elevated him to a level never seen before in the world of intelligence for an African American. He received Commendation for Meritorious Civilian Service after the Second World War, but there is no evidence to say the women received any recognition. Coffee went on to join the Armed Forces Security Agency which later became the NSA.

It was not until 1944 when Eleanor Roosevelt and Mildred McAfee broke through the barrier for black women to join the WAVES. Racial experimentation in the NAC, however, was still considered a step too far by top officials. Persons with an 'unorthodox' background were simply considered a security risk. Commander J.N. Wenger wrote, 'there are many other activities in the Navy where experiments of this sort can be carried on without so much danger in the event that difficulties arise.'[20] There were patches of unrest everywhere as civil rights activists claimed their share of fair and equal treatment, more than a hundred years after the abolition of slavery in America. Instead, keen African Americans – potential WAVES – took their intellect and talents elsewhere.

Secret Service: Segregated African American (mostly female) SIS Codebreakers, led by William Coffee, at Arlington Hall. Seen on the front cover of the National Cryptologic Museum's brochure *Invisible Cryptologists: African Americans WWII to 1956*. (Courtesy of the NSA/National Cryptologic Museum)

After the destruction of black neighbourhoods and homes to make way for the Pentagon, Eleanor Roosevelt declared 12-15 per cent of the workforce should be black. The percentage figure was a poor substitute, but when the new war office was dedicated in January 1943, in accordance with the racial segregation laws for the state of Virginia, President Roosevelt instead, ordered the 'Whites Only' signs to be removed. Until then sets of racially segregated lavatories were positioned side by side, and dining areas for black people were in the basement. The Pentagon had become the only building in Virginia where the laws were not enforced. Segregation was abolished in 1965 and the side-by-side restrooms are now used by all.[21]

JN-25 and Bookbuilding

The most secure communications for command and control of the IJN during the Second World War was given the name JN-25 by western codebreakers. Originally with the reference AN-1, this was a research project rather than an important cipher for daily decryption. The cipher, in 1939, replaced what America called BLUE and produced five-numeral groups for message transmission. But the US couldn't read a single message within a useful time frame. If they did catch something it was weeks old. British, Australian, Dutch and American cryptanalysts co-operated on tackling JN-25 well before the Pearl Harbor attack, but because the Japanese Navy was not engaged in significant battle operations before, there was little traffic to provide 'depth'. The Japanese move to silence their radio signals seemed deliberate, but messages had been picked up through Diplomatic codes before the Japanese embassies were blanked out two weeks before the attack.

Naval Officer Joseph Rochefort was a cryptanalyst also under Captain Laurance Safford, who also worked with Agnes Meyer Driscoll. As Rochefort was a Japanese linguist, Safford as chief of OP-20-G, sent him to run Station Hypo in Hawaii, also known as FRUPAC (Fleet Radio Unit Pacific), early in 1941. He had the best cryptanalyst team there, but they were denied access to PURPLE, the diplomatic cipher, by the Army US War Plans Division. The attack on Pearl Harbor, and his naval office, had been devastating and retaliation was in most people's minds; America would repay Japan in the most forceful way.

British Signals personnel at FECB (Far East Combined Bureau), in Hong Kong, were also crucial in this arena, but two weeks later Japan overran the Hong Kong base, and its staff swiftly escaped to Singapore, only to be uprooted again in February 1942 when the IJA rampaged into Britain's Crown Colony. Churchill said it was, 'the worst disaster in British military history', but this was mainly due to lack of sufficient British defences. Almost 150,000 Allied troops became Far Eastern prisoners of war under the Japanese.

Codebreakers of FECB went to Anderson Station in Ceylon (now Sri Lanka) – known as FRUEF – Anderson, then transferred to Alidina School in Kilindini, Kenya, before returning to Colombo. There was also a small US Navy cryptanalytic unit in the Philippines, who were smuggled out with General MacArthur before Corregidor fell. They went to Australia, to join the combined Fleet Radio Unit, Melbourne (FRUMEL) exchanging intelligence between the US Army and Navy (in Guam), Bletchley Park, Australia and other communication stations. Japanese troop and shipping movements were reported,

THE SECRET LIFE OF AN AMERICAN CODEBREAKER

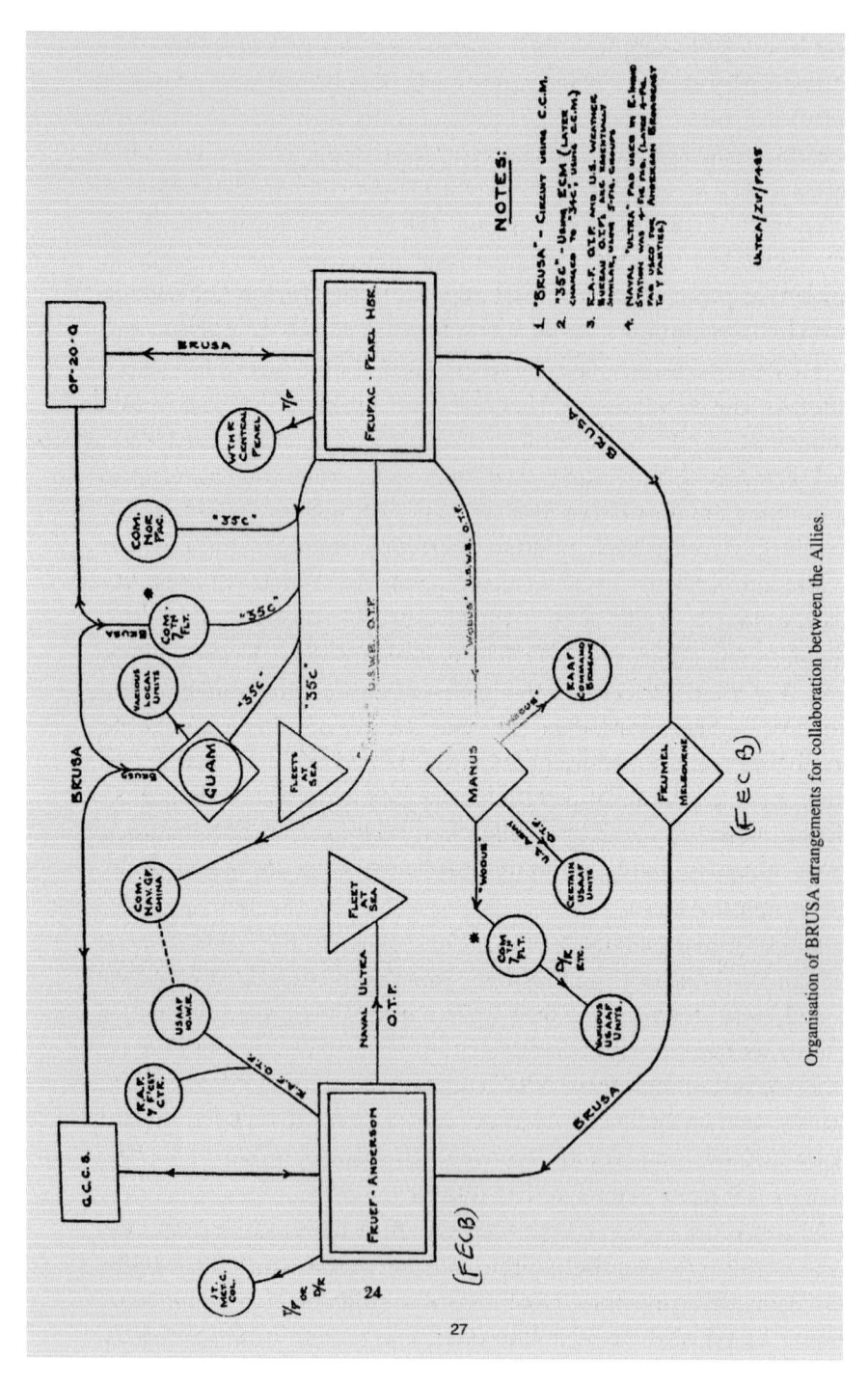

Organization of BRUSA arrangements for collaboration between the Allies. (Bletchley Park Trust - Japanese Codes by Sue Jarvis, by kind permission Director GCHQ)

including to the United States Fleet, but there was a mix of headstrong personalities who often clashed, resulting in a reluctance to share information.

Operators at the overseas outstations transcribed Morse code onto message pads and piled them up for a weekly dispatch to their captains who then passed them securely via passenger ships to the West Coast of America. Pan American Airways with their stronghold boxes ensured the confidential papers reached Washington. Similarly, the Diplomatic Bag from Britain's colonies would securely wing its way to London and Bletchley Park. When the BRUSA agreement was ratified the secure communications systems of ECM and CCM between Washington and Bletchley relayed urgent messages.

Joseph Rochefort often spent days in his Hawaiian bunker without shaving or changing his clothes in order to decode Japanese radio traffic with his staff, all of whom predicted another Japanese attack in the Pacific. The US Navy at OP-20-G agreed this would be early June, but did not know where, except for a clue indicating the objective was 'AF'. Rochefort thought 'AF' meant Midway, an island with an American base in the Pacific defending Hawaii and the west coast. Others thought the Aleutian Islands near Alaska, or Hawaii. The conundrum gripped the team, but before long a cunning plan was hatched. They agreed to ask the signals men on Midway to radio a message in plain text English indicating their water purification plant had broken down and that they were short of water. The team hoped the Japanese would intercept the message and pass it on.

Fortunately, a local Japanese unit performed admirably. It picked up the message and sent its own message saying 'AF' was short of water. Clearly, 'AF' was definitely Midway. The trick also provided access to other intercepts and vital information, including a small decoy fleet being sent to the Aleutians and a huge flotilla assembling of over 200 warships. Admiral Yamamoto believed Admiral Nimitz would respond to the first attack and the way would be clear for Japan to ambush Midway. He would fight Nimitz when his fleet returned.

But Midway was simply reinforced and waited to ambush the Japanese instead. With essential help from codebreakers, Nimitz, knew more about the offensive than most Japanese officers. The attack came on 4 June – an air strike but, unlike Pearl Harbor, their bombers were met by a retaliatory force of heavy ground fire pushing them back, while four squads of US bombers headed toward enemy vessels. Fuel and ammunition crowded the decks which created even larger explosions, destroying four Japanese aircraft carriers. After constant bombardment, the shocked Japanese troops withdrew and abandoned the operation. The US Pacific fleet lost 2 ships, 145 aircraft and 307 men. Japan lost 4 aircraft carriers, nearly 300 aircraft and 2,500 men. The four-day battle was an American victory.[22]

Allied codebreakers were ecstatic with their work. They had recovered the meanings of over 30,000 numbered code groups via overlays of random additives, enabling the intercepted messages of the Japanese Naval Fleet Codes, JN-25 a) and b), to be read and help break other codes. Steeled not to dwell on the carnage, they did their best to limit destruction through deeper examination and reconstruction of codebooks with consistent results. A year later the plane of Admiral Yamamoto, responsible for the attack on Pearl Harbor, was shot down in Operation Vengeance, while other diplomatic message intercepts revealed Japanese 'Orders of Battle' and troop locations. A bounty of information, including valuable 'header' or 'address' codes gave allied military intelligence crucial information to pinpoint and reconstruct the Japanese military set up. This emulated the Western Front Committee at Bletchley Park who, meanwhile, worked on revealing Hitler's strategies.

* * *

After the Allied victory at Midway in June 1942, the volume of messages soared when Japan split their fleet code over five channels, giving certain regions individual codes and additive books. These changeover periods were described as 'when the code went dark', meaning no messages or a brief period when intercepts became unreadable. When naval codebreakers recognised a change, they scurried around on both sides of the Atlantic to build teams, mostly women, to face the new challenges. More than 18,000 intercepts per month were received in the first half of 1942 which doubled to 37,000 by the end of the year.

Recovering additives required endless mental maths every day, week after week. The women worked on large sheets of paper, 3 feet by 2 feet, with rows of five-digit numbers lined up in columns. Each message (lines of five-digit numbers) was aligned over the groups to subtract one from the other, using false maths. The listed groups on the paper rolls already had the additive enciphered and this exercise could then be turned into plain text. Each time a calculation made sense the new code group/word was added to the reconstructed code book by the women. At Bletchley Park they were known as 'Stoppers' for stopping up 'holes' in the code book. In Tiltman's Bookbuilding or emending process, one tries to figure out the number groups; a time-consuming task relying on statistical analyses and groups of numbers to recreate the code book. It was painfully monotonous, the same routine day in, day out. Codebreakers always said they didn't know what happened next. But they knew what they were doing.

* * *

Intelligence experts agree that early JN-25 was only functioning at around 10 per cent and that was predominantly in stripping away the additive of the super-encipherment. At the beginning of 1941 JN-25 was provided with additional resources to collect additional traffic and by April 1942 it was readable at 20 per cent. This meant one in five words had become more useful. Gradually Tiltman's book was being built in Bletchley Park, assisted by America.

Tiltman, builder of relationships and a persistent supporter of cooperation between British and USA cryptanalysts, helped achieve a smooth exchange of information throughout the Second World War. He was promoted to brigadier and became Deputy Director of GC&CS in 1944. After the war he was director of GCHQ, and later held a position in American intelligence at NSA, as part of 'the special relationship'.

Chapter 19

The Workings of Secret Codebreaking
Structure, People, Processes, Machines

In order to attain a crucial degree of secrecy to protect sensitive information of national importance, the government of the United Kingdom had already passed laws, by the royal assent of Queen Victoria, in the Official Secrets Act of 1889, where it became an offence to disclose official information and breach official trust against the interests of the British State. Twenty years later the Official Secrets Act of 1911 was introduced in a response to public alarm – some said hysteria – as widespread espionage fomented, perhaps by popular novels and dramatised threats of spies hailing, supposedly, from Germany as their naval fleet rapidly increased. The added provisions in the United Kingdom were extensive, with heavy penalties for harbouring spies, gathering information, photographing or sketching military installations.

Civil service employees, contractors and military personnel signed a form saying that they abide by the rules of the Crown. The Acts of 1911 and 1920 made it an offence to communicate any military or naval information, documents, models, plans etc., to anyone to whom it would not be in the public interest to make such communication, or to spy in a 'prohibited place', arsenal, dockyard, office etc. belonging to the King.[1] Up to and during the Second World War this included the British Empire, to protect state secrets, overseas crown territories and colonies and applied to all British subjects anywhere in the world. It was no different at MI5 and GC&CS. The structure ensured that all groups worked under strict security. A similar system was introduced in Washington when, two months after entering the First World War, the United States passed into law The Espionage Act of 1917, making it a crime to interfere with or attempt to undermine the efforts of the

THE WORKINGS OF SECRET CODEBREAKING

armed forces during a war, or to, in any way, assist the war efforts of the nation's enemies.

When US Army and Navy were at odds with each other and it was mooted to expand the workforce into their domains by hiring temporary civilians, the Navy objected, saying that the Army would hire reckless and undisciplined rogues who could not keep a secret. But most women came from a loyal generation where they did not expect to receive credit for achievements in public life. They were not combative or competitive and took their Secrecy Oath seriously (under the Espionage Act), swearing that they would never discuss government work or activities with anyone outside their official duties. Never meant forever. To disobey meant prosecution, with a $10,000 fine or ten years in prison, some even felt the penalty might be death.

The process seemed frightening for new recruits, but once their official photograph was taken and fixed to an official badge with their unique ID number, permitting them to certain parts of their work complex, they were part of the 'in crowd' and found they could discuss some work with each other, which helped alleviate any worries they might have had. When asked by outsiders what they did, nonchalant answers were usually given about 'filing' and 'clerical work'.

While it would be difficult to confirm the US Army and US Navy relied on everything from the architects of Bletchley Park to organise their Washington codebreaking operation, certainly British methodical systems were used, some stemming from London's War Office and the First World War. However, parts of British rigor may well have become stuffy and staid, which led new recruits to offer fresh innovative ideas, far more acceptable in the growing American 'can do' society. 'Let's try it and see.' One idea, instead of initially categorising by a reference number, was a simpler system to first categorise messages by date and time. This eliminated duplicate messages from the start and became known as 'de-duping'.

The architect of Bletchley Park was Gordon Welchman. Without his logical mind, vision and attention to detail, War Office mantra, Room 40 pen and paper systems and GC&CS might have just muddled along, and the war might have been lost. The industrial system he devised – which in Britain included the Army, Navy and Air Force in one place, or at least talking to each other under one umbrella – might have seemed at first a confusing mass of different departments, huts and sections, but the developed 'workings' of Bletchley Park were straight forward. After the war his success continued to become Britain's GCHQ (The Government Communications Headquarters).

America, however, had no effective central security agency until 1952. There were some protections put in place during the First and the Second World Wars but sharing analysed information was patchy, especially when the military sections seemed to be at war with each other. The Munitions Building which held the war office and all military units had been inadequate for expansion between the two wars, and though the Pentagon was a great idea, it was not ready until 15 January 1943 (ground was not broken on the Potomac River floodplain in Virginia, south of central Washington, until 11 September 1941). The US Army and US Navy had separate Intelligence facilities – Arlington Hall and the Naval Communications Annex. One could say competition between the two was a good thing, but their duplication of work often reached the same conclusion on the same intercepted messages, when crucial time might have been better spent on a different problem.

Eventually, with Britain smoothing out the ruffles – helped by Denniston, Welchman, Tiltman and Foss to name a few – Washington was able to, at least for the latter part of the Second World War, lose its disparate look. Welchman's spoke and wheel system was applied to all intelligence units for the Army, Navy and Air Force (and to some extent the Coast Guard and OSS), and their listening stations. Around this were new WAVES and WAC recruits, and G-girls – Government employees, also known as Civil Servants. They were smart, trainable, diligent, trustworthy and able to undertake detailed, often boring, work in secrecy.

As the British system had successfully expanded on a grand scale during 1941-1943, the same model was implemented in Washington – unofficially from 1941, then formally during 1942. Britain had the nous while America replenished the might, and between the two it was working. There was a need to share information; the security of British intelligence had to be cloned to a faraway friend, but close enough in spirit should Hitler invade Britain. The invasion of Poland and the codebreakers' ability to pass on machines and secrets (albeit late) had set a precedent.

* * *

THE WORKINGS OF SECRET CODEBREAKING

John Herivel's codebreaking tip also crossed the Atlantic. The Herivel Tip was a 'Let's suppose' theory. An alternative sort of 'lateral thinking'. One evening when sitting by the fire, in England, mulling over a difficult code problem, he surmised that not all operators would follow 'the rules' for enciphering. *What if he was lazy? Would he decide to take short cuts?*

The next day, in the office, codebreakers were advised to ask themselves the same questions and not assume the rules were followed. The tip started to be applied to challenging messages and, sure enough, many codes were broken faster; some German operators had, indeed, become lazy. This method was successfully employed by Hut 6, when the difficult encryption of Code Red, used by German air and land forces, was broken. It was a pivotal moment in the war and Herivel was heartily celebrated for this important tactic for the continuity of code breaking. By 1940 he had gained much experience and admiration. He was young, confident, and still only 21. By 1943 he moved from Enigma to a different department working on new technology and the codes of German and Japanese High Command, in the Newmanry.

Hollerith and IBM

The punch card system used in codebreaking was used to compare the different code groups and speed up the sorting of categorised intercepts: information to co-ordinates, 'cribs' – 'headers' indicating addresses or locations – and salutations at the bottom called 'kisses', which often gave important clues. The machine was invented by American, Herman Hollerith, son of a German immigrant. At 19, he graduated from New York College in 1879, and joined Massachusetts Institute of Technology (MIT) in 1882 to teach mechanical engineering, where he experimented with punch cards. In 1890, he won an important competition to tabulate information for the US Census Bureau, but little did he know his invention would later be used as part of a secret weapon in global conflict.

His invention, which quickly summarises information, is regarded as the start of the semi-automatic information retrieval process. His mechanical system dominated the data scene for nearly a century via

THE SECRET LIFE OF AN AMERICAN CODEBREAKER

The Tabulating Machine Company which, in 1924, became International Business Machines (IBM). The machines were successfully marketed throughout Europe by the British Tabulating Machine Company (BTM) and well established by 1940, with royalties paid to IBM in America.

The invention was based on the binary method of collecting information and was introduced to Bletchley Park in 1940 around the same time William Friedman endured the machines' incessant clanking as his team searched for clues to break PURPLE. Certain values were input to the electro-mechanical system which cranked through many punch cards to find the information that fitted the requested values.

At Bletchley, two brothers from British Tabulating Machines (BTM), Ronald and Norman Whelan, were recruited to Bletchley's 'Freebornery' by Freddy Freeborn. Their task was to elevate information sorting to an industrial scale, the much needed 'depth' to attack many ciphers. By 1943

Hollerith punch card sorting machines at Bletchley Park. American businessman Herman Hollerith led the way in punch card machines using electricity. His concept utilized earlier mechanical 'hole and hook' punch card technology from eighteenth-century French textile designer Joseph Marie Jacquard and the later counting machines of English mathematician Charles Babbage. These early data processing technologies were later enhanced by IBM during the twentieth century. (By kind permission Director GCHQ)

the vast collection of manually classified and filed cards was mechanised, sorting different categories of different ciphers, combining and tracking information, including intercepts which at first might have seemed irrelevant. A slight change in a regular message could mean a change in military operations, something Army, Navy and Air Force commanders needed to know. The database was invaluable in gauging enemy strategy. Manual and Hollerith data was used by all codebreaking sections of the armed forces throughout the war, and though humans could also search through the manual system, Hollerith accelerated the task.

* * *

Before the war, while the US government used Hollerith/IBM machines to capture information about race, the German government used the same technology to record locations and status of Jewish populations.

When the Second World War started, Nigel de Grey was re-assigned to Intelligence at Bletchley. As a Foreign Office civilian, he concentrated on German Enigma traffic. In September 1941, he provided a report to Winston Churchill with the first references of mass destruction by German police battalions, where villages were being systematically levelled and populations 'removed'. Most consisted of Jewish families and their sympathisers. One signalled message boasted over 30,000 executions 'in the central area'. Following a veiled warning from Churchill to Germany in a speech to the British Parliament 'to end such atrocities', a German circular cautioned that no further references to 'sensitive operations' should be made on German wireless channels. It was difficult for Churchill to be candid without revealing his intelligence source – that Britain was listening to the enemy's wireless channels and that Bletchley Park could read all the German messages – but the Allies did little to save the Jewish people in 1941. Not until 1945 were the full horrors of the Holocaust known. Did the codebreakers at Bletchley know more? Could they have done anything?

Typex and Sigaba

Typex and Sigaba are electromechanical clones of Enigma, that incorporate additional security elements eliminating weaknesses in the

Scherbius machine. Neither have been successfully attacked in terms of being broken by an enemy. Both were used after the war, and into the 1960s, until other technologies took over.[2]

The idea of producing a replica of Enigma germinated in the early 1920s, when the British government created an inter-departmental Cipher Committee to investigate replacing message book systems – used by the armed forces, Foreign Office, India and Colonial Offices – with cipher machines. Hugh Foss (Navy) in Room 40 studied the German Enigma's small model C and, recognising its flaws, designed a more secure machine. This was the first standard Typex machine, a later version of which was used at Bletchley Park.

Because Enigma was on the commercial market as a businessman's 'secrets writer' – many had access to the base machine and looked for ways to improve its security, especially for military use. It was not easy. Foss's Typex Navy version had existed before 1937, then Eric Earnshaw-Smith, a First World War veteran of the WTID and War Office's MI1b signals intelligence operation, assisted RAF signals officer O.G.W. Lywood in developing another version for the standard British Typex machine. This incorporated parts from Creed teleprinters to produce text.

Throughout 1941 Signals had struggled to keep up with transmission of intercepts to and from Britain, until Typex adaptions helped bolster security for the Special Liaison and Special Communications units of military personnel. These operators carried ULTRA messages to consumers including commanders in the field who knew the source, could read the message, but could not keep the printed text. Typex could defend Britain's central communications most of the time, but not all; instead, a one-time pad[3] system (which the enemy never penetrated) provided absolute security for the most important messages.

Unlike the German military Enigma machine, Typex had a *minimum* of 120 different wheels or inserts from which to choose. Five-rotor inserts could be selected from a set of twenty-eight. Operators could arrange the wheels inside their machines 7,687,680 different ways compared to Enigma's 60 or 336. German military counter-intelligence would have needed to find electrical wire pairings for 120-150 wheels, an insurmountable task at the time. Typex model II, version 3 – known as Typex 23 – eventually became the main decoding and encoding

THE WORKINGS OF SECRET CODEBREAKING

'imitation' apparatus of many young women in communications intelligence on both sides of the Atlantic.

From 1939-1941, analysis of intelligence for the Axis powers was low on their agenda, but it was high on the Allies' list. By 1942 the USA and Britain had rallied with unmatched power in collecting signals and arial photographs as evidence of enemy movement and matériel, all of which was securely and rapidly distributed via the SLU and SCU. The Typex cipher and its American counterpart Sigaba remain unbroken.[4] The British Commonwealth and the United States had more knowledge and respect for the significance of intelligence data and therefore applied more resources and brains to intelligence mining than the enemy. Even when they did catch on and employed machines such as Hollerith, they were used only to attack low-grade Western codes. Ultra cracked the hardest problems for the richest results.

But the Allies' transatlantic relationship was not without angst, affecting development of US Sigaba which did not become fully effective until mid-1943. Until then Typex was the only high-grade cipher system available for combined operations.

Eventually the BRUSA agreement standardised unofficial procedures, and American Special Support Activity and Op-20-G liaison officers were assigned to GC&CS. Straight off the US nominees understood how much was to be learned from this powerful and innovative organisation, and that they needed to catch up. They were 'absolutely amazed' by what the British had built 'beyond all imaginings'. Friedman credited the success of Bletchley Park to its intellectual staff of dons and professors, and the highest business directors who 'are accustomed to getting much done in a very quiet way without fuss and feathers'. Telford Taylor, US Army and civilian lawyer noted that 'two elderly and practically palsied British ex-civil servants, produced as much from one secondary Japanese system (JN-20), as twenty young men doing it at Arlington'.

Increasingly both sides communicated developments freely, though some technical advances were not obligatory for sharing. In this way America gained more from GC&CS, who also had more to offer than they could gain from the USA, but this helped remove American suspicions of Britain. Gradually, the exchange grew into respect, at least for the task in hand, though both sides managed risk solutions should the alliance change. American chiefs thought a complete breach of relations was possible, but GC&CS had a better line to Churchill who cared far more about intelligence than Roosevelt. This was an issue for US Military Intelligence, who instead could only station its representatives at Bletchley Park to get a 'foothold' in all cipher attacking techniques and acquire every diplomatic system GC&CS had ever mastered. As the MID looked forward their plan was aimed at *'securing the most advantageous (from our standpoint) basis for British-American collaboration.... The long-term interest of the United States requires the greatest possible self-sufficiency in the field of signals intelligence.'*

Taylor further said toward the end of the war: *'diplomatic signal intelligence will be a premium. And the closer the end of the war appears to be, the less eager the British will be to share their diplomatic secrets with us. When the parting of the ways comes...the United States must be in full command of the art as it then stands.'* US Army Signals Intelligence (SIS) would acquire cryptanalytic skills equalling Britain's, but also outweigh OP-20-G.[5]

With this acquired information William Friedman was able to expand the Typex system which randomised rotor movements and included a punched paper tape reader from a teleprinter, a small device with metal 'feelers' so that electricity would pass through the holes. When a keyboard letter was pressed, an electric signal would be sent through the rotors to encrypt the letters (as with Enigma), but the paper tape would then add one more rotor turn, twisting the cipher through one more barrier to decryption. Rowlett then came up with another way to advance the machine using another set of rotors.

Prior to 1942 there was little money or official capacity to expand the British idea, but Friedman and Rowlett built several 'add-on' devices instead of a paper tape reader. The external combination add-ons contained a three-rotor set up in which five of the inputs (rotors normally have one output for every input) were live. It simulated five keys being pressed together – say A-E – and the five signals on the input side would be randomised through the rotors and come out in one of five lines. Now the movement of rotors could be controlled with a daily code, and the paper tape was eliminated. They called the M-134-C combination machine Sigaba. It was larger and less portable than Enigma, perhaps adding to its mystery, instead America kept this under strict lock and key with only trusted American operators. Despite sharing their secrets on the development of Typex, Britain was not party to the mechanics of the new design, at least not wholly.

THE WORKINGS OF SECRET CODEBREAKING

During 1943 pockets of distrust came from officials at the War Office in Whitehall, who did not believe America would refrain from attacking and breaking Typex.

> 'The greatly increased efficiency,' Cabinet Minister Edward Bridges warned Churchill, 'which has been built up with the help of our own cryptographers, who have passed on all our methods and skill, combined with the passing of unparaphrased traffic and "numberless" Plain Language "cribs' to our cypher traffic,' in his and his committee's view, compromised Typex.

This resulted in a British system of absolutely protected messages for rare communications where America was 'never to know'. It was called 'Guard'. Typex covered most traffic against enemy attack but where Britain and America did not see eye to eye certain signals were given absolute security. Protection from enemies was one problem, but certain protections against friends, and for friends, required an additional shield. Churchill accepted the report, with reservations:

> 'I wonder, however, whether it would not be as well for me to suggest to the President a self-denying ordinance by which on a gentlcman's agreement both the British and American Governments would refrain from trying to penetrate each other's cyphers. This would enable the existing easy circulation of messages to proceed without prejudice to the "GUARD" arrangements. I have not authorised the decoding of an American message since they came into the war with us, and I told the President so. I have little doubt that they would say the same.'[6]

In the friend relationship, Typex and Sigaba machines, used the ECM and CCM attachments to communicate across the Atlantic. Both decoded to plain text but had an additional reversing feature to produce encoded messages. Both types of machine were the last element in the code-breaking process, before crucial information was passed to military chiefs at the Admiralty in London and Chiefs of Staff in Washington. The black machines were unusual, but looked similar to typewriters, with additional wires and keys. Once a code solution had been revealed by a Bombe machine, Typex operators in Block E Communications at Bletchley Park typed thousands of 250-character messages into the machines. The clattering devices were under high security in vast and noisy cigarette smoke-filled rooms, resembling a typing pool with 10-15 women per shift. A similar scene could be observed in Washington.

The machines were stiff to use and the elevated touch-typing speeds of the specialist typists were never reached. On some Typex versions an operator only reached 60 characters (20 words) per minute. It was slow work – like typing with a heavy weight on each key – but the message printing out in plain text had to be accurate. Advantages of Typex were that only one operator was needed versus two for Enigma; Enigma messages had to be written, enciphered, transmitted (in Morse), received, deciphered and written again, while a coded message on Typex was automatically enciphered and transmitted when typed in; Typex was linked to a teleprinter on Typex I and Typex II and could print text automatically, if required.[7]

Typex operators generally, were not trained linguists. They were decoding but didn't necessarily understand German or other languages. However, when workloads increased substantially, they always knew an event of major strategic importance was taking place. Typex operators often toiled late into the night to complete their work.

Once translated, high-level and strategic messages to Allied military chiefs, were re-written and re-enciphered by paraphrasing. People who paraphrased outgoing messages were skilled at pulling the wool over the enemy's eyes, but the recipient also had to be skilled at reading between the lines. The messages were rewritten in such a way that the original message was conveyed without the enemy (if he intercepted) suspecting their messages had been read. It was an incredible skill.

One British ATS officer who paraphrased outgoing messages was Charlotte Vine-Stevens. 'Betty', as she prefers to be called, left college in September 1941 during her Home Economics course, and after an interview at Devonshire House, London, found she was on her way to Bletchley Park. She had learned German reasonably well in 1938 at the age of 15, after an exchange trip with a German family organised by her mother. This experience led her to Major Tester's department at Bletchley where she registered Morse code messages, but by 1943 she was transferred to more challenging work in the Japanese Section paraphrasing messages in English.

An intercepted original text example might have been: 'The road between Meiktila and Kohima will be blocked on Monday to Thursday by tanks.'

Which Betty paraphrased to read, 'Road from Meiktila to Kohima to be out of use for 4 days due to tanks assembling.'

The subtle change deflected the enemy should they re-intercept (or not, if the message was meant to be fake). Since it was not an exact copy the enemy could not detect the Allies had read their original message.

Paraphrased texts in Bletchley and Arlington, were produced regularly. There was always another way to say it; re-sending parallel texts were to be avoided at all costs. With paraphrasing, the cipher order was also distorted and bore no resemblance to the enemy's original message. The added security of Typex and the ECM and CCM adapters between Bletchley Park and Washington also helped.

PURPLE

Foss and Oliver Strachey had successfully broken the Japanese Type A Cipher machine in 1934, which they referred to as Red. Frank Rowlett and Solomon Kullback for the US Army achieved this in 1935, and Agnes Driscoll for the US Navy, was credited with breaking the M-1 or Orange cipher. In the end Rowlett's Red and Agnes' Orange machine ciphers were almost the same and broken simultaneously. OP-20-G claimed the army (SIS) benefitted from technical information they provided but the army said they received no naval help. The dispute ran on, almost impossible to settle, and both cryptologic units became reluctant to share any information with each other. Safford propagated the divide with SIS but when he was moved again, OP-20-G was far more accommodating under the leadership of Joseph Wenger. These were precursors to the cipher America called PURPLE.

The Japanese encryption machine was based on a reverse-engineered version by the Swedish inventor Boris Hagelin, where the internal wires were scrambled in a 5 x 5 matrix controlled by 4 pinwheels. It was thought to be more secure than Enigma, but this was not the case.[8]

Japan continued to send diplomats' reports and chatter from Japanese agencies using PURPLE and, before long, Allied interceptors noticed references to an invasion in northwestern France. Hitler needed to defend his gains and worried about a certain counter-invasion. He just didn't know when or where this would happen. Then in November 1943, PURPLE broke through with a valuable contribution to the Allied attack on Diplomatic Codes through Colonel Hiroshi Oshima.

Oshima had been the Japanese military attaché in Berlin since 1934 and spoke perfect German. He was a trusted friend of Joachim von Ribbentrop, a former champagne salesman, who became Hitler's favourite foreign policy advisor. Oshima was thought to be instrumental in constructing the Anti-Comintern Pact of 1936, before the Japanese Ministry of Foreign Affairs became involved, and in September 1940 for the Tripartite Pact. His rapid progression led to the IJA rank of lieutenant general and appointment to Berlin's Japanese ambassador, twice. His fascination and support for Nazi ideology gave the impression he was 'more Nazi than the Nazis'.[9] Hitler held Oshima in such high esteem he was one of few recipients to receive a gold version of the Grand Cross of the Order of the German Eagle, after Japan's attack on Pearl Harbor.

The problem for him and the Axis powers, was that most of his dispatches from Berlin were intercepted by the Allies. One, in January 1942, revealed Ribbentrop's concerns regarding Japanese diplomatic cipher security after it was agreed by Oshima that intelligence reports would be sent to Tokyo daily: 'Any leakage of these reports due to our fault would be of grave consequence, so all handling of these should be strictly secret.'

Despite concerns, Oshima assured the Nazis that the Japanese system was safe – a serious error on their part. In November 1943, he was invited on a four-day trip to inspect German fortifications around the coasts of western and northern France. On return to Berlin his detailed report was radioed to Tokyo using their diplomatic cipher. The Japanese ambassador's numerous missives, about twenty pages, rattled through several Allied interceptors' teleprinter machines, including Arlington via Vint Hill Farms,[10] giving the Allies much to analyse, including German defences, the 'Atlantic Wall', locations of German divisions, manpower and weaponry.[11]

Places where there really was a wall, saw prisoners and forced labour build port and quay barriers constructed of grey reinforced

THE WORKINGS OF SECRET CODEBREAKING

cement, poured into moulds of metal meshes and shuttered wood. Most structures were 4-5 feet thick and 12-15 feet high ascending from the water and sandy beaches below. They were strong and slick, compared to walls of brick or rock, and difficult to climb, providing strong coastline fortification ledges and bunkers from which to repel attackers. Germany knew America would attack and had employed the autobahn engineer Fritz Todt to oversee the building of fortifications.

This information and meticulous detail of tank ditches, shore-line turret armaments and mobile forces were virtually handed to the Allies on a plate, including astounding and valuable intelligence for D-Day. Air Force photographic reconnaissance also provided vital proof and contributed coordinates for Allied plans. From Belgium to Bordeaux, including the Channel Islands, the German wall of defence was a reality, however, the Allies now also knew the weaknesses of their wall.

Tunny Fish and Colossus

Janice was not directly involved in reading Hitler's messages via the diplomatic cipher but she had a good grasp of what was going on. It was almost as if some codebreakers were on the front line, especially when cryptanalysts at Bletchley Park were tasked to tackle another cipher.

Hitler personally commissioned the new Lorenz SZ-40, an electro-mechanical wheel-based cipher machine for teleprinter signals. The machine was also called his 'secrets writer', considered unbreakable by Hitler and his high command. Among other things Hitler had established good relations with the Berlin-based Lorenz family's independent-run Standard Elektrizitatsgesellschaft, a subsidiary of the American ITT corporation, who supplied military materiel including airborne radar beams, radio sets and secure communications equipment. The system was far more complex than Enigma, with twelve rotor wheels instead of four or five in Enigma, and its plugboard. The new encryption system was one of the most advanced. Improved with SZ-42a and SZ-42b, around twenty German stations communicated across occupied territories in Europe and every morning a different key was used, to hinder codebreakers. However, in an off-guard moment, a German operator referred to the codename, *sägefisch* (sawfish), which gave British codebreakers an advantage. From then on codebreakers in Bletchley's Testery department named the codes Tunny – as in tuna fish – and slowly a few messages were read.

They had success after the Battle of Stalingrad, during the frigid winter of 1942/1943. The period was known as the 'turning of the tides', and four months later the Testery team deciphered a stream of messages about another German attack, involving vast numbers of men and weapons approaching the city of Kursk. Russians were warned – through 'a reliable source' – of the exact details of the enemy's fighting power and planned pincer movement. The massive attack in the flat cornfields of Kursk, was one of the largest tank battles of the war, when Russia defeated Germany.

Ralph Tester's domain, the 'Testery', had joined the new initiative of Gordon Welchman and Max Newman to mechanise codebreaking efforts on the Lorenz teleprinter cipher. The department became known as the 'Newmanry', which also incorporated a direct link to Tiltman's team. Under this new arrangement construction of a faster codebreaking apparatus commenced, leading to the Heath Robinson machines and Colossus.

Max Newman was a Cambridge graduate whose dissertation considered the use of 'symbolic machines' in physics, which later became a precursor to his thoughts on computerised machines. His studies and publications built a reputation in modern topology and mathematical logic. He achieved distinctions in Maths Tripos and as a lecturer in 1935, inspired Alan Turing to pioneer his *Entscheidungsproblem* – Decision Problem – using a hypothetical computing machine.

In 1937 Newman accepted an invitation to Princeton University for six months. After the lecturing assignment he returned to Cambridge, but when war was declared and Nazi-ism against Jewish people was on the rise, his young wife and children evacuated to America in 1940. Newman remained at Cambridge. In 1942 he began to assess his involvement in war work and after several discussions agreed to joined Bletchley's research section. At first, he was concerned the work would not be sufficiently interesting or useful, but his worries were dispelled, and he was invited to work on Enigma; however, he chose instead to join the Testery to work on Tunny.

He worked with Bill Tutte, another 'brilliant mathematician', who graduated from Cambridge, who in 1941, was able to comprehend and appreciate the whole structure of the complex twelve-wheel Lorenz cipher without seeing a machine. With his genius and the combined talents of Tiltman, Newman and the Testery team of linguists, Tutte went on to read a 4,000-letter intercept. This was a massive breakthrough and

THE WORKINGS OF SECRET CODEBREAKING

the beginning of deciphering top-level and highly secret 'Fish Code' messages. From this experience Newman convinced his directors that Tutte's manual method could be mechanised and soon after December 1942, was asked by Commander Travis to lead additional research into mechanising the manipulation of the Lorenz cipher.

At that time, America knew little of the success on breaking Hitler's 'Secrets Writer'. The Newmanry's initial staff consisted of Donald Michie, two engineers and sixteen Wrens who developed a machine for faster code breaking. It was known as Tunny (the British Tunny). After a couple of versions, with some success, improvements were still needed and another prototype, was ready by June 1943. Wrens applied the nickname 'Heath Robinson' to this after cartoonist William Heath Robinson, whose amusing drawings of maze-like machines and inventions were popular at the time. With its twists and turns the machine filled a room. There was a thin paper tape that wove through at high speed and the Wrens had to make sure it ran smoothly over every cog and wheel. If it broke, they had to stick it back together. If the code wasn't revealed with the first reel of tape, another spool was chosen until eventually, a result was found.

The Newmanry in Bletchley's Hut 11, increased to more than 100 people, supplying menus and operating the machine in shifts. But another version of the German Lorenz machine delayed their work, when it added a random stream of codes using six wheels, instead of five, making intercepts more difficult to decipher. Now Heath Robinson was too slow and unreliable; a different machine was needed and alongside Newman, Tiltman and Michie, came Tommy Flowers, an engineer with new ideas.

The son of a bricklayer from East London, Flowers, took a mechanical engineering apprenticeship, which led him to evening classes at the University of London. There he earned an electrical engineering degree, and in 1926 at the age of 21, he joined the General Post Office (GPO). The GPO controlled all communications and wireless outstations in Britain and, with their engineers, were able to intercept and listen to German messages.

From 1935 Flowers explored electronics for telephone exchanges at the GPO Research station in Dollis Hill, north London and by 1939, he was convinced an all-electronic system was possible. Recognising his talents and enthusiasm, GPO director, W. Gordon Radley, asked Flowers to join the secret government establishment at Bletchley Park and by February 1941, with his GPO security clearance, he was tasked to help Alan Turing design and build a decoder for the Bombe machine.

THE SECRET LIFE OF AN AMERICAN CODEBREAKER

That project, however, moved to America, but Turing, impressed by Flowers' work, introduced him to other key cryptanalysts working on the German Lorenz cipher. It was obvious to Flowers, in 1942, that electric motor synchronisation of the German machine which produced the Tunny Fish code teleprinter tapes, was, 'very slow and could be many times faster by using electronic radio valves'.

When the first functional replicas of the Lorenz machine (British Tunny, and Heath Robinson machines) appeared to be redundant, Flowers expanded his electronic plug board expertise and designed a better and faster code breaking machine. By February 1943 he was experimenting with his deep knowledge of thermionic valves to build the first electronic version replicating the high-level German Lorenz cipher. There were some near and complete disasters, but valve failures were not as common as one might imagine since they had performed well through 1943. Eventually, Flowers and the Newmanry team successfully produced a digital electronic computer. It was an astonishing achievement and the world's first. Flowers and his team named their invention 'Colossus', a large sounding name, for a large invention, which filled a huge room. The machine accelerated the deciphering methods for numerous daily codes, and output of Tunny Fish Code decrypts increased twenty to thirty times. Its success is even more amazing when you remember that Tutte, Newman, Flowers and their team never saw a real Lorenz SZ-40 or SZ-42.

A further ten of the new computer processors were built, all slightly different, depending on the usage requirements of codebreaking teams. Colossus would play an important part in helping to bring the Second World War to a close. Decrypting a vital D-Day message was its most successful achievement.

Few knew of the German Lorenz cipher machine and its British mirror invention. Colossus was the only electronic computer in existence during the war, but due to Bletchley's high level of secrecy and Top Secret classification, its purpose or presence could never be disclosed, and those involved with this incredible achievement complied with British law. The invention of Colossus as the world's first programmable electronic computer with automated processing, remained secret for more than thirty years under the British Official Secrets Act. After the war Churchill ordered all machines to be dismantled; he was afraid this useful tool would fall easily into Russian hands and be used against Britain and her Allies. However, plans and bits of the machine survived.[12]

THE WORKINGS OF SECRET CODEBREAKING

Colossus at Bletchley Park. The world's first programmable electronic valve computer with automated processing – fully operational and crucial to breaking enemy ciphers and message reading during the D-Day landings in June 1944. (By kind permission Director GCHQ)

Colossus was decommissioned in 1959 and 1960. Gordon Welchman, whose strong personality clashed with Flowers, advanced the science in America under high security at MIT, with permission from the British government. This led to the computer systems we know today including data storage, word processing, search engines and Google, but the first working electronic computer in the world was Colossus: a British invention, designed and built during the Second World War by scientists, GPO engineers and Tommy Flowers, the general post office engineer, who defied opposition.[13]

The machines developed in the 'wartime factory of intelligence' re-opened the door for people such as Grace Hopper, after it was slammed in her face when she was a professor at Vasser College. She was too old to be a WAVE or WAC at the age of 34, despite her PhD in mathematics from Yale University. Discrimination prevailed. Instead, she joined the Navy Reserves and created a 'linker' system to convert English terms to machine code, leading to the FLOW-MATIC and COBAL computer languages.[14]

Chapter 20

Alien Codes?

A Newmanry Wren kept a forbidden address list for her department on which is one intriguing, almost anonymous, American from Minnesota, Lieutenant Commander Howard H. Campaigne from the University of Minneapolis.

In a 1983 oral history interview with Bob Farley of the NSA, Campaigne, a maths professor for the university, recalled how, before the war, he wanted to invent an enciphering and deciphering machine and had submitted his thoughts to the US Army. The Army said they

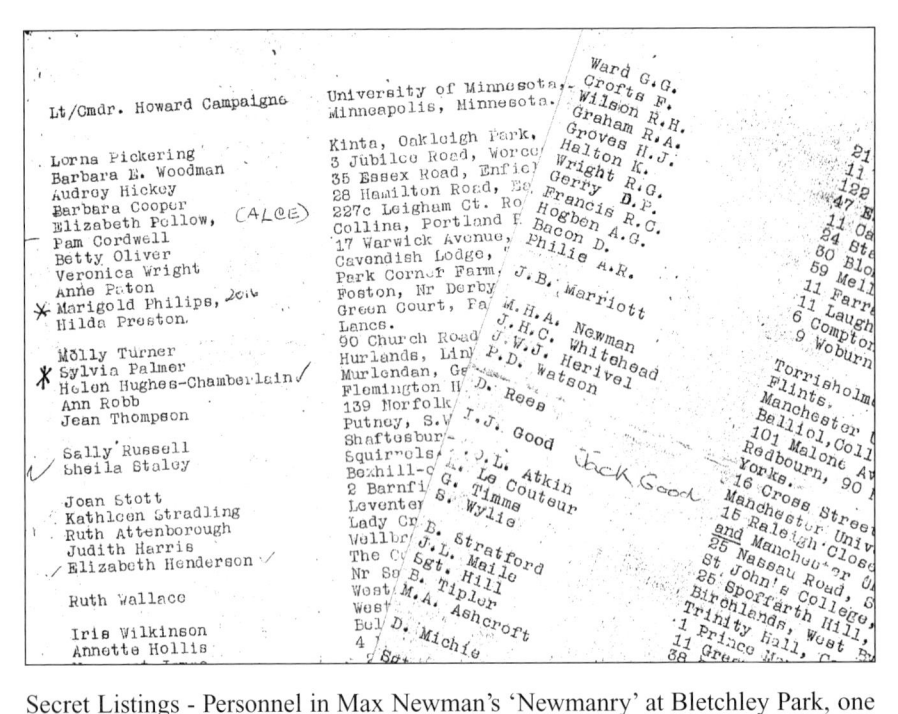

Secret Listings - Personnel in Max Newman's 'Newmanry' at Bletchley Park, one of whom was Lt. Commander, Howard Campaigne. (Author's private source)

worked with the Navy on this subject and that he should contact them. At the time Commander Laurance Safford was leading OP-20-G, who said they didn't need any more crypt systems but needed analysts instead and, 'Would I be interested in taking a cryptography correspondence course?'

Campaigne said yes and took the course but, 'things were heating up and it looked like we'd get into the war,' he remembered. The Navy wrote to him to see if he would be interested in a Reserve commission to which he consented, completed the application and eventually received his commission on 5 December 1941. 'Two days later the balloon went up,' and America was at war. He reported for duty at Main Navy, Washington, on Monday morning 5 January 1942. They said, 'come back at midnight'; he was on the mid watch shift from the off. They did that to everyone. People from all sorts of backgrounds and places, reported in hourly but 'that mid watch shift was quite a time as nobody could keep their eyes open, since they'd travelled so far and were not accustomed to night work'.

Campaigne was assigned to Commander Ford, who worked on JN-20. 'A good bit of the (code) book was known and some additives were known,' and 'some people were very skilful and could recover twenty or thirty groups a day,' where as he, as a beginner who new little, could only recover three. 'Some people could just run rings around me.' His training was on the job and no attention was given to the fact that he'd earned a PhD in 1938; his ranking was based on age. He admitted his work on code recovery was not that effective in recovering additives; he only had hours of experience whereas others had months, but his PhD led him to a research reassignment under Howard Engstrom and Commander Wenger.

After an OP-20 rearrangement, where Safford and his department became OP-20-S preparing complete cryptography, the cryptology work of OP-20-G was then under John Redman. As the research group readjusted, Campaigne found himself on communications delivering messages between Redman and Wenger for release approval. 'Friedman had been in touch with the British and we began to cooperate with them.' They worked on Enigma and after a while began to work on other codes. There was a group that went to England and a British group that went to America, 'and they were able to tell us a great deal about the Naval Enigma and we began to exchange keys so that we were able to read some of the traffic and thereby learn a great deal about it'.

Campaigne knew of the Sinkov quad trip to Britain which relayed feedback to Engstrom. They provided information on the Bombes and how they worked. 'There was a critical fact which we didn't appreciate for a long time, which had to do with the diagonal board…, worth a factor of 26 in the effectiveness of the Bombe.'

But they couldn't see that because they had overlooked something, and Prescott Currier, for some reason, was unable to tell them, which meant they were in the dark for a long time. The solution depended on the reciprocal plugging the Germans used. 'That is, if A went to Z, then Z went to A,' which made the diagonal board feasible, but they hadn't understood that, 'or at least hadn't understood how important it was'. Secrecy was cautioned and re-cautioned, so it's possible this was lost in the coyness of spreading secret information, 'but we eventually had a deep understanding…, and deep respect for the British for perceiving how useful that was'. They just hadn't begun that way.

Campaigne confirmed that Leon Rosen bought back useful information too, though he didn't know much of it since he was in the 'other building, or in Arlington Hall, when they moved…' Cryptanalytic problems that were not broken were called 'research' on either side – army and navy – and resulted in both sides visiting each other to make an attempt at breaking stubborn keys. 'Solomon Kullback was in charge of that.' But each service still employed the sensible system of odd and even days so as not to duplicate work.

In 1944 America considered 'the *Geheimschreiber* to be the future', a different German crypt system, which the British, since 1942, had some success in attacking and had been working with William Friedman since at least May of that year. Friedman wrote to Tiltman:

> 'Among the books I have sent, you will find three orange-colored pamphlets on the Hittite hieroglyphics …, provided me by…the Oriental Institute at a 15% discount…totals $4.04…if you can reimburse me by way of sending me some items that you may find over there, I shall be most appreciative and in this way the exchange can be made without any red tape.'

He was referring to ancient Anatolian scripts (from Syria). Friedman's assistant, Miss Chaplin, continued typing: 'By the time this letter reaches you … Capt. Kullback will be with you and he can bring you up to date as to the status of our work on *Geheimschreiber*. This looks like a most interesting problem and has us quite stymied at the moment.'[1]

Friedman indicated he had ideas, 'suspicions', and would appreciate an exchange with Tiltman on his ideas to reach a valid conclusion. Kullback was at Bletchley Park from May to August that year.

> May 13, 1942
>
> Dear Col. Tiltman
>
> I got together some material for you as per our conversations and it is being shipped together with a good deal of other material from other sources. Among the books I have sent, you will find three orange colored pamphlets on the Hittite hieroglyphics. These were provided me by one of the members of the staff of the Oriental Institute at a 15% discount, which brings the total for the three to $4.04, which same I have already transmitted. At any time that it is convenient, if you can reimburse me by way of sending me some items that you may find over there, I shall be most appreciative and in this way the exchange can be made without any red tape.
>
> I have another book by Gelb which contains photographic plates of the Hittite material. The cost of this book is $8.50 and I have not undertaken to purchase a copy for you unless you really wish to have it. I have a copy of it and while I think it is a worthwhile publication, it is a bit expensive.
>
> By the time this letter reaches you, I suppose that Capt. Kullback will be with you and he can bring you up to date as to the status of our work on the Geheimschreiber. This looks like a most interesting problem and has us quite stymied at the moment. I am beginning to suspect certain things and will communicate with you as soon as we reach what appear to be valid conclusions. We will be most appreciative if you will similarly keep us informed.
>
> I was very glad to learn of your safe arrival, notice of which was communicated to me by Miss Chaplin. I cannot begin to tell you how much I enjoyed your visit and how beneficial it was. Please give my very best regards to Comdr. Denniston and tell him that I still have some letters of his crying for answers.
>
> With very best regards, I am,
>
> Sincerely yours,
>
> William F. Friedman
> Head Cryptanalyst
>
> Approved for Release by NSA on 07-15-2014 pursuant to E.O. 13526

'I cannot begin to tell you how much I enjoyed your visit and how beneficial it was….' William Friedman's letter to Col. John Tiltman, May 1942. 'By the time this letter reaches you, I supposed Capt. Kullback will be with you….'. (Courtesy of the NSA/National Cryptologic Museum)

THE SECRET LIFE OF AN AMERICAN CODEBREAKER

Campaigne and four or five others from the US Army and Navy went there, arriving on 1 August 1944. Al Small (BP listed), Arthur Levinson (not listed in BP records) and George Vergine (Newmanry) were part of the group of army cryptanalysts. They all lived in Little Brickhill, an idyllic English village close to Bletchley Park. A liaison officer, Al Clifford (who superseded Joseph Eachus when he returned to Washington), meshed the sections together.

'I was there, not as a liaison officer but as a working member on this *Geheimschreiber* thing, which we called "Fish" or "Tunny". Colossus was built for that.' (Farley – his interviewer – had said Colossus was for something else and did not know about its success re D-Day then.)[2]

The T-52 *Geheimschreiber* (secrets writer) was developed around 1930 by Siemens & Halske. An electro-mechanical cipher machine for a teleprinter (telex), alongside Enigma and Lorenz S-Z40/42, it was one of the main cipher systems used by the German Army. Its official name was *Schlüsselfernschreibmaschine* (cipher teleprinter) and known as SFM. But its traffic was called *Sägefisch* by Germany, and Sturgeon by British codebreakers. Like the Lorenz machine it was used over landlines as well as over radio. It was a cipher that was occasionally broken.[3]

Campaigne continued with his day-to-day description of the workings of Colossus which was 'built for the Tunny system'. The Colossus he worked on was designed for the key to change every month, but then the Germans changed the key every day. The British first thought it would be impossible, but they discovered by redoubling their efforts they could read everything every day. 'In fact, they got to where they were reading more than ever. They became very effective.' Because of the change to 'daily' keys it was decided to build more Colossi. Campaigne learned how to use the second machine which appeared shortly after and was assigned to Colossus for a while. 'We could only set messages…, we had to make a run for every message to find the key settings…. It wasn't really a message. It was a transmission.' He explained that the German cryptographer 'would get on the circuit and they (BP) would synchronise the two ends of the circuits. And once they got in synchrony they'd keep running and then put message after message after message.'

This sounds remarkably like synchronised mechanical 'depth'.

'So, you just got a basket full of stuff out all at once.' But if they couldn't break the key, they didn't get anything. At times they had to run Colossus for thirty-six hours on one day's traffic to recover something.

ALIEN CODES?

But it wasn't unusual not to succeed and rather than waste time on two-day old traffic they would abandon that and turn to attacking fresh transmissions.

Was this correct and did Campaigne carry his knowledge of Colossus back to America? He was at Bletchley Park for a year but is not mentioned in David Kahn's book.[4] Neither was he listed on Bletchley's Roll of Honour for a while, but since the BP Trust had access to the list in 2016, he is included. Additional research reveals that his crypto career for the US government indeed started in the Second World War, and that he was an integral part of American security and intelligence services, eventually joining a small select group calling themselves the 'cream of the crop in Cryptology'.[5]

Campaigne trained in codes and ciphers under Agnes Driscoll who he recalled, 'after her automobile accident in October 1937, never seemed to get over the traumatic experience.' She had seriously broken her leg and jaw and took a while to recuperate. People who knew her well said her personality changed and her excessive pride only provoked rebuff

Howard H. Campaigne's Draft registration card preparing to aid the Allies in 1941 and after VE Day as part of the British and American intelligence TICOM group in Europe after VE Day, May 1945. (Courtesy of the NSA/National Cryptologic Museum)

THE SECRET LIFE OF AN AMERICAN CODEBREAKER

Howard Campaigne with the postwar Target Intelligence Committee (TICOM). All are American unless otherwise indicated. Bletchley Park personnel (as so far known) are underlined. This photograph was taken by Lt. Paul Knowlton Whitaker during a rest stop. Radio communicators are Signals Intelligence: (L to R) PFC Willliam E. Hoin, driver; LAC L. H. Howells, British radio communicator; F/Lt. George H. Sayers, (British); Lt. Cdr. Howard H. Campaigne; Sgt. H. G. Anderson (British radio communicator); Capt. Louis T. Stone; First Lt. Selmer S. Norland; Major Angus McIntosh (British); Major Ralph P. Tester (British); Capt. Edward Rushworth (British); W/Cdr. Oscar A. Oeser (British); Sgt. Clarence L. Ray, driver.

from most of her colleagues. Campaigne felt she was insecure because, 'she became fearful she wouldn't be able to do things'.[6]

After the war he went to Germany, as part of TICOM[7] a fact-finding team, where, he said, 'we found the Germans were well aware of the way Enigma (ciphers) could be broken, but they concluded it would take a whole building full of equipment to do it. And that's what we had. A building full of equipment. Which they hadn't pictured as really feasible.'[8]

Campaigne's 1983 government reports (including an update in 1955 of William Friedman's *The Index of Coincidence* unclassified by the NSA having been 'taken from WFF's home') investigated Extraterrestrial Intelligence via 'radioed' astronomical signals of aliens through Extraterrestrial Communications, where familiar codebreaking alpha/mathematical methods are applied to break codes of 'received' transmissions said to be from outer space![9] Agnes had died in 1971; what she would have thought of this futuristic world?

Chapter 21

D-Day

Returning to August 1943, a conference in Quebec, known as 'Quadrant,' between Churchill, FDR and Admiral King took place and a date was set for a major escalation in 1944, as well as re-organisation of the Far East and South East Asia Command. Secret agreements also limited sharing of nuclear energy information. Other conferences followed in Moscow and Cairo where declarations of support and plans for postwar USSR and Asia were made.

At the November 1943 Tehran Conference, Averell Harriman, then US Ambassador to the Soviet Union, had to placate a suspicious Churchill while Roosevelt attempted to gain Stalin's confidence. It was the first meeting of the 'Big Three' to finalise strategy against Nazi Germany and its allies, but the conference exposed divisions between America and Britain for a postwar world; Churchill was intent on maintaining Britain's empire and carving the future world into spheres of influence, while the United States upheld the principles of self-determination laid out in the Atlantic Charter. Harriman opposed the Soviet leader's intentions and the spheres approach as it would give Stalin a free hand in Eastern Europe. Plans for Operation Overlord were agreed and a few days later in Cairo, Churchill, Roosevelt and President Inonu of Turkey agreed to complete Allied air bases in Turkey. But Operation Anakim, to recapture Burma from the Japanese, was postponed.

May 1944 brought together prominent Prime Ministers of the British Commonwealth: Winston Churchill (Britain), John Curtain (Australia), Peter Fraser (New Zealand), William Lyon Mackenzie King (Canada), and General Jan Smuts (South Africa). They agreed to support the earlier Moscow Declaration and settled their respective roles in the overall war effort.

* * *

THE SECRET LIFE OF AN AMERICAN CODEBREAKER

On both sides of the Atlantic, a flurry of activity and optimism brewed as the quantity of intercepts increased in the lead up to the secret Operation Overlord – D-Day. All leave was cancelled. Over 18,000 intercepts from Listeners came into Bletchley, with similar ratios in Washington. But not only were messages intercepted, deciphered, paraphrased and re-enciphered, they were created as fake decoys for German Listeners to purposely intercept. Dummy traffic was also 'confirmed' by bogus forces strategically placed (fake landing craft and headquarters in Dover, England, under General Omar Bradley, which 'doubled in size' when General Patton's fictious army and leadership was employed, to intimidate the Germans), together with double agents working to convince Hitler and his generals that the Pas-de-Calais would be the site of the invasion.

It was a busy time for the message processors, human and mechanical, as preparations took place around Britain. Map plotter Wrens and WAVES worked with flatbed plans of the English Channel, not just for the real invasion but also for a false assault. All vessels in the Channel were recorded, including French fishing boats. At times it was so busy they had to work two watches; it was that important to keep the plot up to date. As part of the secret plan southern England's coastal waters concealed temporary Mulberry Harbours (Phoenix Caissons). British engineers had developed these floating jetties of reinforced concrete for the rapid transfer of cargo, troops and trucks to Northern France. They lay hidden beneath the sea crests but on D-Day they would rise untethered and float into place to create a harbour – another amazing feat of engineering first mooted by Churchill in 1917.

Technology aligned when on 4 June 4, 1944, codebreakers in the Newmanry using Colossus intercepted and deciphered Hitler's Lorenz message which revealed he had fallen for the faux orders of the Allies. It was one of the most crucial contributions to the planned operation. His intercepted radio-transmission contained secret orders of battle for Field Marshal Rommel. Through his spies Hitler received information that the Allied invasion was planned in Normandy but, as he informed Rommel, Hitler thought (because of Patton's army) it was a trick to draw German troops from Calais and the main Channel ports. The Führer's instruction to Rommel was not to move his troops.

As the US commander in chief, General Eisenhower, took time to think – over half a pint of beer in the Golden Lion pub, next to Southwick House HQ, Portsmouth – a Typex message was delivered by a Special

OPERATION OVERLORD

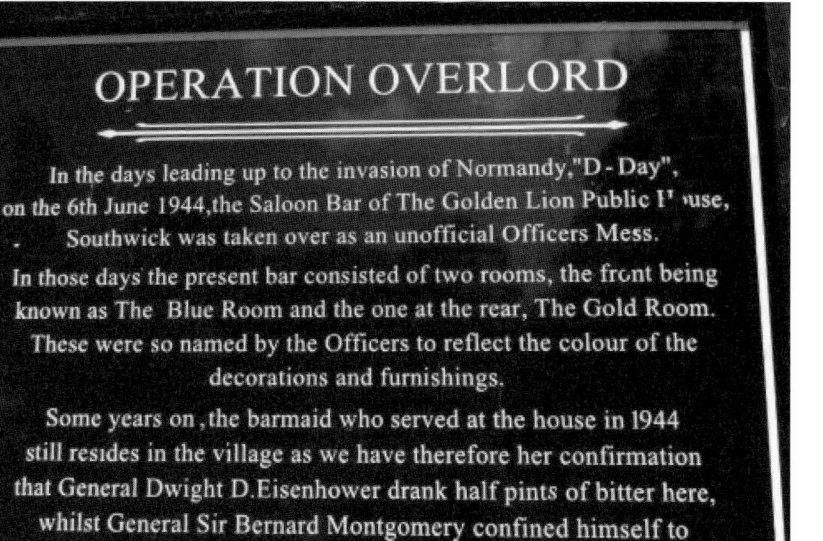

In the days leading up to the invasion of Normandy,"D - Day", on the 6th June 1944, the Saloon Bar of The Golden Lion Public House, Southwick was taken over as an unofficial Officers Mess.

In those days the present bar consisted of two rooms, the front being known as The Blue Room and the one at the rear, The Gold Room. These were so named by the Officers to reflect the colour of the decorations and furnishings.

Some years on, the barmaid who served at the house in 1944 still resides in the village as we have therefore her confirmation that General Dwight D. Eisenhower drank half pints of bitter here, whilst General Sir Bernard Montgomery confined himself to grapefruit juice.

The beer dispensed to the General was brewed in the brewhouse at the rear of this property.

The Golden Lion Plaque at Southwick, Hampshire, UK. Eisenhower's local watering hole. (Author Public Domain)

Liaison Unit officer. The operator moved with haste to hand the message directly to Eisenhower, as he prepared to meet with Allied commanders. He asked Eisenhower, to read the message and keep the contents to himself, 'Sir!' He saluted. It was Hitler's intercepted message read via Colossus at Bletchley Park.

Careful to absorb and correctly understand every word of the message, the Supreme Commander knew he had five clear days for the Normandy invasion. He could not tell his staff and other commanders what was written in the message, nor could he keep the paper. Under orders, he handed it back to the courier and made his decision. There was no room for error: 'We go tomorrow.'

He could tell Hitler thought the plan was a trick and that Allied convoys would move east along the Channel coast of northern France, to start the invasion at Calais, close to where the German Panzer divisions awaited combat. But it was the opposite strategy, and the secret invasion of Normandy on the west of northern France was safe. However, bad weather played a part with high winds and heavy seas, and so D-Day, the Allied invasion of Normandy, went ahead a day later under cloudy skies, on 6 June 1944.

* * *

Beneath a waning crescent moon and clear skies in Washington, Janice woke early for her morning shift. The air was cool. She was well practised in getting the timing exactly right for 7.00am, with plenty to spare for 8am. Again, from Dupont Circle, she hurriedly walked the three miles to work, but there was something about the sunrise that Tuesday. She knew it was an important day. Op-20-GYI-2(A) had been busy the last few days, and she knew American forces were about to act, but did not know where. She saluted the marine guard at the front of the building and showed her ID, then tapped in the security code. A buzzer announced her arrival and the door opened; she walked past the blank temporary wall into a hive of activity. Her colleagues coming off the midnight shift told her she was in for a busy day – the invasion had started.

By now the Allies had control of the Atlantic and U-boat traffic was low. German meteorologists, therefore, had less information than the Allies on incoming weather patterns. The Luftwaffe's imprecise meteorological office in Paris predicted two weeks of stormy weather and as an invasion at any point in the Channel seemed unlikely, German commanders went off to Rennes, it is said, to play war games or rest. The average age of the German army was around six years older than the average age of the Allies, and feeling war weary, they lacked the commensurate strength to keep going. Rommel, very sweetly, even returned to Germany for his wife's birthday, though the official line was that he was meeting with Hitler to bolster his Panzer division in Calais.

The weather of course was vastly different in Washington. The English Channel was often prone to poor weather, no sun and bad visibility, but early that morning in Portsmouth harbour the weather was milder than the day before, with high cumulus cloud. British Wrens on watch at 'Fort Southwick', as Americans called this house, had been confined to barracks and not permitted to travel more than five miles. But from their dormitories, they saw the country lanes and surrounding fields fill with troops and tanks, some passing beneath their second-floor windows. Troop and artillery movement went on for more than 24 hours which meant sleep was almost impossible, but some Wrens bucked the rules and borrowed a bicycle to ride to their billet in civilian clothes, simply to get sleep.

After a delay of one day the Special Duty Wrens, who were Listeners and plotters, were excited to go down the tunnel to their workplace; they knew this was the big day. Wrens coming off the previous shift were mortified at having to miss 'the party'. 'Even if you had been dropped from Mars that day you would have known something very big was about to happen. All of Portsmouth Harbour and Spithead, in fact all the water usually seen from the Portsdown Hills, was utterly invisible, covered so thickly with ships it was impossible to see any space between them.'[1]

As Washington was waking up, the invasion was underway. WAVES on the 'graveyard' (midnight to 8 am) and morning shifts at the Naval Communications Annex, WACs and codebreaking civilians on duty at Arlington Hall, were inundated with intercepts. The flurry of activity was spellbinding and worrying. A message to all U-boats from German Central command was decoded and translated: 'Enemy landing on the mouth of the Seine.' The German chatter was repeated over and over; Bletchley Park and Washington were reading the messages just as fast as, or earlier than U-boat captains. Operation Overlord – the Allies were attacking the enemy fox-holed on land in occupied North-western France.

The Germans knew as well as the Allies that a perfect tide in the Channel would either be the 5th, 6th or 7th of June, indeed they had been on full alert around those dates in May. Clouds do not affect tides but the wind they bring with them affects the sea's tranquillity. Wind would hinder the Allies, and clear skies would jeopardise their element of surprise, though it would benefit accuracy in hitting artillery targets. Mists and low cloud would help mask battleship silhouettes on the horizon and a smooth crossing would be preferable; German meteorologists estimated the Allies would not attack if wind reached force 4 or higher, ergo, no invasion.

But they were wrong, despite the moderate breeze (wind force 4 on the Beaufort Scale) and 6-foot swells in the Channel, 160,000 American, British and Canadian troops crossed at night. Cloud cover was low. Some voyages took seventeen hours to cross the 100 miles or more. Troops were herded into landing craft and other combat vessels without stabilisers, but many could not control seasickness; the smell of vomit started a chain reaction. Within hours the land battle was on as they waded waist high or swam to the shore of Normandy's coastline with frogmen, military armour, tanks and fire power. Allied battleships and destroyers discharged long-range artillery overhead as troops ran across the beaches. The German army responded with machine-gun fire and mortars. The friendly soldier the sapper had just met on the boat was hit, but the sapper carried on, dodging the bullets. Bodies were strewn across the sand and hands reached out for help. Still, he had to advance, firing his weapon high at the enemy on the cliffs above him.

* * *

Corporal Helen Kogel watched events from the sidelines, she could see the whole picture before her. Just a few days before when hundreds of Allied planes flew over London heading south toward the coast, she knew the invasion was about to begin, but divulged nothing, not even to her friends in the forces. When Allied troops stormed the Normandy beaches, she had to prepare, she would be going to France with General Eisenhower and the rest of his staff when the Allied forces reached Paris.

She had wired her parents in America a few days before asking them not to send any more mail until she contacted them again from her new location – she couldn't tell them where, but anywhere would be safer than London. That day, the telegraph office she stood in was hit by a German V-1 bomb and knocked her out. She came to screaming, covered in shards of glass, as someone shook her and told her she was going to be OK.

From Woonsocket, South Dakota, Helen joined the WACs and after training found herself part of the US Army, on the *Queen Mary* for a four-day voyage to England. From there she and other WACs were billeted in a hotel in London's Berkeley Square, near Piccadilly, and told to report for duty the next day. The office she was assigned to, in a grand building, was small at 10 feet square. It had a fireplace, a door and one long window with a blackout curtain constantly drawn to prevent light from filtering out during Luftwaffe bombings of the capital. Five officers, two Americans, one Canadian, one British and an Australian worked at a long table by the window and she had a small desk in the middle of the room just big enough for her Royal typewriter and a stack of papers to type. She also took dictation from some of the officers in the morning. There was little talking, just the crackle of the fire in the ornate fireplace and the clacking of her typewriter. Nobody discussed what she was doing, but she understood. A Military Policeman guarded the office door.

She had three carbon copies to make of each page. It was meticulous typing. Mistakes were irritating and time consuming, but for eight hours, five days a week, her routine was identical. Every completed sheet of paper threaded through her typewriter was rubber stamped TOP SECRET in red. At the end of her working day, an officer placed the original document and its copies into four separate folders and took them to another office. The military policeman would then confiscate the carbon papers and her typewriter ribbon and together they would watch the inky secret paper and spools flare and burn to ash on the fire. The MP would then walk her back to her hotel on Berkeley Square, where she would join other WACs for dinner. Nobody there asked what she did, and nobody revealed their tasks. All were part of General Dwight D. Eisenhower's confidential staff.

One day in April 1944, she had just typed the last page of her assignment and the officer compiling the folders asked if she would like to go with him to take the now-thick file to General Eisenhower. Prior to that she had only saluted from afar, but after a year of working for him she felt honoured to be asked and said yes.

'Corporal, do you know what you've typed?' asked General Eisenhower. 'Yes, sir. These are the battle plans that you will use for the invasion of France.'

Twenty-three-year-old Corporal Kogel, was suddenly part of history. She had typed the complete battle plans of Operation Overlord, and the liberation of Europe. But she couldn't tell a soul. She was told to forget what she had typed. The number of troops, ships and aircraft; the units to be deployed, where they would land and the movements of all; the landing airstrips to be seized, where bombs would drop, the first bridges and railways to be destroyed. She hadn't known the date but guessed it would be soon.

A few days later, Kogel's London unit left for Southampton and Southwick House, where shortly after they embarked on a navy transport ship and sailed in complete darkness across the English Channel. As they neared Utah Beach they were told to put on their knapsacks and disembark by way of a hefty rope ladder over the side railings to a smaller landing craft that would take them closer to the shore. Surprised, but with a certain amount of inevitability, they found themselves like troops before, wading in waist high water crossing the flat beach and, once there by the cliff wall they were told not to move. There were no bombs detonating around them, but in the distance was the sound and red glow of heavy guns.

They waited until daybreak for a truck to take them to base camp and food at the mess. Still damp from their wet and salty arrival, Corporal Kogel wondered out loud to a friend as to where their personal bags were – she'd heard they were floated ashore. Standing behind was a young sergeant who offered to find a jeep to help search for them. His name was Noel Denton, a staff sergeant in the Signals Corp. He was also waiting to go to Paris to set up communications with London and Washington, but that was the only detail he could give. Kogel and the other twenty-nine women camped on Utah beach in two-person tents for approximately six weeks before Paris was liberated, and during that time Noel and Helen fell in love.[2]

Chapter 22

Final Battles

As gliders dropped parachute regiments behind enemy lines, 7,000 men descended into the fields of France, aided by Allied ships, minesweepers, landing craft, Mulberry harbours, destroyers, cruisers, amphibious tanks and support vessels of all kinds. American, Canadian and British, 160,000 allied soldiers with heavy weapons crossed the Channel. Codebreakers watched the battle unfold from the German intercepts but could say nothing. They felt excitement, relief and horror.

At the end of June, France flew the Tricolour on its northern shores, as Normandy was liberated. The invasion lasted well into August when German forces finally retreated across the Seine. Allied deaths in the first fifteen days of the battle totalled 40,549 according to figures issued by Supreme Headquarters. Britain lost 1,842 with 8,599 wounded and 3,131 missing; America lost 3,082 with 13,121 wounded and 7,959 missing; Canadians lost 393 with 1,359 wounded and 1,093 missing.[1] The total combined German casualties at their retreat was around 215,000, but it was several more months and many more deaths before the war ended in Europe. More American troops were needed.

Meanwhile, Hitler continued to send his 'miracle' weapon over London to terrify its citizens, the V-1 flying bomb – 'buzz bombs or 'doodlebugs'. The jet propelled 'secret weapon' was a low-altitude pilotless aircraft capable of 400mph. It was noisy, fuelled by compressed air and petrol, crammed with nearly a ton of explosives and controlled by a gyroscope. When the fuel expired there was a silent lull of approximately 15 seconds before the missile hit the ground and exploded on impact. If you could hear the noise you were safe, but if sudden silence, there was a good chance it was about to land on you. The attacks prompted another mass evacuation in London and south-east England.

In Room 149 on the upper floor of Block B at Bletchley, the Western Front Committee continued to meet. Formed in October 1942, a small select group of mostly Air Section personnel kept track on war related information destined for military chiefs at London's War Office. The group of about six, was chaired by Professor T.S.R. Boase,[2] who was also a Director of the Courtauld Institute while on BP duty. Their question was, 'Is there a military Battle Order for the Western Front?' There was no active fighting in the Low Countries of France and Belgium then, but the committee's aim was to keep abreast of the mass of German troops and fortifications being built along the North and Western reaches of France (aided by Colonel Hiroshi Oshima's reports through Allied interception of Japanese Diplomatic messages). Such installations indicated that Hitler knew the Allies would retaliate with a sea and land invasion on the western coast.

Before D-Day the committee provided information, and some say advice, to military chiefs regarding troop movement, weaponry, supplies and barrier developments, for what became known as Hitler's Atlantic Wall. Their meetings were behind the scenes and strictly confidential under Ultra but after the invasion, they found themselves, metaphorically speaking, right on the front line. As well as a mass of intelligence via Enigma intercepts, fast messaging Signals and Typex operators of the SLU and SCU were providing a minute-by-minute account of events on the battlefield.

Now Bletchley Park could exploit their expertly mastered techniques, and the committee found it was almost running the war from an hourly plot chart of immediate outcomes and counter strategies. That's not how it was supposed to be, but it was working. Allied chiefs had so much information on which to act, they came to rely on the intelligence received from Bletchley Park – who could see the bigger picture – 'especially with MI14 and CIS who had gone from being one of "delivery service" and "customer" to intelligence partnership and collaboration.'[3]

* * *

A new influx of American troops prepared for a 'boat ride', a euphemism for crossing the Atlantic on a troop ship, where they ate canned apricots and slept on hammocks slung from pipes in the hold. The journey for thousands of young, newly trained soldiers of the 112th Infantry Regiment of the 28th Infantry Division, took ten days to reach England. By September, American commanders aimed to pin down German forces 5 miles across the Belgian-German border, to prevent reinforcements from reaching other front lines.

FINAL BATTLES

Meanwhile, the women at Arlington Hall worked overtime that December keeping up with the German offensive via Enigma messages, but they despaired at the carnage later reported. Some had young brothers who had taken that 'boat ride'. But worse was yet to come. Germany successfully defended its position to maintain a staging area for a winter offensive, using the surrounding mountains to command access to the Rur Dam and the *Rurstausee* (the Rur Reservoir). The Allies already had heavy losses and setbacks, when another offensive took place in the Ardennes on 16 December, and Hitler decided his mobile reserves would split the Allies once and for all to retake Antwerp.

Wacht am Rhein (Operation Watch on the Rhine) or the Ardennes Counter-offensive (known as the Battle of the Bulge), was a complete surprise for American forces. A combination of overconfidence, preoccupation with allied plans, a weak defence, poor aerial reconnaissance due to bad weather and insufficient understanding of Allied intelligence by the military were blamed for their unpreparedness. Consequently, America bore the brunt of the largest and bloodiest single battle of any operation in the war. Overall, 140,000 American personnel were lost. But the battle also depleted Germany's armed forces, which by then were becoming hard to replace.

The Wallonia area of Belgium's Ardennes region saw the Allies put up fierce resistance in freezing temperatures to the north at Elsenborn Ridge and south at Bastogne, blocking key access roads to the west and northwest which Germany was counting on. After another month of skirmishes, Germany eventually retreated to the defences of the Siegfried Line.

* * *

The German concentration camp at Auschwitz was captured at the end of January 1945, as Russia's Red Army moved through Poland toward Germany. It was known as the 'death factory' but when their forces smashed through the gates, they were horrified to see piles of emaciated corpses and people so weak they were simply left to die. Jews from all over Europe were either slaughtered or worked to death with many dying from starvation and disease.

* * *

THE SECRET LIFE OF AN AMERICAN CODEBREAKER

Churchill, Roosevelt and Stalin, the "Big Three" at the Yalta Conference (codename *Argonaut*), February 1945. Behind them are Field Marshal Sir Alan Brooke, Fleet Admiral Ernest King, Fleet Admiral William D. Leahy, General George Marshall, Major General Laurence S. Kuter, General Aleksei Antonov, Vice Admiral Stepan Kucherov and Admiral of the Fleet Nikolay Kuznetsov. (National Archives Public Domain)

At the Yalta conference on 11 February, Allied leaders demanded unconditional surrender for Germany and Japan. Intelligence provided evidence to military chiefs that the Allied air offensives in the Ardennes had reduced German fuel production levels to a few tons a month. The plan then was to increase Bomber Command attacks on German communications and other oil installations. On 14 February, after a day and half of constant bombing, the RAF and US Air Force razed Dresden in the east of Germany to a pile of smoking rubble. The German population had increased to around a million as many people thought the city safe, but estimates said 60,000 to 130,000 died. Shortly before midnight Lancaster Bomber Pathfinders had led the trail, laying marker flairs for bomber targets – a risky mission especially for the navigators who sat in

FINAL BATTLES

the bottom cockpit of the plane pinpointing target coordinates. Air Chief Marshal Sir Arthur 'Bomber' Harris came under great criticism as he championed his theory that terror bombing would destroy the enemy's will to fight. As well as the loss of civilian life many 17th and 18th century art treasures were also destroyed. Over 800 Lancaster Bombers took part in the midnight raid, followed by 400 American B-17s at noon.

Meanwhile, 750 miles from Tokyo on 23 February, a platoon of marines hoisted the Stars and Stripes on the highest point of Mount Surabachi on Iwo Jima in the Japanese Volcano Islands. Bill Montgomery of the US Marines 5th Division, then only 18-years-old, remembered the first day, around noon:

RAF Bomber Command. (Wikimedia Commons, Public Domain)

'I turned around and looked up at the top of the mountain. I wondered what they were doing. And as I looked the flag went up. That was a good feeling because we thought the battle was over. But it was just the beginning.'

February 19 – March 26, 1945, the 'month of hellish combat' was supposed to only take three days. Pulling supplies up through volcanic ash, the US soldiers struggled to keep control as 21,000 determined Japanese troops fired from a network of underground tunnels and pillboxes armaments to defend the island. They fought a savage battle for days to gain strategic advantage.

Bill Montgomery had wanted to be a scout sniper, but he was assigned to intelligence instead with the 2nd Battalion forward observation unit. He was part of the second wave and one of the very few who landed and wasn't hit. 'I don't know why; all my buddies were hit or killed. All of us assumed and expected to be hit. Everybody else was being hit. And our hope was it wouldn't be fatal.'

Being 18 helped him and other young troops, because they didn't have combat fatigue, and didn't 'crack up'. 'Several times I came across men sitting on the ground, they were usually older guys, sobbing their heart out, shaking all over…; that was one of the saddest things of the battle.'

By Day 5 Montgomery was the only surviving member of his three-man forward observation unit and reassigned to rifles. Both sides lost many men and endured many casualties in one of the bloodiest battles of the war.[4]

The flag of the United States of America is raised at Iwo Jima, February 1945. (Public Domain)

* * *

FINAL BATTLES

Back in Europe, after defeat in Wallonia, German defences were pushed back and Operation Plunder was launched two months later under Field Marshal Montgomery, Lieutenant General Sir Miles Dempsey and US Lieutenant General William Simpson. By 25 March Allied advancing armies prepared to thrust deeper into the urban industrialised Ruhr Valley after a dramatic crossing of the Rhine and capture of the Gothic cathedral city of Cologne. At one vital crossing point a railway bridge had been spotted at Remagen that had not been demolished by the Germans and a quick-thinking American sergeant raced across with his platoon under German fire, dodging booby traps, and hiding in bomb craters to await reinforcements. Montgomery, further north in Wesel, meanwhile, prepared his crossing in meticulous detail, with massive supplies of ammunition, amphibious craft and bridge-building equipment. He was also aided by heavy smoke screens and Allied bomber attacks under Operation Varsity, using several thousand aircraft, gliders and 16,000 paratroopers. The Rhine crossing took place at midnight after a 2,000-gun bombardment, followed by a fast installation of 1,152 feet of pontoon treadway, to build a floating bridge. In record time the first trucks crossed at 4pm. The scale of the operation almost equalled D-Day.[5]

As groups of German youths calling themselves 'Werewolves', carried out acts of murderous sabotage against supporters of the Allies, Italian partisans plotted the capture of Mussolini and his aides. Asking for mercy, he was found under a pile of coats and arrested. A brief trial ensued and Mussolini and his supporters, including his mistress, Clara Petacci, were condemned to death by firing squad. On 28 April their bodies, tied from their heels, hung from the façade of a petrol station in Piazza Loretto, Milan. The war with Italy was over and ended Operation Sunrise, where the remnants of their Axis forces surrendered unconditionally to the Allies. Negotiations had been initiated in secret three weeks earlier by the SS Commander, General Karl Wolff, who had offered to capitulate via the Archbishop of Milan. The surrender was to be signed 26 April but there was a delay of three days under orders from Germany. The document was finally endorsed on the afternoon of 29 April 1945.[6]

For more than twelve years Hitler, once an Austrian street artist, had hypnotised and fooled millions of ordinary Germans along with many so-called intelligent industrialists. Now it was the end, everyone knew he had lost, but he wouldn't take the blame. He truly believed it was not his fault. As the Soviet Red Army seized the central government area of Berlin, Eva Braun, his longtime companion, model and photographer raced to the Führer's reinforced bunker under Reich Chancellery Gardens. On 29 April they married in the bunker sitting room, which that night became the grim scene of their suicide pact. Braun bit into a cyanide capsule and Hitler shot a bullet through his head.

Goebbels committed suicide in the bunker the next day, remaining loyal to the end, but one questions this when recalling his role as propaganda chief, and his claim, 'a big lie was more likely to be believed than a small one'. In the hours before his death Hitler chose Grand Admiral Karl Dönitz as his successor *Staatsoberhaupt* (Head of State).

'Hitler Dies, Doenitz takes Helm' reads the headline in May 1945. (Boston Daily Record)

An Enigma interception received at Janice's Naval Communications Annex to Dönitz' troops read: 'You have fought like lions…you are laying down your arms after a heroic battle.'[7]

Chapter 23

War's End in Europe

An excited voice in the office shouted, 'The War's Over! The Nazis had surrendered to Field Marshal Montgomery at a schoolhouse in Rheims on Lüneburg Heath, Hamburg, on 4 May 1945.

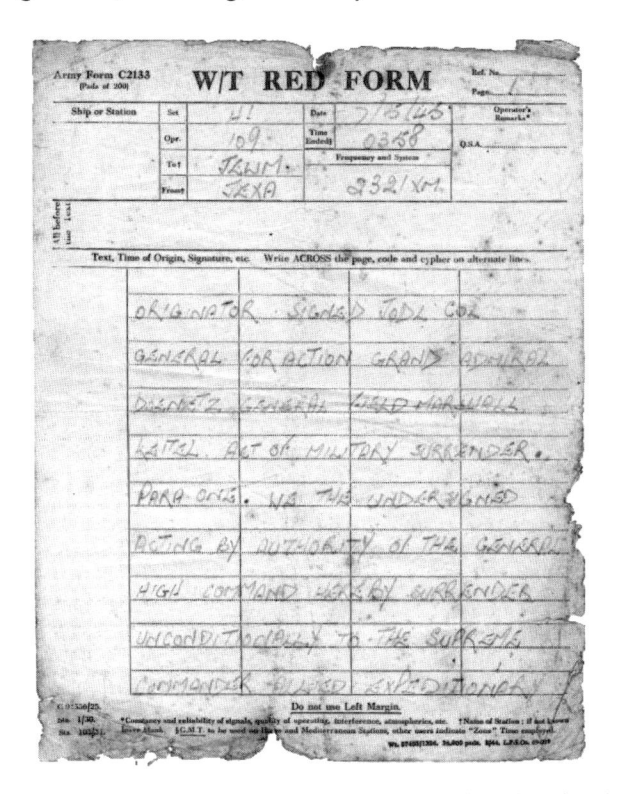

Army Wireless Telegraphy form, No. C2133. "Originator signed Jodl Col. General for action Grand Admiral Dönitz General Field Marshal Keitel. Act of Military Surrender. Para one. We the undersigned acting by authority of the general high command hereby surrender unconditionally to the Supreme Commander Allied Expeditionary." (Crown Copyright 2021. Original document donated to Bletchley Park Trust by ATS Royal Signals operator Netta Curd.)

THE SECRET LIFE OF AN AMERICAN CODEBREAKER

War in Europe was finally over! In England codebreakers rejoiced wildly, but codebreakers in Washington were more subdued. However, all glowed from their clandestine teamwork as they reflected on their contributions and celebrated as peace was officially confirmed by the new President and Britain's Prime Minster. President Roosevelt had died less than a month before on 12 April 1945.

After several days, personnel began to be reduced. The end of the war was becoming real.[1]

There was immense relief on many continents around the world. Weary Britain had been at war for five and a half years, America, two years less. The tides of war had turned. In New York, a cacophony of noise lashed its busy streets as ships in Manhattan ports blasted their sirens and all around were festooned with white tickertape and yards of colourful drapes thrown from the open windows of tall buildings. Conga lines formed as festive crowds danced, drank, cheered, sang and laughed. Some felt such emotions had not been sensed for an eternity.

But even though church bells rang in both countries, it wasn't the end of Britain and America's war as they could not forget the prisoners of war in the Far East. Now Bletchley Park prepared to send another consignment of new codebreaker recruits to Colombo. There were still Japanese codes to decipher. Nazi communications also had to be monitored to ensure all their forces surrendered. On 4 May Hut 3 at Bletchley Park translated and read an intercept from Generalfeldmarschall Keitel 'to fight to the last. The Führer has given his life to the German people.' A week later Germany had surrendered, but there was a failed last-ditch attack at Cuxhaven, on the German North Sea coast, 75 miles east of Wilhelmshaven, after it was captured by the Polish First Armoured Division eight days before. In a message decoded at Bletchley Park, German military radio codenamed BROWN, signalled the arrival of British troops and ended with, 'Closing down forever – all the best – goodbye.'[2]

*　*　*

It was the President's birthday and Mother's Day was the next weekend. Truman held a press conference in the early hours of 8 May:

> *'This is a solemn but glorious hour. General Eisenhower informs me that the forces of Germany have surrendered*

WAR'S END IN EUROPE

> *to the United Nations. The flags of freedom fly all over Europe. For this victory, we join in offering our thanks to the Providence which has guided and sustained us through the dark days of adversity. Our rejoicing is sobered and subdued by a supreme consciousness of the terrible price we have paid to rid the world of Hitler and his evil band. Let us not forget, my fellow Americans, the sorrow and the heartache which today abide in the homes of so many of our neighbours – neighbours whose most priceless possession has been rendered as a sacrifice to redeem our liberty..... We must work to finish the war. Our victory is only half over.'*

President Truman also promised that if 'If Japan doesn't surrender, atomic bombs would be dropped on her war industries.' The world watched and waited as he promised 'a rain of ruin from the air'.

* * *

Janice listened to the news on the radio and President Truman's speech. She had, of course, known in advance that the war had ended from NCA messages received the day before and wondered what she would do next.

After VE Day, 8 May 1945, for those working on German intercepts some were reassigned to the Pacific war for Japanese intelligence, but Janice was assigned to BuMed, the government Bureau of Medicine and Surgery. With nearly a year still to serve, she undertook secretarial work for that department at the Old Naval Observatory in Washington and in her spare time tutored Latin.

* * *

In London the British Coalition government was dissolved and an election was planned for 23 May. The question was: 'Would Churchill survive to run Britain in peacetime?'

The next month the European Advisory Council apportioned sections of Europe to Russia – part of the Allies' deal with Stalin for Russia's help to defeat Hitler. Germany was divided, East and West, and American troops moved back westward 150 miles. Not everyone agreed. Meanwhile, German citizens faced the grim evidence of Nazi death camps in their country.

The European war was over for many and 750,000 war-weary American troops on SS *Queen Elizabeth* sailed home to New York where, after six days at sea, they received a rapturous welcome. But in the Far East, 300 miles south of Japan, vicious combat raged between 50,000 American soldiers and the Japanese for the strategic island of Okinawa. By 21 June, bloody hand-to-hand fighting on land and in caves culminated in full Japanese ritual when their commander admitted defeat by committing hari-kari at dawn in front of his staff. There were 12,000 American casualties with 110,000 Japanese dead. Days later delegates from fifty countries signed the World Security Charter on 26 June, appointing the United Nations committee as international peacekeeper.

'We All Went To Washington'

While Janice was familiarising herself with her new position at BuMed, a group of women from Bletchley Park went to the Pentagon, as British Staff. The department was set up in 1941 and later became the British Joint Services Mission[3] where around 437 staff linked various Allied government sections to liaise with the British War Office and the US War Department. Their tasks covered a wide area. Charlotte Vine-Stevens (Betty) was one of the ATS officers selected, together with Commander Denniston's daughter, Margaret, and his former assistant Barbara Abernethy.

Betty, who paraphrased messages at Bletchley, was one of the honoured few to be posted to Washington, 'a humble staff sergeant', as she describes herself. After short embarkation leave, and an expensive visit to a London hair salon (for a 4 guinea (£4.4s.0d.) perm which, she'd heard would combat the humid weather in America), she found herself conveyed in a small boat through choppy waters in Poole Harbour on the south coast of England. There she climbed up over the wing of a flying boat to find her seat.[4] At the age of 22, it was her first flight and with recent aerial combat she was understandably nervous they might crash into the sea. After a stop in Ireland for food and fuel, she transferred to a small Sunderland plane, where the seats converted to sleeping areas for

WAR'S END IN EUROPE

the thirty-six VIP passengers. The night flight seemed endless, complete with turbulence and air sickness, but ended safely when they descended through the morning mists at Botwood airport, Newfoundland. The last leg of the journey followed a few hours later after a hearty breakfast of eggs and bacon and Grapenut cereal, which as Betty pointed out, are neither nuts or grapes, but wheat and barley.

Relieved to finally be in America, she was met at Baltimore airport by Captain John Burrows from GC&CS's Japanese section. He had recommended her for the transfer. Exhausted, she collapsed for twenty-four hours in the Cairo Hotel, a designated billet that she was to share with another ATS girl for five months, Pip Wallace, from Hull. The following day she boarded an official Pentagon bus for her first day of work. She felt like a tourist, taking in Washington's amazing sites; the White House and the Capitol building, the monuments, the Mall,

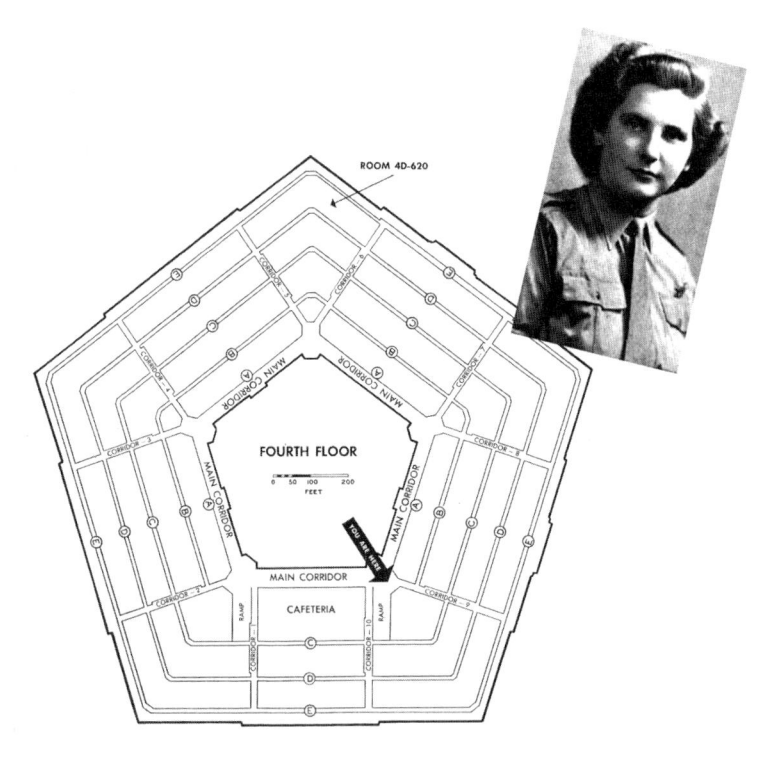

ATS Officer Charlotte Vine-Stevens, aka Betty Webb. At Bletchley Park she paraphrased secret messages before being transferred to the Pentagon mid-1945 as part of BJSM. Escorted War Department visitors found there were several routes to their destination. In this case, Room 4D 620. (Betty Webb and BookTower Publishing)

THE SECRET LIFE OF AN AMERICAN CODEBREAKER

eventually crossing Arlington Bridge and the Potomac River to the newly built Pentagon. The heat was stifling, especially in her thick British uniform, but fortunately she was provided with lighter attire, courtesy of Canadian forces.

Betty soon discovered America was in complete contrast to the wartime austerity of England, and that the new Pentagon building was enormous, far larger than the fusty operation at Bletchley Park. Escalators from the car park took the 32,000 employees to the multiple levels where they worked in large open plan offices; a 'metropollis' on 34 acres serviced by banks, shops, restaurants, a medical centre and even a church.

As one would expect security was tight 9-5pm, and Betty's ID pass was checked 2-3 times each day. She was presented with a desk, a chair and a typewriter, and continued paraphrasing intercepted Japanese

An inside look at the Pentagon, revealed in a 'souvenir' instructions pamphlet retained by Betty. (Betty Webb and BookTower Publishing)

WAR'S END IN EUROPE

messages. From time to time she was also a 'Special Courier' carrying top-secret papers. It was a scary task, 'I was always relieved when the package was signed over to the correct department, without incident.'[5]

* * *

In July, Dwight D. Eisenhower wrote to Major General Sir Stewart Menzies, Chief of MI6 from his HQ in England.[6]

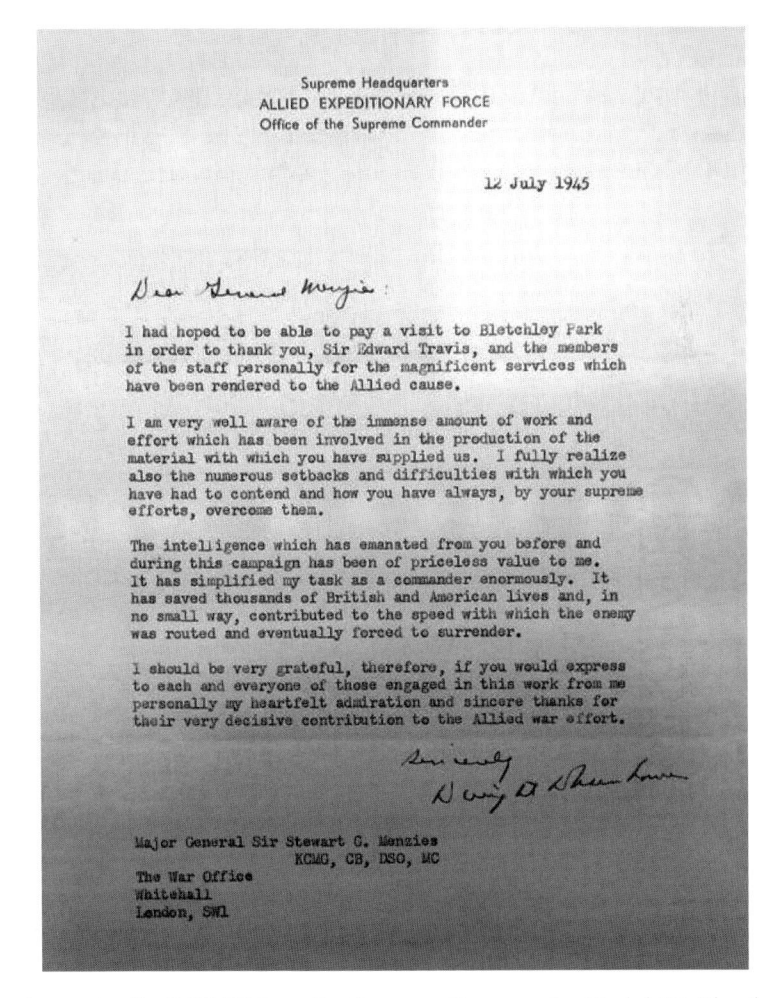

> Supreme Headquarters
> ALLIED EXPEDITIONARY FORCE
> Office of the Supreme Commander
>
> 12 July 1945
>
> Dear General Menzies:
>
> I had hoped to be able to pay a visit to Bletchley Park in order to thank you, Sir Edward Travis, and the members of the staff personally for the magnificent services which have been rendered to the Allied cause.
>
> I am very well aware of the immense amount of work and effort which has been involved in the production of the material with which you have supplied us. I fully realize also the numerous setbacks and difficulties with which you have had to contend and how you have always, by your supreme efforts, overcome them.
>
> The intelligence which has emanated from you before and during this campaign has been of priceless value to me. It has simplified my task as a commander enormously. It has saved thousands of British and American lives and, in no small way, contributed to the speed with which the enemy was routed and eventually forced to surrender.
>
> I should be very grateful, therefore, if you would express to each and everyone of those engaged in this work from me personally my heartfelt admiration and sincere thanks for their very decisive contribution to the Allied war effort.
>
> Sincerely
> Dwight D. Eisenhower
>
> Major General Sir Stewart G. Menzies
> KCMG, CB, DSO, MC
> The War Office
> Whitehall
> London, SW1

Glowing praise for GC&CS from The Supreme Commander, Dwight D. Eisenhower, July 1945. (Public Domain, from copies held at the NSA/National Cryptologic Museum and Bletchley Park Trust)

Meanwhile, President Harry Truman maintained his interest in nuclear fusion and 'Project Y'. From 1942 the Manhattan Project was also supported by Britain and Canada. The main research was undertaken by American universities, but mostly in the 'Rad Lab' at the University of California.[7] Then Oak Ridge, a hidden valley 25 miles from Knoxville, Tennessee, became a highly classified testing and production site to develop many of the weapons, along with Los Alamos in New Mexico and Hanford, WA. Women were also secretly employed in explosives chemistry manufacturing including WACs for administration duties. Research and production took place at more than thirty sites in America, Britain and Canada, where over 130,000 people were employed at a cost of US$2 billion (2018 equivalent of US$23 billion). More than 90 per cent of the cost was ploughed into building factories, while 10 per cent was apportioned to weapons development. Defecting scientists from Germany also helped in providing the Führer's missile secrets.

Chapter 24

Waiting for VJ Day

While the world anxiously hoped for peace in the Far East, Allied leaders insisted on unconditional surrender at the Yalta conference in February 1945, after the Nazi defeat in May and at the Potsdam Conference in July. Concede defeat 'or meet prompt and utter destruction'. Emperor Hirohito had to step down, but the Allies' emphasised their demand was 'not intended to enslave the Japanese people'.

That month a powerful Royal Navy task force joined the United States Third fleet and the Royal New Zealand Navy in bombarding Japanese industrial and military facilities. It was the strongest fleet ever assembled in the Pacific and caused heavy damage to targeted factories as well as civilian neighbourhoods. Shortages of fuel had confined most of the surviving Japanese ships to port, together with the Army Air Service, which stood in reserve in the event of an Allied invasion. The Allies had predicted an aircraft counterattack but there was no retaliation or serious combat leaving the fleet of Allied warships undamaged.

Still Japan refused to concede. On 12 July, Foreign Minister Shigenori Togo sent a message to the Japanese Ambassador, Naotake Sato, in Moscow: The word, 'unconditional' was the only obstacle to peace. If they agreed Allied terms the Japanese feared their emperor would be tried as a war criminal and executed. Since the emperor held a god-like status, his execution, said General MacArthur, would be comparable to 'the crucifixion of Christ'.

Togo's aim was to enlist the USSR as mediator, but Allied intelligence had known for months that Soviet involvement would force a Japanese capitulation. While Japan tried to arrange Soviet help, Truman, and his advisors decided to officially enter the nuclear age. This was despite earlier dissent from seven of his eight United

THE SECRET LIFE OF AN AMERICAN CODEBREAKER

States five-star Army officers who, on record, had previously stated that atomic bombs were either militarily unnecessary, morally reprehensible, or both.[1]

* * *

The alternative decision was prolonged combat against 2.5 million Japanese, who were motivated by 'Bushido'. They were prepared to fight to the death. In response Operation Downfall could take months, not to mention the loss of half a million American and Allied lives. But then signals intelligence raised the chilling alarm of preparations for imminent mass slaughter of prisoners of war, when they intercepted Japanese military commanders' messages. These revealed they had orders on their desks to 'dispose of' all prisoners of war and civilian detainees 'without trace'. The date of terror was 23 August.

Meanwhile, codenamed 'BOWERY', the USS *Indianapolis*[2] transported uranium and weapon parts for final assembly to Tinian. The skies in the beautiful Pacific Mariana Islands were clear that sunny morning as the US Army B-29 super-fortress aircraft, *Enola Gay*, secretly loaded LITTLE BOY and her crew of twelve. At 14 feet tall and 5 feet wide, the world's first atomic weapon had been tested in July in New Mexico and was ready for battle. It weighed almost five tons. Now called Operation Centreboard the assignment's Captain William Sterling Parsons was in charge of releasing the drop. On 6 August at 8.16 am, the bomb hit its mark annihilating Honshu, the capital of Japan's largest island, Hiroshima. As the pilot swung away from the target, Parsons observed and signalled back the previously arranged secret reporting code: 1, 2, 6 and 9, four of the agreed twenty-eight coded lines. 1. Clear cut, successful in all respects, 2. Visible effects greater than TRINITY (the previous test), 6. HO (Hiroshima, primary target) and 9. Conditions normal in airplane following delivery, proceeding to regular base.[3] The face of war had changed forever.

Allied listeners twiddled the dials of their radio equipment to locate the Hiroshima station. Usually, the signal was strong but that day there was nothing. One operator, Alethea Chamberlain at Two Rock Ranch near San Francisco, couldn't understand the silence either and laid her headphones on her desk to investigate. But in the Pacific Islands Brigadier Farrell had received Parson's message loud and clear and immediately communicated to Washington. Within sixteen hours the rest of the world reeled from news – how could one bomb cause so much destruction?

Before Hiroshima, the earlier fleet attacks hurt the Japanese, and most believed the war was lost, but civilian opinion, including the zaibatsu – the huge conglomerates of Japanese industry – had little impact in forcing the Japanese government to surrender.[4]

A second bomb was dropped on Nagasaki three days later, obliterating the Japanese city on the island of Kyushu, as USSR declared war on Japan and invaded its puppet state of Manchukuo. Was the second bomb to tell Japan, and the rest of the world, that America had unlimited nuclear weapons and would use them? Or to show Russia that America had infinite power over Japan? Thousands of civilians died and tens of thousands would later die of radiation poisoning – 146,000 on Hiroshima, 80,000 on Nagasaki. Over half died within the first day of each bombing. Smoke plumes hovered over the dead and dying and complete devastation for days. No longer secret, the British-American led Manhattan Project was the work of 100,000 international scientists who researched and created the most devastating weapon of all time. The debate continues as to whether Truman's decision was justified.

Field Marshal Prince Morimasa Nashimoto urged Japanese reservists 'ultimately to destroy completely the "strong enemy"', but the *New York Times* stated that some observers saw 'a serious split' among Japanese factions. The surrender of Japanese forces overseas was 'a most delicate task…having a direct bearing on their honour'. Broadcasts in Japanese-occupied territories stressed the danger of 'fatal dissension' among the people and exhorted all to obey the decision of the Emperor as 'final and beat'.

The Emperor ordered the Supreme Council for the Direction of the War to end the fighting and agree to the Allies' Potsdam terms. Similar requests were sent to the governments of Great Britain and the Soviet Union through Sweden, as well as the Chinese Minister in Switzerland, through Berne.

The *New York Times* reported, 'The world passed another anxious day waiting for the word from Tokyo that would signal the end of World War II'. It was sixty-two hours after the first communication with Japan and the Allies immediate 240 word reply from Secretary of State James

Byrne. He had also on 11 August, outlined again three other conditions as part of the surrender agreement:

1) Direct prompt cessation of hostilities and the effective date and time.
2) Japanese emissaries to be sent at once to the Supreme Commander with information on the disposition of Japanese commanders and forces, and fully empowered to enable him and his accompanying forces to arrive at a designated place to receive the formal surrender.
3) Designation of Army General Douglas MacArthur to decide on place and time of formal surrender.

But the White House had not received a reply by midnight, 13 August. Then Japan claimed both messages were received on the morning of Monday, 13th, which a Swiss Embassy spokesman said was a lie, prompting suspicion that Japan was 'stalling for time'. There was no longer a Japanese Embassy in Washington, which meant messages to the president were sent via neutral Swiss Embassies.

Finally, on 14 August, a message was received from the Japanese Government transmitted, via Swiss embassies in the low-grade JAH cipher (the LA bigram and tetragram code of Herbert Yardley days), accepting the Allies' terms.

* * *

Units in Australia and on both sides of the Atlantic were ready to pounce on anything that indicated the end of the war, and Cover Management Y was first at Bletchley Park to hear the news. But nothing could be said. The low-grade cipher, JAH, was read quickly and the head of department, Cyril Williams, known as 'Bungy', was delighted to announce to his team that Japan had surrendered. 'Well done girls!' he said. 'I think I am going to tell you the war is over, a signal has just been intercepted between Tokyo and Geneva, but we cannot announce until Switzerland has relayed to London, meanwhile the King and the Prime Minister know.'

The women sat and stared at him in complete silence, to which he responded, 'Well, bloody well get on with your work then!' The Glassborow twins[5] and their colleagues were first to know in Britain, but they couldn't utter a word, not until the news became public, 'otherwise they would have known we were listening,' said Bungy.

WAITING FOR VJ DAY

America, six hours behind Switzerland and five behind Britain (GMT -5), saw Virginia Dare Aderholdt in Washington as the first American to hear. After college she spent four years in Japan and JAH was her responsibility. She 'owned' the all-purpose code with its mundane information on utilities, commodities, vacations and pay, but it also carried a wealth of first-rate material in terms of personalities, problems and documented materials such as speeches, various papers and orders. In addition, it gave seeds of economic and political data for occupied territories and was used to disseminate propaganda. Another transportation cipher, called JBB, was also part of her remit where she and other translators cross-referenced events in occupied islands and territories. While Britain and Australia had scholars of Japanese, analysts like Virginia and Arlington's group of young 'j-boys' were fresh with energy. The young officers had been sent to California and Colorado to specifically learn Japanese, returning with modern ideas, a love of the culture, the land and the language. Every intercepted Japanese conversation and military manoeuvre was followed with detailed intensity. As few Americans spoke Japanese, they were crucial to Arlington Hall.[6]

Rumours began and Rowlett and Kullback asked for discretion. The surrender would not be official until the President accepted the final terms, but soon everyone in Arlington Hall was summoned to raise their right hand in a vow of silence. At 7pm, President Truman announced the surrender. By now it was midnight in London, and the rest of the Far East was waking to hear the official news, on Wednesday, 15 August.

Janice and her colleagues at BuMed and the Naval Communications Annex celebrated. They knew before but when the announcement came, they expressed their excitement with the rest of the city. Thrilled was an understatement. Cars were gridlocked and streets were mobbed. Some people in movie theatres saw a bulletin flash across the screen 'JAPAN SURRENDERS'. Everyone hurriedly left their seats and surged onto the streets. Car horns blared continuously. Betty Webb from England joined a throng of people shouting. 'We want Harry, we want Harry.' Thousands had crossed the Potomac river from Virginia and Arlington and ticker tape 'rained' from every office window. Others sang 'Happy Days are Here Again' and the President declared a two-day holiday. They had done it. The war was now well and truly over.

***

Emperor Hirohito had surrendered unconditionally, and 15 August became known as VJ Day (Victory over Japan). The Supreme Commander for the Allied Powers, General Douglas MacArthur, led the occupation of Japan from 28 August, and formal ratification of the *Instrument of Surrender* by the Japanese Empire took place in a ceremony aboard the aircraft carrier *USS Missouri* on 2 September – VJ Day in America.

Chapter 25

Aftermath

Thousands of Allied Prisoners of War in the Far East were saved, together with many lives projected for combat. The Second World War was the most devastating and destructive conflict in human history, affecting over sixty countries. It is said that dropping the Atom Bomb shortened the war by at least two years and ultimately saved many more lives than were lost. If this was Churchill's 'wizard war', then it was true, though perhaps not straightforward 'magic'. Intelligence collection and analysis by administrative staff, brainpower and developing technologies, significantly aided commanders and their brave troops, who would have had a tougher time if not for Allied codebreaking and security efforts. From 1939 to 1945 the distinction between military and non-military became blurred, as vast resources of entire populations were mobilised to conspire and protect, but also allowed a brutal and hurtful assault on civilians. Raw truths – war hurts.

Over time, estimates increased indicating that more than 60 million people lost their lives (some say 70-80 million from all causes). More than a trillion dollars was spent on the conflict and a huge shift in international status moved to a new age of superpowers, accelerating the decline of the French and British empires. Disagreement between the United States and Soviet Union grew, and Japan and Germany nurtured new democratic governments. Chinese communists led by Mao Tse Tung defeated Chiang Kai-Shek's nationalist party, and a new era of the People's Republic of China commenced in 1949.

* * *

Janice, still bound by the rules of secrecy, could never talk of her war-work in Washington, but as a civilian she took advantage of the higher learning offered and kept herself occupied. In May 1946, she was

THE SECRET LIFE OF AN AMERICAN CODEBREAKER

released from active duty, discharged as Lieutenant, Junior Grade, US Navy Reserve by Disbursing Officer V.G. Finney. Her initial mustering out pay was $100, plus insurance, but no travel allowance.

Janice's Notice of Separation from Service, including her right index fingerprint. (Janice Benario Archive)

AFTERMATH

'After BuMed I had four years of GI Bill, which paid for all my studies at Johns Hopkins and gave me a graduate's education, a Masters, a PhD in the classical languages Latin and Greek, and paid for the typing of my dissertation.'[1]

The 'Servicemen's Re-adjustment Act of 1944, the 'GI Bill of Rights', was signed into law on 22 June 1944, by Franklin D. Roosevelt. Though initially ridiculed, the legislation for veterans is now recognised as one of the most important acts approved by Congress. Enthusiastic participant response signalled a move in world attitudes from an Industrial Society to a Knowledge Society, and offset a post-war economic collapse as seen after the First World War in the Great Depression. The American Legion is credited for the bill's design which provided investment of billions of dollars in education and training for veterans. With this foresight America now earns more in employment tax revenues and peoples' lifestyles are greatly improved as they better provide for their families. The law also made possible billions of dollars of loans to veterans for them to purchase their own homes, converting the majority of the population from renters to homeowners[2] – now widely phrased as 'Living the American Dream'.

As they looked to a new future the past was pushed behind and Janice and her peers moved into a group that would later be described as the 'Silent Generation' – the secrecy, the devastation, the Atom Bomb – nobody wanted to remember or talk about what had happened to them – the silence between them was understood.

Janice knew she wanted to be in a college atmosphere and worked in Johns Hopkins library for a year. The ancient histories of Romans and Greeks continued to be a safe haven for her, and where she met her husband.

'I met Herb in 1950 when I just happened to sit next to him in a Latin Seminar at JHU. We married in 1957.'

'During that time,' she continued, 'The Ford Foundation gave grants to certain schools for "Beginning College Teachers" and I received one for St Johns, near Baltimore.'

She taught there for a year under the grant which amounted to around $3,000 per year.

'I would say that was my first job, but St Johns was the College of a *100 Great Books* and had a very peculiar curriculum. After a year I'd had enough and was lucky to receive an offer to Sweetbriar College, Virginia. It was a normal girl's school; I taught Latin and History.'

Above: Post war graduation from Goucher. Janice with her parents, J. Elmer Martin and Gladys Kathryn Martin. (Janice Benario Archive)

Left: Janice with her husband, Herbert. (Janice Benario Archive)

AFTERMATH

Among Janice's other academic honours was a Fulbright Award to the American Academy in Rome, and a National Teaching Award for Excellence in the classics from the American Philological Association. Janice and Herb moved to Atlanta in 1960 to successful faculty positions at Georgia State and Emory Universities. When asked about the Baltimore house on North Calvert Street, she reflects on its passing.

'I lived there until 1957 when I married age 34. I had been away to the WAVES and away here and there, but my father died of a heart attack in 1955, and my mother lived alone in this monstrous three-story house, so she sold it. I believe a Hopkins Fraternity bought it and it is now a fraternity house.'

'I was never able to tell my parents what I did during the war.'

Recognition

Major General Stephen Chamberlain from the United States Army, serving under General MacArthur in the South West Pacific, stated: 'I believe that our cryptographers in the war with Japan did as much to bring the war to a successful and early conclusion as any group of men'.[3] No mention of thousands of women.

Bletchley Park was the basis for America's equally industrious intelligence operation - a willing and very able student. Allied Air, Army and Navy signals intelligence gathered some of the finest intelligence in history which contributed enormously to the defeat of the enemy and shortened the war by no less than two years, saving many thousand lives.

However, in 1946 when American civilians left their wartime assignments, they only received letters from the US Army Security Service (the new name for Signals Intelligence at Arlington Hall), thanking them for their service and warning them again never to reveal details of their work to 'unauthorised persons'.

> 'Information you are privy to should not, now or at any time in the future, be revealed.'

With little recognition, US codebreaking women could not secure other jobs or accommodation easily in Washington due to the influx of people leaving wartime employment, and because nearly all positions were reserved for men returning from war. Some stayed at their Agencies in important positions, such as 'Mathematician', however, they were expected to leave if they married as women become pregnant. There was no inkling of childcare.[4]

'When I was discharged from Active Duty, I was given three ribbons to wear,' said Janice. 'The World War II Victory Ribbon, the Atlantic Theatre Ribbon; all thirty-five people in our office received a Navy Unit Citation ribbon, the highest honour the Navy can give to those not in combat, we received all three.'

'People often ask if I kept my uniform and the answer is no, but I wish I had kept that hat! My name is inside so maybe it will turn up somewhere. I have my discharge papers of course, but I kept the ribbons only until recently. I thought *'why keep those ribbons?'* So, I got rid of them in 2012. I didn't give them to anyone – I just threw them away! Sometime later I gave a talk to residents in my apartment building. It was the Fourth of July, and there was a man who was interested. He happens to be one of the few living there who also has a PhD; he calls me Professor all the time. He heard me say I'd gotten rid of the ribbons and found a place in California that could make them. I gave him a copy of my discharge papers, which say I am entitled to the ribbons and he had them re-made for me.'

At Bletchley Park there were no medals for codebreakers, encouragement to continue codes and ciphers, nor any GI-style educational opportunities. The clandestine operation simply disappeared from British public records, forgotten and erased from history. Churchill referred to them as 'my most secret source'. But they knew who they were, and never said anything, not until they had permission to do so.

Ann Caracristi, from Bronxville, New York – who admitted that northern staff at Arlington were condescending and not as kind as they should have been to African American women arriving from the south – eventually received public recognition, but only after forty years' service in the intelligence world. Neither did African American women receive recognition.

After the war and a short period in journalism, Ann returned to Signals Intelligence at Arlington Hall, (US Army Security Service) and faced some of the trickiest challenges of her life. The Cold War, known as 'the Soviet problem', stretched to many troubling corners for Ann and her team, followed by serious issues in East Germany. The work was difficult and critical in dangerous times. She retired in 1982 and, as

AFTERMATH

Janice's remade WWII Ribbons. (Janice Benario Archive)

a senior member of the NSA, received the National Security Medal and the Distinguished Civilian Service Award. She died in 2016, aged 94.

Helen Kogel and Noel Denton married soon after the war ended. They adopted a son Jon, and raised collies in Noel's hometown of Atlanta, where he continued in communications with Southern Bell. Helen worked for Delta Airlines for fifteen years and often took the opportunity to return to Europe and Normandy. Sadly, Jon accidently died in his early thirties and Noel died from a heart attack a few months later. But Helen never told Noel or Jon what she did.[5]

* * *

By the end of the war of 84,000 American women served in the WAVES, 8,000 of whom were officers.[6] The WACs reached its peak of 99,388 women in active duty, with 140,000 serving in total throughout the Second World War. Most served in the Armed forces, but large numbers also served as 'Air WACs' (Army Air Force) and the Army Medical Corps. Only 2,000 however, served in heavy combat with Army Ground Force. WACs not on the battlefield were awarded the Distinguished Service Medal, the third-highest US Army decoration and highest award for non-combat service.

The initial bill called for women in service to be discontinued six months after war ended, but women were now seen as more than capable. Dwight Eisenhower said, 'During the time I have had WACs under my command they have met every test and task assigned to them…. Their contributions in efficiency, skill, spirit and determination are immeasurable.' General Douglas MacArthur called them 'my best soldiers'.

With the urgency to send men home, WACs were in demand to help maintain peace in recently liberated lands.

Eisenhower supported the act to maintain a Permanent Nurse Corps and establish a specialist women's medical section which led to the Army-Navy Nurses Act of 1947, Public Law 8036, granting permanent status to females in the forces. But the House Armed Forces Committee amended the bill to restrict women to reserve status only. Eisenhower objected to this vehemently writing 'the women of America must share the responsibility of the security of their country in a future emergency as the women of England did in World War II'.

The debate for all women's permanent status service continued into the summer of 1948 with much support, including that of Elizabeth Nourse Rogers, until finally the bill passed giving women that right and President Harry Truman signed the 'Women's Armed Services Integration Act' into Public Law 80-625.[7]

Epilogue

Instinctively, other people did not ask about the war. At least not until younger generations became interested, but most older people hid under a cloak of secrecy protecting information too sensitive to admit. Now the NSA and Bletchley Park want codebreakers to talk. Their stories are fascinating and compelling.

'I kept in touch with Jane Thornton Apostol, who I worked with at OP-20-G,' confirmed Janice. 'She was also from Goucher and we've been friends since 7th Grade, through high school and the navy'.

Janice and Jane spoke of their WAVES days, 'We always laughed that we never actually used that cryptology course.'

Their work instead was after the processes of interception, registration, codebreaking and decoding, as they tackled the important task of traffic analysis in translating, indexing, categorising, paraphrasing and writing reports for commanders on crucial military strategy. The data they produced, filed in a central library, was also used by codebreakers and decoders for future reference when they sought clues to trickier intercepts and ciphers.

Janice continued talking about Jane: 'She was a year older than me and married a man who was a professor at Cal. Tech., and for her 90th birthday he put together all the things she had written. She was a good writer, A+ in English composition, but no advance degree, only the degree from Goucher and turned to writing about Southern California. They sent me one. The book is very thick; I can hardly lift it. Inside there is a picture of her as a WAVE, similar to mine. We kept in touch with Christmas cards, but I only saw her once after, when I visited Los Angeles and went to Pasadena in the nineties'

'Nobody ever did say anything, at least not until the seventies,' said Janice.

Thirty years after the war, American writers, journalists and codebreakers started to speak about intelligence in the Second World War, especially in the world of computer technology, but codebreakers in Britain were horrified. They had been told never to mention their work.

David Kahn's first book in 1967, giving much of Friedman's story, was kept low-profile in Britain, but some codebreakers were able to obtain copies only to find neither they nor Bletchley Park were mentioned. Apart from a few supposedly fictitious (but partially true) accounts, Frederick Winterbotham was one of the first to write his version and Gordon Welchman next, but the British government kept the shutters closed. Welchman lived in America by the time he wrote *The Hut 6 Story*, avoiding extradition to the UK and a jail sentence. He moved to Massachusetts after the war bringing his Bletchley computer knowledge to assist MIT and the Mitre Corporation, but the US National Security Agency also disapproved of his publication and Welchman lost his security clearance and his job. Governments had stepped in to gag the informers. Even Friedman thought some of the NSA's postwar security ridiculously over classified and took papers home. Unfortunately, this meant his career with them did not end well either.

Not until Peter Wright's *Spycatcher* in 1987, and immense pressure from politicians, did Prime Minister Margaret Thatcher, finally concede that after forty years it was time to be more candid. The British public wanted to know, and codebreakers wanted to tell. 'What would the government do? Surely they couldn't put us all in jail?' 10,000 codebreakers and more behind bars? It was unlikely.

* * *

From European roots to the amazing feats of signals and codebreakers, including the complex Agnes Meyer Driscoll, Elizebeth Friedman, Genevieve Hitt, Ann Caracristi and Mary Prather, Janice Martin walked in the aura of these great women (and men) who helped put American codebreaking on the map – the seeds of Homeland Security.

Gradually, their history was declassified on both sides of the Atlantic, and publications started to appear in the 1970s but still, while raising her family and a successful career at Georgia State University, Janice refrained from saying much of anything about her Second World War Top Secret work. Then in 1984 Professor of Classics, Dr Janice Benario, retired from her Latin and Greek lecture responsibilities and re-kindled her love of needlepoint. She proudly presented the

EPILOGUE

beautiful dining room seat covers she made. Then in 1991 as the fiftieth anniversary of Pearl Harbor approached, Herb bought a copy of David Kahn's *Seizing the Enigma, The Race to Break the German U-boat Codes 1939-1943*.

For so long the story had been buried, but she eagerly read through the pages, immersing herself into the backgrounds of other departments she recalled but had not fully understood. Then halfway through, as the story unfolded, she was shocked to suddenly see an image of herself staring back in a glossy black and white photo of OP-20-GI 2(A). There she was with her entire office! Unable to contain her excitement, she was now free to talk to everyone.

In 1992 the *Goucher Quarterly* magazine published her personal account. At the same time, Goucher claimed its contribution to victory in the Second World War, inducting students into the cryptologic correspondence course. From then on, Janice presented her story to many groups, gave radio and television interviews, as well as personal recordings for this book. She even discovered that many Classicists in both England and America worked on Ultra, including Denys Page, Leonard Palmer, T.B L. Webster, Hugh Trevor-Roper and L.P. Wilkinson. Her first Greek professor, John B. McDiarmid had also been in charge of the submarine tracking room in Ottawa, Canada. They would have had much to talk about had they known! In the early part of 2000 Janice visited Bletchley Park where it all began, and she was pleased to report, 'I was treated like royalty and felt like a film star; they looked after me very well.'

In May 2010, sixty-seven years after majoring in Latin, Janice returned to Maryland and the campus of Goucher College, Baltimore. That day she received another degree, Doctor of Human Letters, *Honoris Causa*, in recognition of the secret wartime role she began at the college as a student. Janice's family is proud of the fact that she was one of an elite group during the Second World War that received a Presidential Citation for its success.[1]

Recognition was also given in England in 2011, when Queen Elizabeth II, spoke of her 'deep sense of admiration and gratitude for the men and women who served in Allied intelligence, and the debt our nations owe to them for their achievements.'[2]

* * *

The NSA National Cryptologic Museum and Bletchley Park are shrines to Allied codebreaking achievements. Arlington Hall was listed on the National Register of Historic Places in 1988 by the National Park Service and is used for training. The former 'gym' at Washington DC's Naval Communications Annex on Nebraska Avenue hosted important presidential events as part of the US government's expanding Department of Homeland Security (since 2003). The navy vacated in 2005 but let us hope one day this historic building will publicly honour their codebreakers, and the little girl who once splashed in the sea under the watchful eye of her father, J. Elmer Martin. Years had passed since their visits to Atlantic City beach and the ocean they both loved. How could they have known then that Janice's work as an adult would be crucial in saving lives in the Battle of the Atlantic and the Second World War? Sadly, she could never tell him.

Afterword

GCHQ and NSA Directors meet at Bletchley Park

The Codebreakers were small cogs in two huge wheels, connected by a well-oiled chain of command, performing their duties efficiently and diligently to help the Allies defeat the Axis powers. In this special relationship a foundation was laid for future generations for a new framework in technology and electronic communications.

On 9 February 2016, the directors of American and British signals intelligence services met at Bletchley Park to celebrate the 75th anniversary of the beginning of the countries' Special Relationship. Admiral Michael S. Rogers, Director of the NSA, joined GCHQ Director Robert Hannigan, in the same Bletchley room as the original meeting, 75 years before, to tell the story of how a late-night sharing of secrets began over sherry and cigarettes; a Special Relationship crucial to both nations today.

It was in 1941, on 8 February, ten months before entering the war, that four US signals intelligence officials secretly made their way under cover, toward the Buckinghamshire countryside. They were expected, but it was a secret and dangerous assignment. The four men were Abraham Sinkov and Leo Rosen from the Secret Intelligence Service (SIS), Lt. Prescott Currier and Lt. Robert Weeks from the US Navy. Delayed, diverted and even shot at as they travelled, they eventually arrived, late and dishevelled, and were offered drinks in the Mansion office of Alastair Denniston, Head of the GC&CS. Small talk ensued over icebreakers of cigarettes and sherry, before each felt comfortable to share their code breaking achievements against Germany and Japan's secret communications systems.

Denniston smoked a pipe; the others' cigarettes – as was commonplace those days – most adults smoked, ill-informed of the health risks then.

One can imagine the smoke clouds puffed slowly around the Commander's office, as they talked; cross-exchanges of secret messages and methods, in the front room of the Mansion with the bay window; the room where Daisy Lawrence would sit when she first arrived at Bletchley two years later. Were they the Americans who stayed, and played tennis on the lawn tennis courts? Were they the ones who were teased by the Budd children 'D'ya 'ave any gum chum?' Nobody was supposed to know the Americans were there…

No sherry or cigarettes this time. Admiral Rogers said: 'I would encourage people to come here, because Bletchley Park represents an entwined history between our two nations and shows what we can do when they come together.'

Robert Hannigan added: 'Standing in this room is a reminder that it all comes back to people in the end; brilliant, dedicated people working together, taking risks, as we have between us. That partnership can do fantastic things against threats today, as it did 75 years ago.'

The two directors were given a tour by the Chairman of Bletchley Park Trust, Sir John Scarlett, and CEO Iain Standen. Sir John said: 'As you go into the room, which has now been restored, you have a strong sense of what it must have been like on that evening 75 years ago.'

Iain Standen added: 'The directors were like any visitors, in awe of the Bletchley. When they watched the introductory film, where it says "it happened here" they got the hairs-on-the-back-of-the-neck feeling as everybody does. Standing in Alastair Denniston's office where this important event took place; they were moved.'

Based on press articles from Bletchley Park's announcement February 2016.

AFTERWORD

Author's Note on Navajo Code Talkers

When I mention Codebreakers, people in America often immediately refer to Code Talkers, 'the Native Americans from the Navajo tribe.' Of course, I'm quick to correct since Code Talkers are not Codebreakers – although they did make a code – nor were they solely Navajo Indians.

Code Talkers' history, quite rightly, is now documented in publications and films, particularly after the death of Chester Nez, in 2014, the last Second World War Navajo Indian code talker. However, in 2002 I hadn't heard of Code Talkers either, so I can relate to the initial confusion. That year, after visiting Monument Valley, Utah, my family and I came across an unusual Navajo Code Talkers display in a Burger King.[1] I knew my mother had something to do with codebreakers and was instantly drawn by the word 'code' and the interesting photos on the restaurant walls. We were on the edge of the Painted Desert in Kayenta, Arizona, on a dusty crossroad. Burger King and the gas station were the only two buildings with facilities before our next stop, the Grand Canyon visitor centre, 155 miles west.

I found the Native American Code Talkers' story intriguing, going back to the First World War, when eight Choctaw[2] men served in Europe in the US Army's 36th Infantry Division. The company, blended with people from Texas and Oklahoma, was under the command of a Captain Lawrence, who heard two men converse in their Native American tongue. Telephones were becoming 'An exceedingly convenient way to communicate', according to David Kahn in *The Codebreakers,* and paying customers could settle everything in one conversation rather than several messages, letters or telegrams. The same was true on the battlefield when, after telegraphic codes and ciphers, speech and field telephones started to be used. However, these were insecure and the radiotelephones, even more so. Therefore, a system developed using obscure dialects and languages, with an additional layer of code.

Solomon Louis was one of the two Choctaw men and he was put in charge of training others using their unique language, plus the layer of code. Their missions, some behind dangerous enemy lines, were successful, including on 26 October 1918 when they were pressed into action. After 72 hours the Allies launched a full attack that resulted in German surrender on 11 November.

THE SECRET LIFE OF AN AMERICAN CODEBREAKER

During the Second World War Assiniboine, Cherokee, Choctaw, Comanche, Cree, Meskawi, Mohawk, Muscogee and Navajo soldiers all took part. Twenty-seven of the Meskwaki enlisted together in January 1941, representing a huge 16 per cent of Iowa's Meskwaki population. All were trained to use their native language or sub-set language, and a code. Comanche[3] code talkers took part in the invasion of Normandy, having compiled a vocabulary of over 100 code terms, in their own idiom. It was a substitution method similar to Navajo, where descriptive sentences were used for things that did not have a translation in their language. The word for tank was *turtle*, bomber was *pregnant machine*, machine gun was *sewing machine*, and Adolf Hitler was *crazy white man*.[4] All their stories can be heard at the Smithsonian National Museum of the American Indian.

The use of Navajo in the US Marine Corps was proposed by Philip Johnston, a civil engineer from Los Angeles, and a First World War veteran. He was raised on the Navajo reservation, where his father was a missionary, and was one of few non-natives fluent in Navajo, then an un-written language. Johnston believed their numerous dialects, complex syntax and phonology would be indecipherable to anyone without intensive exposure and training. It was estimated that fewer than thirty non-Navajo understood the language. Immediately, after Pearl Harbor, Johnston tested and demonstrated that Navajo men could, under simulated battle conditions, encode, transmit and decode a three-line message from Navajo to English in 20 seconds, versus the 30 minutes required by a machine at the time. The idea was approved, and 200 Navajo were recruited to the Marines, eventually rising to more than 420. The first 29 attended Camp Pendleton in Southern California, May 1942, where the Navajo Code was created. This was modelled on the joint Army/Navy phonetic alphabet using standard English words to represent letters, though some military terms, letter by letter during combat were too cumbersome, therefore, some terms and instruments of warfare used unique Navajo nomenclature. Navajo for destroyer was the equivalent of *shark*, while lieutenant colonel became *silver oak leaf*.

New recruits would, at first, have no idea what their Navajo colleagues were discussing until they learned the code. A classroom code book was written, but it was never to be taken into the field. Instead they had to memorise and practise under multiple rapid testing, to emulate stressful

AFTERWORD

conditions. Skills of speed and accuracy were demonstrated to the full throughout the war. It is said that, 'If it were not for the Navajo, the Marines would never have taken Iwo Jima.'

Sadly, discrimination within the forces meant some Native Indians needed protection from their American colleagues and were assigned bodyguards. Conversely, however, if a Navajo was in danger of revealing the code to the enemy the secondary duty of the bodyguard was to shoot him to protect the code. Fortunately, this never happened.

* * *

Returning to Kayenta in 2018, the Navajo Code Talkers museum has expanded into a larger building behind Burger King. It is worth a visit but relies on donations.[5] Janice would have read about the Code Talkers, but what would Sacagawea (Lemhi Shoshone) – the first and only Native American female translator on the Lewis and Clark expedition (1804-1806) – have made of this? Perhaps she spoke in code too?[6]

Code Talkers – The Choctaw Eight. (Public Domain)

Memorial Day 2021

Writing this on Memorial Day Weekend 2021 and reading Herbert Benario's comments at The Greatest Generation Foundation, he remembers that when Janice's secret past was revealed he wasn't surprised. 'I knew she was in the WAVES, but I didn't know exactly what she was doing.' Fred, their eldest, first remembered learning about her work in the early 2000s. 'I was already 40 years old, so her Second World War escapades aren't, and weren't ever, part of the family story or mythology, especially not when I was growing up. I always knew she was both very bright, and very meek and docile, which made her unlikely to talk about it out of turn.' Following the academic life of his parents, Fred went on to study law and finance. 'Finding out about it didn't change my relationship with her at all,' he said.

John, two years younger, first heard of his mother's code breaking at the same time as Fred, when Janice showed them the OP-20-G photo in David Kahn's book *Seizing the Enigma*. He wasn't surprised and believes there would have been nothing remarkably different in his childhood.

> 'I grew up knowing she was an officer, which had nothing to do with my choice, but when I became a naval officer it seemed like a reasonable succession. Both my mother and my father came from very smart families. My mother was a naval officer in the Second World War and my father was drafted during Korea (though prevented from becoming an officer because of his eyesight), and I was a naval officer at the end of the Cold War. It seemed to me simply the obligation to serve one's country. I was a naval nuclear propulsion officer in DC and one time when she visited, in the 80s, she talked about where she lived and worked

during the war (meaning literally the location, not what she did). I remember commenting that I would not have wanted to wear the woollen Navy dress blues during DC's summer humidity, before air conditioning became common. Being in the WAVES was a normal part of her past to me and when I was in the Navy, I had the picture of her in her Navy uniform on the wall of my office. There is, however, one aspect of our story I find very interesting. There was a woman in Hamilton, Ontario, now passed away, who kept up the family tree on my father's side. My father had no interest in this, but as a pilot, I flew for free up to visit with her in 2004. My father, being German, had many distant relatives who were killed in the camps in the Second World War. Between the family tree and *The Ultra Secret* by F. W. Winterbotham, my mother identified a distant relative of my father's, who worked at Bletchley Park at the same time my mother was in DC. They worked on the same codes.'[1]

– Intriguing! JS

Acknowledgements

I am eternally thankful to Janice Martin Benario who in November 2012 gave me the opportunity to research this project. Through her willingness to have her story recorded I have been able to discover much of my mother's important wartime work and beyond, regarding my adopted country the United States of America. My sincere thanks also go to Dave Barasoain, radio programme producer at NPR Atlanta, WABE 90.1 FM, and Steve Goss, whose velvet voice in the mornings introduced me to Janice. Without all three I would not have discovered the intricacies of codebreaking during the Second World War. Thank

Janice Martin Benario and Jan Slimming, February 2015. (Author)

ACKNOWLEDGEMENTS

you to the many authors whose works I could not do without during the time of not being able to travel due to Covid restrictions. A BIG THANK YOU also, to my husband, Allan, and our children Harry, Jonathan and Rebecca, for their patience and in helping me finish this project. Also to the Atlanta Writers Club and many writing and history friends who were my invaluable 'critiquers', Kerry Howard and Howard Craston, Valerie Biggerstaff at the Dunwoody Crier, and my first editor Philip Parker (when my story was one). Generous thanks to Paul Reid for agreeing to write an engaging Foreword, to my editors at Pen & Sword especially Heather Williams and Irene Moore, The Winston Churchill Society of Georgia, Codebreaker Charlotte Vine Stevens (Betty Webb) for her help and enduring interest in my work, Dr David Sherman of the NSA for his suggestions, GCHQ and NSA/NARA for their permissions and as ever the staff at Bletchley Park. Finally, sincere thanks and appreciation to the Benario family for their support, and to the Robertson family, especially my nephew Christopher Robertson who helped with reproduction of the photographs.

Abbreviations

AEF	American Expeditionary Forces
ASDIC	Anti-submarine division/sound experimentation using quartz
ATS	Auxiliary Territorial Service
BEF	British Expeditionary Forces
BJSM	British Joint Services Mission
BP	Bletchley Park
BRUSA	British and USA agreement 1943
BuMed	Bureau of Medicine and Surgery (USA)
CCM	Combined Cipher Machine
CCS	Combined Chiefs of Staff
CIA	Central Intelligence Agency (USA)
CIS	Combined Intelligence Services (British Army and Navy)
CMG	Companion Order of St. Michael and St. George (Ambassador award)
COMINCH-CNO	Commander in Chief, of United States Fleet and Chief of Naval Operations
COMINT	Interception of enemy communications
ECM	Electric Cipher Machine also known as SIGABA or Converter M-134
FDR	President Franklin Delano Roosevelt
FBI	Federal Bureau of Investigation
FO	Foreign Office
FRUEF	Fleet Radio Unit Eastern Fleet – HMS Anderson, Ceylon

ABBREVIATIONS

FRUMEL	Fleet Radio Unit, Melbourne
FRUPAC	Fleet Radio Unit Pacific
GC&CS	Government Code & Cypher School/Bletchley Park
GCHQ	Government Communications Headquarters
GI	Government Issue (USA)
GMT	Greenwich Mean Time (Z Time – USA)
GPO	General Post Office
IJA	Imperial Japanese Army
IJN	Imperial Japanese Navy
JAH and JBB	Low-grade utility codes, Japanese
JN	Japanese Naval codes and ciphers, multiple numbers
MI	Military Intelligence
MI1	British Military Intelligence
MI5	Military Intelligence, Sec. 5, UK domestic counterintelligence & security agency from October 1909
MI6	British Secret Intelligence Service (SIS)
MIT	Massachusetts Institute of Technology
NCR	National Cash Registers
NID	Naval Intelligence Department
NSA	National Security Agency/National Cryptologic Museum (USA)
OIC	Operational Intelligence Centre (Admiralty Citadel in London)
OP-20-G	US Naval Communications Signals Intelligence Operation (20th division, Section G)
OSS	Office of Strategic Services
OTP	One-time cipher pad
POWs	Prisoners of War
RADAR	Radio Detection and Ranging
RAF	Royal Air Force (UK)

R/T	Radio Telephony
SCU	Special Communication Unit
SFM	Schlüsselfernschreibmaschine (cipher teleprinter)
SIGINT	Signals Intelligence
SIS	Signals Intelligence Service (USA) and Secret Intelligence Service (MI6 – UK)
SIXTA	Hut 6 at BP, Traffic Analysis
SLU	Special Liaison Unit
SPARS	US Coast Guard Women's Reserve
SSU	Strategic Services Unit (USA - post OSS and pre-CIA)
TRR	Two Rock Ranch, California
TICOM	Target Intelligence Committee
ULTRA	"Most Secret" and "Top Secret" Intelligence
USASC	United States Army Signals Intelligence
USS	United States Ship (Steamship or Steamer)
WAC or WAAC	Women's Army (Auxiliary) Corps (USA)
WAAF	Women's Auxiliary Air Force (UK)
WASP	Women Airforce Service Pilots (Civil USA)
WAVES	Women Accepted for Volunteer Emergency Service (USA)
WOYG	War Office "Y" Group
WRNS	Women's Royal Naval Service (Wrens) (UK)
W/T	Wireless Telegraphy
XU	Examination Unit
Y	Wireless Listening Service (UK)
YMCA	Young Men's Christian Association
YWCA	Young Women's Christian Association
Z	00Z midnight in Greenwich. Greenwich Mean Time (GMT)

American Personnel at Bletchley Park

(derived from the Bletchley Park Roll of Honour and Top Secret U document – The American 6813th Technical History, reformatted by Tony Sale, original founder and former curator of the Bletchley Park Trust Museum.)

Allred, Fred
Auerbach, Herbert
Bicher, George
Bijur, William
Biorman, Charles
Black, David
Bruce, Alfred
Bundy, William
Burke, William F.
Campaigne, Howard
Carl, Ralph
Carroll, Benjamin
Carroll, James
Collins, Thomas
Currier, Prescott
Donahue, Charles
Dixon, George
Edgerton, William
Egleston, Oliver
Enzdbeck, Louis
English, John
Evans, Gwynne
Fehl, Alfred
Fischer, LeRoy
Frank, Maxwell
Frazier, Stuart
Frengel, Alex
Friedman, William
Friendly, Alfred
Fuller, Kenneth
Goldstein, Theodore
Hoydstun, Laurence
Hurley, George
Hyman, John
Jacob, Walter
Jaffe, Sidney
Johnson, Roy
Kidder, Robert
Kirby, Oliver
Kullback, Solomon
Laptook, Louis
Leehy, James
Lewis, Arthur
Levenson, Arthur
Libers, John
Libern, Lt.
Lively, James
Lucas (other names unknown)

Maas, Herbert
Magilavy, Jack
Martindale, Ross
Massarsky, Sergeant
McDonald, Grant
McGeachy, John
Moilien, Tilmar
Morris, Ernest
Morris, George
Mueck, Frank
Nielson, James
Nunn, Robert
O'Donnell, William
Porter, Cecil
Porter, Howard
Possan, Bail
Prengel, Alex
Reckert, Frederick
Rosen, Leon
Rowlett, Frank
Salsberg, Edgar
Seaman, John N.
Sharp, Walter
Sibley, Forbes
Simon, Mathew
Singer, Norman
Sinkov, Abraham
Small, Albert
Spatz, General
Stanton, Francis
Swanson, Earl
Taylor, Telford
Thielbar, Henry
Van der Veal, Elmer
Vergine, George
Vogel, Barnard
Walker, George
Whitaker, Paul
Wossorsky, Irving
Yochelson, Maurice

Endnotes

Chapter 2: Trouble in Europe

1. Anna Huebeck Knipp and Thadeus P. Thomas. The History of Goucher College 1938 en.wikipedia.org/wiki/Goucher_College.

Chapter 3: War UK

1. SS *Athenia*, an unarmed passenger ship, was violated under the Hague conventions and the 1930 London Naval Treaty. Lemp did not follow the rules or advice from the German commanders, but the truth was not revealed until the 1946 Nuremberg trials. Wikipedia.
2. A cipher is where each letter is replaced with a different letter, number or symbol. A code is where each word is replaced with a different word or a symbol. However, it is recognised that in most cases when people say 'code' they probably mean 'cipher'.
3. Dorling & Kindersley *Millennium 20th Century Day by Day*, p.510, 27 August 1939 Conscription news report.
4. *The Codebreakers*, David Kahn p.488.
5. *Citizens of London*, Lynne Olson, p.4 and p.10.

Chapter 4: America Inches Forward

1. *The Codebreakers*, David Kahn p.493. Additional information from www.people.duke.edu/~ng46/collections/crypto-disk-strip-ciphers.htm.
2. *The Codebreakers*, David Kahn p.491. Humourist and cartoonist James Thurber wrote 'Exhibit X', The New Yorker XXIV (6 March 1948) pp.26-28, *Battle of Wits*, Stephen Budiansky, p.27 and www.thurberhouse.org/james-thurber.
3. *The Codebreakers*, David Kahn p.488 The Department of State's code compilation was through the Bureau of Indexes and Archives (Division of Communications and Records). David A. Salmon, its chief, was a career employee with little knowledge of cryptology, code making or codebreaking. His department started the American system of allocating codenames by the colour of their binding, hence RED, BLUE, GREY and GREEN codes.

4. Ellen Cicely Wilkinson was a British Labour MP and journalist from Manchester. She played a prominent role in women's suffrage and the Jarrow March to London petitioning for unemployed people's right to work. In Churchill's coalition government she was a junior Home Security minister and in post war Britain appointed Minister of Education for Labour under Clement Atlee.
5. en.wikipedia.org/wiki/Liberty_ship. Lend Lease. A total of $50.1 billion worth of supplies were shipped: *Citizens of London*, Lynne Olson p.219.
6. *Behind the Enigma*, John Ferris p.328. George Veazey Strong (b. 4 March 1880 – d. 10 January 1946) was a U. S. Army general with the rank of major general, who served as commander of the Military Intelligence Corps during the Second World War. In the First World War he served in France during the Battle of Saint-Mihiel. en.wikipedia.org/wiki/George_Veazey_Strong.

Chapter 5: A Junior in College

1. *Citizens of London*, Lynne Olson, p.3.
2. *Millennium 20th Century Day by Day*, Dorling & Kindersley p.553.
3. *Seizing the Enigma*, David Kahn, p.175-178.
4. *Seizing the Enigma*, David Kahn, p.179-186.
5. *Solving the Enigma: History of the Cryptanalytic Bombe*, Appendix. Information provided by Commander Gilman McDonald USNR(R), a senior watch officer of Bombe operations at the Naval Communications Annex on Nebraska Avenue, Washington.
6. *Seizing the Enigma*, David Kahn, p.222-225.

Chapter 6: War USA

1. *Millennium 20th Century Day by Day*, Dorling & Kindersley p.553 and 554
2. First Naval Ship Lost in World War II, US Naval Institute and en.wikipedia.org/wiki/USS_Reuben_James.
3. en.wikipedia.org/wiki/Tyler_Kent, and *The Codebreakers*, David Kahn p.494
4. *The Codebreakers*, David Kahn, p.495.
5. *The Codebreakers*, David Kahn, p.496.
6. www.history.com/topics/world-war-ii/pearl-harbor-attack-video: Reporter H.V. Kaltenborn and www.history.com/topics/world-war-ii/us-home-front-during-world-war-ii. One Japanese message gave a clear indication of impending war and was to be delivered to the US State Department only hours prior to the attack on Pearl Harbor. Controversy on whether the US had fore knowledge of the Pearl Harbor attack, has rolled well into the 21st century.
7. From the pedestal plinth below the bust of Winston Churchill donated by the international Churchill Society to US Congress.

ENDNOTES

Chapter 7: Chosen

1. en.wikipedia.org/wiki/John_Dill.
2. *Citizens of London*, Lynne Olson, p.150.
3. *The Codebreakers*, David Kahn p.490.
4. www.Classified information. 'Most Secret' and 'Ultra' were British government classification terms, changed during the war for interoperation clarity to blend with American classification 'Top Secret' and 'Top Secret Ultra', *Code Girls*, Lisa Mundy p.38.
5. *Millennium 20th Century Day by Day* Dorling & Kindersley, p.56l: Tōjō Hideki, prime minister of Japan (1941–44). He was tried for war crimes and hanged on 23 December 1948.
6. *The Second World War,* John Keegan (2005), p.275. en.wikipedia.org/wiki/Battle_of_Midway.
7. Janice Martin Benario and Cryptologia Volume 35 issue 1 January 2011 (Taylor & Francis ISSN 0161-1194 article Secret Keeping 101 – Dr Janice Martin Benario and the Women's College Connection to ULTRA by Robert Edward Lewand.
8. en.wikipedia.org/wiki/Ola_ElizabethWinslow. Classical Bulletin of Georgia State University Volume 74 1998 #1Top Secret Ultra by Janice M. Benario; Bletchley Park Roll of Honour.

Chapter 8: A Brief History of American Codebreaking

1. Janice Martin Benario and Cryptologia Volume 35 issue 1 January 2011 (Taylor & Francis ISSN 0161-1194 article Secret Keeping 101 – Dr Janice Martin Benario and the Women's College Connection to ULTRA by Robert Edward Lewand. Jaqueline B. Jenkins-Nye's son is Bill Nye "The Science Guy," a popular syndicated TV program for children and their parents. *Code Girls* by Liza Mundy, p.362.
2. Nara records CNSG Historical Review by John Holtwick RG38, NSA, NN3-38-93-001 Box 110.
3. *The Codebreakers and Seizing the Enigma*, David Kahn, pp17-27. en.wikipedia.org/wiki/Room_40.
4. Adaptation *The Codebreakers*, David Kahn, pp 478-479.
5. GCHQ Director Iain Lobban's speech, Leeds University (2012) - Knox simply visited the manufacturing company in Berlin in 1926 and bought one. Mavis Batey (neé Lever) in her biography of Knox, confirmed that GC&CS was in possession of an Enigma Machine in 1929 when Foss' codebreaking work was completed on same. *Gordon Welchman, Bletchley Park's Architect of Ultra Intelligence*, 2014, Joel Greenberg p.266.
6. *The Hut 6 Story*, Gordon Welchman.

THE SECRET LIFE OF AN AMERICAN CODEBREAKER

Chapter 9: Codebreaking in America

1. *The Codebreakers*, David Kahn p.321.
2. *The Codebreakers*, David Kahn p.323.
3. Only magazine or encyclopaedia articles had appeared in America before, plus Mauborgne's pamphlet and an obscure 31-page notebook produced in 1874 in Boston by Harvey Gray entitled Cryptography. *Codebreakers* David Kahn p.324.
4. Price Collier's *Germany and the Germans*, published in New York in 1913, *The Codebreakers*, David Kahn p.371-373.
5. *The Codebreakers*, David Kahn p.488-489.
6. *The Codebreakers*, David Kahn p.490-91.
7. en.wikipedia.org/wiki/Black_Tom_explosion. A German act of sabotage to destroy US-made munitions destined for Allies in the First World War. One of the largest artificial non-nuclear explosions ever, which damaged the Statue of Liberty.
8. The Era of the Black Chambers. In 1628 Huguenot Réalmont was under siege by the royal army of Henry II of Bourbon. An inhabitant, escaping to deliver a message to Huguenot forces outside the embattled area, was captured with an enciphered message. No man could 'unriddle' it until word of a relative of Albi interested in ciphers was found. The young man solved it on the spot; thus, began the career of a man who become France's first full-time cryptologist: Antoine Rossignol. *The Codebreakers* David Kahn p.157.
9. brewminate.com/pioneers-of-u-s-military-cryptology-colonel-parker-hitt-and-genevieve-young-hitt/ The Friedmans later inscribed in one of their copies of Hitt's publication: '*The Manual for the Solution of Military Ciphers* guided our early, halting footsteps in the science and launched us upon our careers in the service of our country (1957).'

Chapter 10: Women in Codebreaking

1. Ada Lovelace - Wikipedia.
2. www.bbc.com/reel/video/p08kdvj0/the-secrets-of-the-mysterious-culper-spy-ring, 190 documents. www.en.wikipedia.org/wiki/Anna_Strong_(spy).
3. www.ancient.eu/article/623/women-in-ancient-egypt/.
4. www.britannica.com/biography/Hatshepsut.
5. *Code Girls*, Liza Mundy p.13, p.383.
6. brewminate.com/pioneers-of-u-s-military-cryptology-colonel-parker-hitt-and-genevieve-young-hitt/ and www.army.mil/article/122935/an_army_wife_doing_her_bit_in_world_war_i_the_story_of_genevieve_young_hitt by Ruth Quinn.
7. *The Codebreakers*, David Kahn p.415-419.

ENDNOTES

8. NSA release 6/12/2009 DOCID:3575740 Cryptologic Almanac 50th Anniversary series. Madam X: Agnes Meyer. Courtesy H. Craston and K. Howard.
9. *Code Girls*, Liza Mundy p.71-73 and www.britannica.com/event/Prohibition-United-States-history-1920-1933.
10. Elizebeth Friedman's work for the Coast Guard, helped design the code-making unit for the Coordinator of Information, a new US spy service – renamed the Office of Strategic Services (OSS). *Code Girls*, Liza Mundy p.88.

   The OSS, at 70 Grosvenor Square, London, was created for all US Armed Forces and their Joint Chiefs of Staff to coordinate espionage activities behind enemy lines. American intelligence efficiency was lacking, and FDR took advice from William Stephenson, a senior Canadian-British intelligence officer, to draft a plan for an intelligence service based on Britain's MI6 and SOE. Colonel William J. Donovan was appointed Coordinator of Information London, July 1941. Britain provided equipment, instructors, training and short-wave broadcasting capabilities to Europe, Africa and the Far East. The OSS was established by 13 June 1942, collecting and analyze strategic information and conducting some special operations. They supplied facts and estimates to policymakers, but never had jurisdiction over all foreign intelligence activities. They employed 24,000 people at the height of the war. Multiple activities and missions included collecting intelligence and spying, acts of sabotage, waging a propaganda war, subversion, organizing anti-Nazi resistance groups in Europe, and providing military training for anti-Japanese guerillas in Asia. OSS Resistance included Mao-tse Tung's Red Army and Viet Minh in French Indochina and areas occupied by Axis powers. US training facilities were Prince William Forest Park, Cacotin Mountain Park (now Camp David), the Congressional Country Club in Bethesda, Catalina Island and Camp X, Ajax near Oshawa, Ontario. OSS preceded the Strategic Services Unit (SSU) for post-war planning, which became the CIA. In August 2008 names and documents of personnel involved with OSS were released by the US National Archives. Among them are Julia Child, Arthur Goldberg, Arthur Schlesinger and Boston Red Sox baseball player, Moe Berg. Sources: CNN and *Wikipedia* 2016.

Chapter 11: Signals, Operators, Poppies and WACS

1. en.wikipedia.org/wiki/Claude_Chappe.
2. en.wikipedia.org/wiki/Flag_signals#Semaphore.
3. en.wikipedia.org/wiki/Samuel_Morse and en.wikipedia.org/wiki/Cooke_and_Wheatstone_telegraph.
4. en.wikipedia.org/wiki/Hello_Girls#/media/File:US_Army_Signal_Corps_Female_Telephone_operators.jpg. Camp Franklin (Fort Meade, Maryland).

5. en.wikipedia.org/wiki/Battle_of_Saint-Mihiel.
6. John Jacob Rogers was a lawyer and member of the House foreign Affairs Committee. He visited Britain in 1917 to see the war conditions first-hand. He enlisted as a private in the 29th Training Battery, 10th Training Battalion, Field Artillery, and 4th Central Officers Training School, September 1981. He is remembered as 'The father of the Foreign Service', due to his sponsorship of the 1924 Foreign Service Act, also known as the Rogers Act. He died from appendicitis complications in March 1925 and was succeeded in Congress by his wife Edith.
7. en.wikipedia.org/wiki/YMCA.
8. en.wikipedia.org/wiki/Edith_Nourse_Rogers.
9. www.alaforveterans.org/features/moina-michael and en.wikipedia.org/wiki/Moina_Michael.
10. en.wikipedia.org/wiki/United_States_Army_Nurse_Corps.
11. *Code Girls*, Liza Mundy pp.159-160.
12. *The Codebreakers*, David Kahn p.545, and www.energy.gov/women-manhattan-project.
13. en.wikipedia.org/wiki/Women%27s_Army_Corps#WAC_ranks.
14. en.wikipedia.org/wiki/Frances_Keegan_Marquis and https://en.wikipedia.org/wiki/Ernie_Pyle.

Chapter 12: WAVES

1. *Code Girls*, Liza Mundy p.161- Quote Professor Virginia Gildersleeve of Barnard College from her book *Many a Good Crusade* Macmillan, 1954.
2. en.wikipedia.org/wiki/1943_BRUSA_Agreement: The BRUSA Agreement came after the Holden Agreement of October 1942 which had given the US overall responsibility for Japanese naval codes, but with continued British participation. The agreement specifically stated that Eric Nave was not to work at FRUMEL, the Australian naval codebreaking establishment run by the US Navy Lieutenant Rudolph (Rudy) Fabian. Fabian thought Nave breached security in his desire to share information with the allied Army Central Bureau, where Nave amicably transferred to.
3. Wikipedia 1943_BRUSA.
4. *Code Girls*, Liza Mundy p.6 and Wikipedia.
5. Playfair Cipher example using information from www.rumkin.com April 2020.

Chapter 13: Going to the Chapel

1. www.history.navy.mil/research/library/online-reading-room/title-list-alphabetically/u/womens-reserve-1943.html.
2. *Code Girls*, Lisa Mundy p.45/49.

ENDNOTES

Chapter 14: Battle of the Atlantic

1. Quote from *Sea Power: The History and Geopolitics of the World's Oceans*, James G. Stavridis.
2. *Seizing the Enigma*, David Kahn, p55.
3. ASDIC en.wikipedia.org/wiki/File:ASIC.png. In 1916, under the British Board of Invention and Research, Canadian physicist Robert William Boyle took on the active sound detection project with A.B. Wood.
4. *Operation Drumbeat*, Michael Gannon p.182. Wikipedia.
5. *Operation Drumbeat*, Michael Gannon p.238 Wikipedia.
6. en.wikipedia.org/wiki/Second_Happy_Time: Cressman (2000) point 10 p.88-46, Alan Boyle point 49, NBC News.
7. *Blackout*, Charles Dickinson, Atlanta, 2015.
8. Janice Martin Benario and Cryptologia Volume 35 issue 1 January 2011 (Taylor & Francis ISSN 0161-1194 article Secret Keeping Dr Janice Martin Benario and the Women's College Connection to ULTRA by Robert Edward Lewand, also *Seizing the Enigma* by David Kahn, photo page 181 paperback edition.
9. en.wikipedia.org/wiki/Hunter-killer_Group.
10. www.historycentral.com/ww2/events/battleoftheatlantic.html.
11. *Millennium 20th Century Day by Day*, Dorling & Kindersley p.584, June 1943.

Chapter 15: Working in Nooks and Crannies and other strange places

1. NSA release 6/12/2009 DOCID:3575741 Cryptologic Almanac 50th Anniversary series. Madam X: Agnes Meyer Twilight Years. Courtesy H. Craston and K. Howard.
2. Nara records *CNSG Historical Review by John Holtwick* RG38 as supplied by NSA, NN3-38-93-001 Box 110.
3. *Code Girls*, Lisa Mundy p.233/234.
4. en.wikipedia.org/wiki/Vint_Hill_Farms_Station and http://www.asalives.org/ASAONLINE/hm2rock.htm.
5. en.wikipedia.org/wiki/Ballistic_Research_Laboratory.
6. *Code Girls*, Lisa Mundy p.232.
7. www.history.com/topics/world-war-ii/pearl-harbor-video. 'Bracero' was a series of laws and diplomatic agreements from 4 August 1942, when the USA and Mexico signed the Mexican Farm Labor Agreement. Farmworkers were guaranteed decent living conditions, and a minimum wage of 30 cents an hour, protection from forced military service, and guaranteed part of their wages would go into a private savings account in Mexico; it also permitted temporarily importation of contract laborers from Guam in the early part of World War II en.wikipedia.org/wiki/Bracero_program.

8. u-s-history.com/pages/h1656.html. A Rosie the Riveter memorial honouring all American women's labour during World War II was created in The Rosie the Riveter World War II Home Front National Historical Park, Richmond, California.
9. *Code Girls*, Lisa Mundy p.233/234.
10. *Code Girls*, Lisa Mundy p.47/48/49.
11. Nara records *CNSG Historical Review by John Holtwick* RG38 as supplied by NSA, NN3-38-93-001 Box 110.

Chapter 16: Handling Top Secret Intelligence

1. Adapted from *Seizing the Enigma*, David Kahn, pp39-43.
2. en.wikipedia.org/wiki/Royal_Corps_of_Signals.
3. en.wikipedia.org/wiki/Napoleonic_Wars#Use_of_military_intelligence and en.wikipedia.org/wiki/George_Scovell.
4. en.wikipedia.org/wiki/Telegraph_troops#Telegraph_Battalion_No._1.
5. *They Listened in Secret*, Gwendoline Page, pp.vii.
6. Google/Bletchley Park: Pat Davies, (née Owtram). WRNS, Y-Service.
7. Based on information from *Seizing the Enigma*, David Kahn, pp268-9.
8. *Code Girls*, Lisa Mundy p.407 British congratulations RG 38 Box 4 COMNAVSECGRU Commendations Received by the COMINT Organization, Jan 1942 -8 July 1948.
9. *Code Girls*, Lisa Mundy p.268.

Chapter 17: Bombe Machines, German Codebreaking and ULTRA

1. *Code Girls*, Lisa Mundy p.187 indicates OP-20-G-L represents Library and OP-20-G-M represents 'machine laboratory,' p.270.
2. NARA RG 0457, 9032 (A1) Box 833 'Security Posters and Miscellaneous Documents', *Code Girls*, Lisa Mundy p.303.
3. Combining three rotors, the settings with twenty-six positions, and the plug board with ten pairs of letters connected, the military Enigma had 158,962,555,217,826,360,000 different settings, (approximately 159 million, million, million (eighteen zeros), an impossibly high number to fathom for most. *Gordon Welchman, Bletchley Park's Architect of Ultra Intelligence*, Joel Greenberg.
4. John Tiltman was stationed at Indian Army Headquarters in Simla from 1921–1929 where he served as Cryptanalyst, and in Room 40 between the wars. tiltman.pdf (nsa.gov).
5. Enigma History (cryptomuseum.com).
6. *Gordon Welchman, Bletchley Park's Architect of Ultra Intelligence*, Joel Greenberg p.24 and p.25.

ENDNOTES

7. en.wikipedia.org/wiki/Joseph_Desch. His high-speed thyratron tube was used for the Manhattan Project.
8. en.wikipedia.org/wiki/C.E. Wynn-Williams.
9. *Code Girls*, Lisa Mundy p.263.
10. RAF Eastcote, also known as Lime Grove, HMS *Pembroke* V and Outstation Eastcote. en.wikipedia.org/wiki/RAF_Eastcote.
11. Bletchley Park Roll of Honor US: www.bletchleypark.org.uk/roll-of-honour/search?page=11&rank=US.
12. www.en.wikipedia.org/wiki/Alfred_Friendly, Bletchley Park Trust and en.wikipedia.org/wiki/Jean_Barker,_Baroness_Trumpington.
13. en.wikipedia.org/wiki/Donald_Howard_Menzel.
14. *Code Girls*, Lisa Mundy p.270-271, NARA RG, Box 113 "CNSG-0P-20-GM-6/GM-1-C-3/GE-1/GY-A-1 Daily War Diary 31 January 1943.
15. www.bletchleypark.org.uk/roll-of-honour/14226.
16. *Code Girls*, Lisa Mundy p.271.
17. *Code Girls*, Lisa Mundy p.279 and Deborah Anderson at Dayton Codebreakers.org.
18. RG38 Box 109 CNSG Report of supplementary Research Operations in WWII. *Code Girls*, Lisa Mundy p.274.
19. *Code Girls*, Lisa Mundy p.280. Bombes first summer RG 38 Boxes 39 & 40, (British) Watch Officer's Log 26 Jun–9 Aug 1943.
20. en.wikipedia.org/wiki/Washington_Navy_Yard; *Code Girls*, Lisa Mundy p.142 and p.276.
21. *Code Girls*, Lisa Mundy p.277.
22. *Sharing the Burden: Women in Cryptology During World War II* p.10. Center for Cryptologic History, NSA, Maryland. Gilman McDonnell interview with author, 9 May 1996. National Security Agency Oral History 39-96.
23. *Code Girls*, Lisa Mundy p.286-7, RG 0457,9002 (A1) Box 84, SRH 306 'OP-20-G Exploits and Communications World War II.'
24. *Code Girls*, Lisa Mundy p.280.
25. *Seizing the Enigma*, David Kahn, p.283-285 and based on discussions with Janice Martin Benario.

Chapter 18: Japanese Codebreaking

1. Wikipedia – The Boxer Rebellion.
2. en.wikipedia.org/wiki/Treaty_of_Portsmouth.
3. *Millennium 20th Century Day by Day*, Dorling & Kindersley pp.407,408,411.
4. *Japanese Codes*, Sue Jarvis (Bletchley Park Trust) and Wikipedia.
5. *Code Girls*, Lisa Mundy p.88 and p.89.
6. *The Story of Magic, Memoirs of an American Cryptologic Pioneer*, Frank B. Rowlett, p.151 and NSA Oral Histories.

7. Wm. Friedman's 27 September 1943 memorandum SPSIS-3, NSA Cryptologic Museum. Recommendations for Legion of Merit Awards and Medal of Merit Awards.
8. *David Kahn 1995 Secret Codebreakers World War II Japan Purple Code* video www.bing.com/videos/search?q=american+codebreakers&docid=608018625332249925&mid=EA61D66C797886B8E586EA61D66C797886B8E586&view=detail&FORM=VIRE.
9. *Japanese Codes*, Sue Jarvis (Bletchley Park Trust) p.24.
10. en.wikipedia.org/wiki/Japanese_army_and_diplomatic_codes#:
11. Frank W. Lewis - US Government Civilian at Bletchley Park 1945-1946 advising GC&CS on US Knowledge of Japanese codes. Employed by The Nation and NSA helping spies to solve top secret codes. BP Roll of Honor and New York Times Obituary 2010.
12. en.wikipedia.org/wiki/Japanese_naval_codes.
13. NSA release 6/12/2009 DOCID:3575741 Cryptologic Almanac 50th Anniversary series. Madam X: Agnes Meyer Twilight Years. Courtesy H. Craston and K. Howard.
14. ibid.
15. ibid
16. *Code Girls*, Lisa Mundy p.217 and Ann Caracristi.
17. *Code Girls*, Lisa Mundy p.219.
18. *Code Girls*, Lisa Mundy p.231 and p.232.
19. Segregation history of recruiting 1943-1944 NARA RG 0457, 9032 (A1), Box 1115, 'Signal Security Agency Report Fiscal year 1944. NARA RG 0457, 9002 (A1), Box 95, 'History of the Signal Security Agency,' Vol.1 'Organization' part 2 '1942-1945'.
20. NSA. Jennifer Wilcox Archives: J. N. Wenger Memorandum of Op-20-126 June 1945.
21. en.wikipedia.org/wiki/The_Pentagon and *Code Girls*, Lisa Mundy p.208-9.
22. *Code Girls*, Lisa Mundy p.145.

Chapter 19: The Workings of Secret Codebreaking

1. *The Daily Express Encyclopedia* OBE-SHA, 1934, p.14.
2. Sigaba was known as ECM Mark II, or Converter M-134 by the US Army, or CSP-888/889 by the US Navy, a modified Navy version was referred to as CSP-2900. Wikipedia. 'The encryptions of Sigaba remain immune to attack.' re NSA National Cryptologic Museum, Fort Meade, Maryland. Re Typex: as stated at Bletchley Park 2016.
3. One-time pads (OTP) with a unique table, had a long cryptographical shelf life and were used for superencipherment, as digits covered each group

ENDNOTES

(plain text or enciphered) only once in a message, thus producing depth of just one. Each message was unique and unbreakable, as opposed to another key that might have been used twenty times over a short period and created a depth of twenty. The more depth – the easier it was to reconstruct a key, which led to 'keystripping' from other number groups to expose book codes. A large staff using brute force or data processing machines easily reinforced this process. The only time the OTP might fail is if tables were reused, as Japan and Russia did between 1941 and 1945. *Behind the Enigma, GCHQ*, John Ferris p.107.

4. *Behind the Enigma, GCHQ*, John Ferris p.335; *Improvisation to Permanence*, Sherman; NSA-OH-OI-85. Telford Taylor interviews 22.1.85, www.nsa.gov.
5. *Behind the Enigma, GCHQ*, John Ferris p.336.
6. *Behind the Enigma, GCHQ*, John Ferris p.336-7, Personal minutes by Churchill to Bridges 27.1.44.
7. www.en.wikipedia.org/wiki/SIGABA.
8. www.cryptomuseum.com/crypto/hagelin/index.
9. *The Rise and Fall of the Third Reich*, William Shirer.
10. NARA RG 0457, 9002 (A1), Box 17 'Achievements of US Signals Intelligence during WWII'.
11. www.en.wikipedia.org/wiki/Hiroshi.
12. After the Second World War the GPO maintained a numbered historical index for each project. The report index began in 1871 and are recognized by UNESCO on the *UK Memory of the World Register*. Colossus is not included as David Hay, Head of Heritage and Archives at British Telecoms discovered. However, he did locate technical drawings for Colossus at London's National Archive, and on a second look found a project number. Checking back at his own archive he confirmed TNA's plans held the missing number in the GPO project Index at Dollis Hill. *Bletchley Park Magazine* Issue No.12, Spring 2019/Joe Townend. Hay explained that all the links had been erased and that Colossus in the index was 'visible by its omission', and that the science of other projects around the missing file number worked on thermionic valve technology. For further reading refer to *Colossus* by Jack Copeland 2006.
13. Tommy Flowers propagated this stance while running future teams, allowing suggestions to be made and heard. 'This was the most important thing I learned from him,' said Dame Stephanie Shirley, a Jewish woman who escaped Nazi Germany as a child in 1933. She was the only woman to work with Flowers on ERNIE (Electronic Random Number Indicator Equipment), the British lottery machine winning numbers selector, after the war. *Bletchley Park Magazine* Issue No.12, Spring 2019/Joe Townend.
14. en.wikipedia.org/wiki/Grace_Hopper.

Chapter 20: Alien Codes?

1. NSA Cryptology Museum A2775364. Friedman to Tiltman 1942. www.nsa.gov/News-Features/Declassified-Documents/Friedman-Documents/Correspondence/#
2. Howard H. Campaigne NSA Oral History 1-17.
3. www.cryptomuseum.com/crypto/siemens/t52/index.htm.
4. However, Kahn's last chapter includes the science that Campaigne moved into, entitled 'Messages from Outer Space.' *The Codebreakers*, David Kahn p.938.
5. Howard H. Campaigne: www.mayinetreeconsciousness.wordpress.com/tag/key-to-extraterrestrial-messages/
6. Howard H. Campaigne NSA Oral History 33-34.
7. TICOM (Target Intelligence Committee) was an Allied project formed after the war to seize German intelligence assets. www.en.wikipedia.org/wiki/TICOM
8. Howard H. Campaigne NSA Oral History 15-16.
9. Extraterrestrial Intelligence report by Howard H. Campaigne approved for release by NSA on 21 October 2004. www.tarrdaniel.com/documents/Ufology/alien_message.html.

Chapter 21: D-Day

1. Shirley Cannicott (née Gadsby), Special Duty Wren, *They Listened in Secret*, Gwendoline Page. p.48.
2. The Citizen.com, 11 December 2013 and Fayette Woman, War Secrets – 60 years later, October 2005 and kelolandblogs.com.

Chapter 22: Final Battles

1. *Millennium 20th Century Day by Day*, Dorling & Kindersley p.618.
2. Prof. Thomas Sherrer Ross Boase was an Oxford historian and Director of the Courtauld Institute from 1937-1947. Miss Diana 'Dinah' Pares was the only woman in the Western Front Committee at Bletchley from 1942, Hut 3, Block A, Air Section. Other members were Lt. Col. A.L. Gadd, Head of SIXTA, Wing Cdr. Oscar Oeser, Enigma and Fish Processing requirements, Jack M. Brown, BP Hut 3, GHQ Home Forces and probably SIXTA, Alan Pryce-Jones, BP Hut 3, and Handel Bowen Edwards, Air Section Blocks A and F, Luftwaffe tactical codes, Jafo (Japanese Forces – Japanese Army and Airforce Intelligence), Block G, Berkley Street and Diplomatic Section, from David Kenyon's *Bletchley Park and D-Day, The Untold Story of How the Battle for Normandy was Won*, p.99, and Bletchley Park's Roll of Honour.

ENDNOTES

3. *Bletchley Park and D-Day, The Untold Story of How the Battle for Normandy was Won*, David Kenyon.
4. *Millennium 20th Century Day by Day*, Dorling & Kindersley p.618. Discussion with Bill Montgomery, Atlanta 1.16.20, AJC article 'The few, the proud who remember Iwo Jima.'
5. www.en.wikipedia.org/wiki/Operation_Plunder, accessed 8/26/20, *Millennium 20th Century Day by Day*, Dorling & Kindersley p.619.
6. *Millennium 20th Century Day by Day*, Dorling & Kindersley p.619 and p.621.
7. *Code Girls*, Lisa Mundy p.320 NSA NARA RG0457, 9032 (AI), Box 623, COMINCH memoranda file of U-Boat Tracking Room Operations.

Chapter 23: War's End in Europe

1. TNA GC&CS Branch Records HW64 April/May 1945.
2. www.en.wikipedia.org/wiki/Cuxhaven and Bletchley Park Trust.
3. The British Joint Services Mission at the Pentagon: ref TNA DEFE 20.
4. This was probably a US-Built Boeing 314 Clipper owned by the British Government via BOAC. It held 68 passengers plus crew, except overnight transatlantic flights permitted only 36 passengers to allow for converted sleeping accommodation. www.pooleflyingboats.com and www.en.wikipedia.org/wiki/Boeing_314_Clipper.
5. *Secret Postings, Bletchley Park to the Pentagon*, Charlotte Webb, Chap.6, by kind permission of Charlotte Webb and Kerry Howard of BookTower Publishing.
6. Bletchley Park Trust, Bletchley Park Research and Forces News.
7. www.atomicheritage.org/location/university-california-berkeley.

Chapter 24: Waiting for VJ Day

1. Included Generals Dwight Eisenhower, Douglas MacArthur and Henry "Hap" Arnold and Admirals William Leahy, Chester Nimitz, Ernest King and William Halsey. www.msn.com/en-us/news/world/op-ed-u-s-leaders-knew-we-didnt-have-to-drop-atomic-bombs-on-japan-to-win-the-war-we-did-it-anyway/ar-BB17Ayn1.
2. www.en.wikipedia.org/wiki/USS_Indianapolis_(CA-35).
3. *The Codebreakers*, David Kahn p.548-549. Parson's Enola Gay secret code had three levels for good, medium and bad results.
4. www.en.wikipedia.org/wiki/Allied_naval_bombardments_of_Japan_during_World_War_II.
5. Glassborow: www.en.wikipedia.org/wiki/Family_of_Catherine,_Duchess_of_Cambridge, www.bletchleypark.org.uk/roll-of-honour/Glassborow.
6. *Code Girls*, Lisa Mundy p.326.

THE SECRET LIFE OF AN AMERICAN CODEBREAKER

Chapter 25: Aftermath

1. The Bureau of Medicine was one of five Navy Bureaux.
2. Adapted Source www.military.com.
3. *Code Girls*, Lisa Mundy p.31 NARA RG 38 Box 4 COMNAVSECGRU Commendations Received by OP-20-G.
4. *Code Girls*, Lisa Mundy p.335-p.336.
5. The Citizen.com, 11 December 2013 and Fayette Woman, War Secrets - 60 years later, October 2005, and kelolandblogs.com.
6. WAVES: Women in the WW2 US Navy Wikipedia.
7. www.en.wikipedia.org/wiki/Edith_Nourse_Rogers.

Epilogue

1. Janice Benario recorded interviews with author, from 6/22/2014, Cryptologia Volume 35 issue 1 January 2011 (Taylor & Francis ISSN 0161-1194 article Secret Keeping 101 – Dr Janice Martin Benario and the Women's College Connection to ULTRA by Robert Edward Lewand, The Classical Bulletin Vol.74 1998.
2. Adapted from 'Dedication of Bletchley Park Memorial by HM The Queen, 15 July 2011', Bletchley Park Trust.

Afterword

1. Originally said to be from Alaska and Canada, Navajo Native Americans live in Arizona, Colorado, New Mexico and Utah.
2. Choctaw Native American people are from Alabama, Florida, Louisiana and Mississippi.
3. Comanche people are from Colorado, Kansas, New Mexico, Oklahoma, Texas, and Mexico.
4. See www.en.wikipedia.org/wiki/Code_talker for more information on these secret operations.
5. Navajo Cultural arts.com.
6. www.en.wikipedia.org/wiki/Sacagawea.

Memorial Day 2021

1. Sources point to Walter and Albert Ettinghausen, 'major' and 'minor', who both worked at Bletchley Park during the war. Walter, as Walter Eytan, became Director General of the Israeli Foreign Ministry in 1948–1959 and Israeli ambassador to France in 1959–1970.

Index

ADERHOLDT, Virginia Dare 241
African American, Segregation 84, 91, 180-2, 248
American Expeditionary Forces 60, 84, 89
Ancient Codes (inc. Hittite Hieroglyphs, Queen Hatshepsut's and Petroglyphs) 58, 68, 208
APOSTOL, Jane Thurston 49, 101, 251
Arlington Farms 124
Arlington Hall 72, 120-4, 127, 171-4, 177-82, 190, 208, 217, 223, 241, 247-8, 254
Authors, Artists, Journalists and TV
    Bob Farley 206, 210
    Al Friendly 147, 267
    David Kahn 15, 41, 52, 54, 59, 63, 68, 211, 252-3, 257, 260
    Ed Murrow 20-2
    NBC's H. V. Kaltenborn 38
    Ernie Pyle 91
    William Shirer 20
    James Thurber 18, 60
    Frank Lloyd Wright 57
    William Joyce 36
    Norman Rockwell 123
    Frederick Winterbotham 252, 261
    Peter Wright 252

BABBAGE, Charles 66, 192
BANKER, Grace 84

Battles
    Atlantic ix-xii, 6, 13, 15-17, 24-8, 29-33, 73-4, 104-16, 133-7, 155-60, 171-6, 200, 213-14, 216, 248, 254
    Blitz, Britain 13, 18, 109
    Bulge 223
    Coral Sea 43
    Cuxhaven/Wilhelmshaven 30, 230
    Dunkirk 16, 37
    Iwo Jima 225-6, 259
    Midway 43, 185-6
    Mukden Incident 161-2
    Okinawa 232
    Saint-Mihiel 84, 270
    Stalingrad 202
BENARIO, Herbert, Fred, Janice, John ii, viii, xi, xii 1, 3, 97, 246-9, 252, 260-3,
BERKOWICH, S.B. 48
BERRYMAN, Wilma 124, 164, 178
British Services
    ATS 110, 122, 130-1, 198, 229, 232-3
    Royal Air Force 12, 18, 40, 43, 94, 109, 149, 194, 224-5
    Royal Navy 51, 61, 73, 92, 105, 109, 112, 116, 237
    Royal Observers 122
    Royal Signals 229
    WAAF, Wrens (WRNS) 92, 99, 110, 203, 214, 216-17

British Joint Staff/Services Mission 42, 232-3
Black Chamber 54, 60-3, 161
Blackout 106, 111-13, 218
Bletchley Park vii-xi, 1, 14, 28-32, 42, 44, 52-4, 63, 69, 94, 108, 110, 119-21, 125-7, 134, 136-7, 142-59, 168-73, 179-206, 209-17, 221-2, 229-35, 240, 247-8, 251-6, 261, 263
American Personnel 267
B. B., Mrs. 141
CAMPBELL-HARRIS (Barker), Jean, Baroness of Trumpington 147
DE GREY, Nigel 51, 59, 193
DENNISTON, Alastair 53, 140, 176-9, 190, 232, 255-6
Government Code & Cipher School 44, 52-4, 63, 94, 108, 117, 120, 132, 136-7, 157, 160, 163, 171, 176-8, 187-9, 195-6, 233, 235, 255
Western Front Committee 14, 74, 84, 186, 221-2, 280
GLASSBOROW twins/CMY 240
Government Communications HQ 187, 190, 255
HEATH ROBINSON machine 202-4
HUT 6 53, 134, 191, 252,
Official Secrets Act vii, xi, 36, 54, 188, 204
BOMBE Machines UK 104, 136-42, 147, 149, 176, 198, 203, 208
Bootleggers 64, 78
Bradley, Gen. Omar Nelson 214
British Military Intelligence 44, 52, 61-2, 71, 77, 94, 131, 139-40, 160, 171, 173, 186, 188, 190, 196, 222, 235
Admiralty (OIC), The 29, 31-4, 49, 51, 53-4, 73, 111, 118-19, 132, 138, 157, 159, 197

Boniface 108
Broadway Buildings 53
SINCLAIR, Rear Admiral Hugh (QUEX) 52, 140
Room 40 50-4, 59, 144, 189, 194
War Office/Cabinet 13, 14, 40, 44, 52, 59, 73, 118-19, 131, 171, 182, 189-90, 194, 197, 222, 232
BRUSA/Holden Agreement 94, 134-6, 184-5, 195
BuMed 231-2, 241, 245
BURCHELL, Janet 172

CAMPAIGNE, Howard 59, 206-12, 267
Canadian Forces 13, 21 ,63, 87, 111, 116, 144, 217-18, 221, 234
CARACRISTI, Anna 178-80, 248, 252
CHAMBERLAIN, Alethia 238
CHAMBERLAIN, Prime Minister Neville 12-19
China ix, 21, 39, 68, 160-3, 243
CHURCHILL, Winston vii, 14-27, 31, 39-44, 50-3, 73, 93-4, 101, 108, 142, 163, 170, 183, 193-7, 204, 213-14, 224, 231, 248
CHURCHILL, Clementine 86
Cipher Machines
Enigma vii, 23, 29-31, 52-3, 63, 104-108, 116, 128-41, 148-57, 163-4, 171-80, 191-202, 207-12, 222-3, 228, 253, 260
Lorenz S-Z 40-42a/b 201-204, 210, 214
M-134-C 196
M-138 18, 37
M4 134
Sigaba 138, 150, 154, 193-7
T-52 Geheimschreiber 208-10
Typex 138, 150, 154, 193-9, 214, 222

INDEX

Civil War 83-4, 132, 144
Codes and Ciphers
   American Codes 59-60
   A-1 B-1 C-1 D-1 37
   AN-1 182
   BLUE 162, 183
   Brown 37, 230
   Codebook 151 50
   CORAL 175
   Diplomatic Codes 19, 59-60, 62-3, 172-5, 183, 200
   Fish Codes 201-204, 210
   Gray 18, 37
   Green 18
   Home Waters Cipher 29-30
   Japanese Naval Codes (JN-20, JN-25 and others) 171-2, 182, 187, 195, 207
   Japanese Dockyard and Water Transport Codes 172-3
   MAGIC 168
   Mexican Ciphers 55
   Morse Code 83, 110, 129-30, 133, 136, 148, 150, 185, 199
   One-time Pad 194
   ORANGE 175, 199
   Playfair 55, 95-6
   Purple 137, 165-71, 175, 183, 192, 199-200
   RED 77, 162, 164-5, 175, 191, 199
   sägefisch 201, 210
   Shark (Triton) 133-4
   Short Weather Cipher 29-30
   ULTRA 18, 94, 101-103, 108, 114-16, 135-59, 168, 194-5, 222, 253, 261
   Vignere Square 94, 96
Colleges and Schools
   Margaret Brent Elementary 5
   Eastern High 5, 8, 9
   Emory 1, 247
   Georgia State xi, 1, 247, 252
   Goucher 8-10, 20, 26, 44-8, 70, 101-103, 155-6, 246, 251, 253
   Ivy-League 10
   Johns Hopkins 26, 245, 247
   Mount Vernon Seminary 102, 114, 119-20
   Roland Park Jnr. High 8
   Seven Sisters 10, 92
   Western High 8-9
COLOSSUS computer UK 201-205, 210-11, 214-15
COMSTOCK, Ada 69
Conferences
   Atlantic 19, 24-5, 116
   Casablanca 93
   CAVIAR 24
   League of Nations 2, 61, 162
   London 162
   Moscow 24, 44, 213
   Munich 15
   Potsdam 237-9
   Quadrant 213
   Riviera 24
   SYMBOL 93
   Tehran 213
   United Nations Declaration 39
   Washington 43, 62, 161
   Yalta 224, 237
Convoys 24, 28, 30-5, 104-109, 111-16, 134-5, 156-9, 161
CORDERMAN, Preston 169, 174
Cryptology Course, Cryptanalysis methods
   Archeries 31
   Bookbuilding 182-7
   Cribs 31, 104, 133-4, 137, 150, 157, 162, 191, 197
   Data Processing 19, 30, 33, 50, 104, 157, 191-5, 205, 241, 251
   Herivel Tip 136, 191
   Hollerith 157, 165-6, 173, 191-5

IBM 137, 145, 157, 162-6, 173, 191-3
Index of Coincidence 59, 212
Kisses 31, 133-4, 191
Manual for the Solution of Military Ciphers 55, 70
Paraphrasing/Parallel Texts 138, 198-9, 234, 251
Culper Spy Ring 67
CODE TALKERS 257-9
CURRIER, Prescott 23, 117, 169, 208, 255
Czechoslovakia 15, 39, 140

D-Day 201, 204-205, 210, 213-20, 222, 227
Depression, The Great 6-7, 120-2, 164, 245
Dill, John 24, 25, 40-2
EACHUS, Lt. Joseph 136-7, 210
Eachus Abernethy, Barbara 136, 232
ECM/CCM 150-6, 185, 197-9
EISENHOWER, Dwight, D. 27, 44, 91, 214-9, 230, 235, 250
Engstrom, Howard 137, 207-208
Ettinghausen, Albert and Walter 'Eytan' 282

Fairfax, Mary Somerville 66
Far East Theatre of War ix, 39, 42, 160, 163, 167, 177, 183, 213, 230, 232, 237, 242, 243
  Emperor Hirohito 237, 242
  Konoye, Prince 37
  Nomura, Admiral 37, 38
  Oshima, Hiroshi 200, 222
  Nashimoto, Prince Morimasa 239
  Surrender 237-42
  Togo 237
  Tojo 163
  Yamamoto 185-6

FLOWERS, Tommy 144, 203-205
FOSS, Hugh 52, 140-1, 159, 163, 190, 194, 199
France
  Defarge, Therese 68
  De Gaulle 93
  Charles Giraud, Henry 93
FRIEDMAN, Elizabeth and William 23, 51, 54, 57-9, 63-6, 70-80, 86, 94, 117, 124, 137, 163-9, 177-9, 192, 195-6, 207-209, 252

General Post Office 49, 203, 205
Germany
  Axis Powers 21, 35, 39, 93, 155, 175, 195, 200, 227, 255
  Dönitz, Admiral Karl, 106-107, 116, 155, 228-9
  Happy Time 108-109
  Hitler, Adolf 7, 12-15, 20, 24, 27, 39, 40, 42, 128, 133, 156, 180, 186, 190, 200-201, 203, 214-16, 221-31, 258
  Lemp, Kapitänleutnant, Fritz Julius 13-14, 107
  Nazi ix, 22, 28, 35-6, 147, 200-202, 213, 229-32, 237
  Siegfried Line 223
  Siemens & Halske 210
  U-boats/Wolfpacks 30-6, 104, 109-10, 155
GI Bill 245
Gildersleeve, Virginia 92
Good Hope, GA 86
Goucher students 48
Gray, Thomas, Elegy 138
Gresham, Lieutenant Commander John 74
Grew, Ambassador Joseph C. 37
Grotjan Feinstein, Genevieve 166-9

INDEX

Guerin, Madam E. 89
Gylden, Yves and Olaf 51

Haines, Captain 29-30
Hall, Marshall 148
Harriman, Averell 22-7, 35, 147, 213
Harris, Arthur 225
Hebern, Edward 75-6
Hello Girls 84-5
Herschel, Caroline 66
HF/DF Dowding System 109
Hindu Radicals 59, 63
Hitt, Genevieve (née Young) Parker 18, 54-6, 64, 70-1, 84-6, 132, 164, 252
Holocaust/Auschwitz/Jewish People 36, 58, 193, 202, 223
Holtwick, Jack, John 175
Hopkins, Harry 21-2, 24-5, 27, 39, 44
Howard, John C. 149-53
Hull, Cordell 37

Iran 35

Kennedy, Joseph P. 15, 22
King, Admiral Ernest ix, 25, 104-105, 111-12, 118, 139, 156-9, 213, 224
Knowles, Kenneth Parsons, John E. 158-9
Knox, Dillwyn 'Dilly' 52, 140-1
KOGEL, Helen Denton 218-20, 249
Kullback, Simon 65, 164, 199, 208-209, 241

Lawrence, Daisy viii, xi, 256
Leahy, Admiral D. 105, 224
Lend Lease 21-2, 27, 159
Liberty Ships 22, 89
Listeners, Y Stations 32, 110, 122, 130-3, 137, 172, 214-7, 238
Lord Lothian 17
Lovelace, Ada 66
Lywood, O. G. 194

Main Navy ix, 41, 101, 114-19, 136-9, 152, 158-9, 207
Manhattan Project 236-9
   Atom/Atomic Bomb 231, 238, 243-5
   Ballistics Lab/Hubble 122-3
   Enola Gay 238
Marquis, Frances Keegan 91
Marshall, George 18, 25, 40, 86, 89, 90, 119, 147
Martin Janice ii, viii, xi, xii, 97
   birth 3
   Gladys Katherine 3
   J. L "Dadaddy" and Grandmother 3
   J. Elmer 3, 9, 20
Mauborgne, Joseph 55, 164, 168
McAfee, Mildred H. 92, 181
Meader, Ralph 150, 152
Menzel, Donald 70, 148
Menzies, Col. Stewart Graham 140, 235
Meyer, Agnes (Driscoll) 70, 72-80, 86, 134, 162, 175-6, 183, 199, 211, 252
Meyer, Major James 132
Michael, Moina Belle 86-9
Michie, Donald 203
Montgomery, Bill 225-6
Montgomery, Marshal 227-9
Muirhead, Murray 55
Mulberry Harbours 214, 221
Mussolini 12, 227
Mustard Gas 40, 113
Myer, Albert J. 83

Naval Communications Annex 101-102, 119-20, 125, 127, 137, 150-2, 172, 190, 217, 228, 241, 254
NEWMAN, Max 144, 191, 202-204, 206, 210, 214
Noyce, William 173
Noyes, Leigh 69

287

Oath of Office/Official Secrets vii, xi, 35-6, 54, 102, 188-9, 204
Oliver, Henry 49-50
On the Roof Gang, Harry Kidder 76, 118
OP-20-G and OP-20-GL xii, 74, 77, 114-15, 117-19, 125, 135-7, 149, 156-9, 161-2, 170-6, 183-5, 195-6, 199, 207, 216, 251, 253, 260

Operations
    Anakim 213
    Bang, *Paukenschlag* or Drumbeat 109, 112
    Centerboard 238
    Downfall 238
    Dynamo 16
    Overlord 213-19
    Plunder 227
    Primrose 108
    Sunrise 227
    Varsity 227
    Vengeance 186
    Wacht am Rhine (Watch on the Rhine) 223
Office of Strategic Services 273

Parsons, Captain William Sterling 238
Parsons, Lt. John E. 158
Patton, General George Smith 27, 214
Pentagon, The 121, 124, 180-2, 190, 232-4
Pearl Harbor, Hypo/Hawaii ix, 38-41, 43, 54, 89, 109, 136, 161, 170,176, 183-6, 200, 253, 258
Pearsall, Louise 149-53
Pershing, General. John J. 64, 84, 90
Polish, Bomba 139-43, 146
Pound, Dudley 24-5, 133
Prather, Mary Louise 166-9, 252
Prohibition 64, 78-80

Radley, Gordon 143
Redman, John 117, 207
Riverbank Research Laboratories/ Fabyan, George 57-9, 63-4, 70, 76, 80
Rochefort, Joseph 183-6
Rogers, Edith Nourse and John 86, 89-91, 250
Roosevelt, (Anna) Eleanor 12, 93, 181-2
Roosevelt, Franklin Delano 12, 14-19, 21, 24-5, 27-31, 37, 39-40, 43-4, 93-4, 108, 111, 117, 142, 170, 182, 196, 213, 224, 230, 245
Roosevelt, Theodore 161
ROSE, E. B. (Jim) 94
Rosen, Leo (Leon) 23, 117, 167, 169, 208, 255
Rowlett, Frank 65, 77, 164-9, 175, 196, 199, 241
Royalty/Crown 12, 20, 26, 58, 183, 188, 240, 253
Rutherford, Ernest 143

Safford, Laurance 77, 117, 176, 183, 199, 207
Scouts, Girls and Boys, Baden-Powell 8, 86, 113, 144,148,
Signals, Telegraphy History 23, 28, 31, 51-2, 54-5, 63-4, 74-7, 81-5, 94-6, 108, 110, 112, 116-17, 119-20, 122, 131-2, 136, 147-9, 155-7, 168, 171, 181-3, 194-7, 212, 220-2, 229, 238, 247-8, 255
Sinkov, Adam 23, 65, 117, 164, 169, 173, 208, 255
Small, Albert (Al) 169, 178, 210
Smith, Lt. Cdr. Leon P. 48-9
South Atlantic Championships, Medals 8-9
Southwick House 44, 214-16, 219

INDEX

SPARS 92, 96
Spies 36-7, 60, 67, 74, 102, 108, 147, 173, 188-9, 214, 252
Stalin 7, 13, 24, 213, 224, 231
Stevens, Major Geoffrey 177
Stimson, Henry and Dorothy 44-5, 62, 90, 162
Strong, General George Veazy 23, 270
Submarine Tracking Room ix, 31-2, 111, 114, 116, 139, 156, 158, 253
Sugar camp (NCR) 144-6, 151-2

TAYLOR, Colonel Telford 94, 195
TESTERY, The, Tester, Ralph 198, 201-202, 212
TILTMAN, John 23, 127, 142, 171-2, 187, 190, 202-203, 208-209
TRAVIS, Edward 23, 53, 94, 142, 203
Tunny Machine UK 201-204, 210
TICOM 211-12
TIZARD, Sir Henry 18-19
TRUMAN, President Harry 230, 236-7, 241, 250
TURING, Alan 108, 139-42, 202-204
TUTTE, Bill 144, 149, 202, 204

US Air Force 43, 92, 110, 113, 160, 190, 193, 201, 224, 250
US Army 42, 51, 57, 61, 63-4, 70, 81-5, 91, 118, 120-1, 132, 136, 147-9, 164-5, 170-4, 183, 189-90, 195-6, 199, 206, 210, 218, 238, 247-50

US Coast Guard 64, 78-80, 92, 96, 106, 110, 116, 190
US Navy 24, 32, 34-5, 42, 45, 48, 69, 72-4, 84-5, 92-3, 99-101, 104, 106, 110, 117-9, 126, 142, 144, 146, 148, 158-9, 164-5, 170-1, 175-6, 183, 185, 189-90, 199, 244, 255
US Bombe Machines 134, 136, 139, 141-9, 151, 154-6, 171, 208, 249

VE/VJ Day 211, 231, 237-42
VINE-STEVENS, Charlotte (Betty Webb) 198-9, 232-4, 241, 263

WAACS/WACS 81, 86, 89-91, 121, 123, 190, 205, 217-19, 236, 249-50
WAVES Uniform 31, 89, 92, 99-101, 126, 234, 248, 261
Weeks, Lt. Robert 23, 117, 169, 255
Welchman, Gordon 53, 132, 159, 189-90, 202, 205, 252
Wenger, Cdr. Joseph N. 181, 199, 207
Winant, Amb. John Gilbert (Gil) 22, 26-7
Winn, Captain Charles Roger Noel 32-3, 111
Winslow, Professor Ola 45-6, 48
Wolff, General Karl 227
Wynn-Williams, C. E. 143

Yardley, Herbert O. 60-3, 76, 240